Praise for Cracking Open

"Your book is absolutely amazing. I can't even begin to tell you how much it helped not only myself, but my family too, as my mother in law was in the process of passing away. You are a godsend, Isabeau. I'm so grateful for you."

Jennifer White

"Compelling story, inside perspective. I have never read an account of someone realizing and experiencing that they are a psychic or a medium. While I still have a hard time imagining the things she describes happening to me, I am certain after reading her book that she is authentic. In reading the book I found myself pulling for her. I would not be surprised if her account got turned into a movie of some sort in the future."

J. McCormack

"I wanted to read more! Isabeau's journey has been written in a very down to earth fashion that makes me want to get to know her as a person. I've personally witnessed her amazing ability and I feel extremely fortunate. I really enjoyed the book and would highly recommend it to anyone."

Andrea

"More than a "must read" and beyond what I would call a "page turner." If you are having things happening, things you can't explain, and you don't know what to do because you don't want to tell anyone for fear of judgment, fear no more. Get Cracking Open and begin the Journey that is the rest of your REAL life."

David

"Entertaining and Enlightening. The author writes on a level that allows the reader to see and feel what she is going through and walk the path that has led her to where she is now. Funny and an all-around great story! It left me wanting to learn more."

Colorado Girl

"Absolutely a must read... a page turner!! "Cracking Open: Adventures of a Reluctant Medium" took my breath away. When I sat down to read it, I felt like everything else around me fell away. I was totally enveloped."

Cmcgarry113

"Cracking Open is a beautifully told, emotional peek into one woman's journey into becoming a medium... what it is like to start accepting the signs and messages that are so often ignored. I highly recommend it!!"

Meghan Harris

"So glad she cracked! With humor, openness and honesty, Beau shows us the "real deal." Not only are we able to witness the doubt and fear that comes with mediumship, we also experience the joy and amazement. I recommend this book not only to anyone who wonders what's on the otherside, but also to those who want to add to their spiritual knowledge. Like Beau, I'm one who needs proof. Beau's story gives me that proof."

Cosmet

"SUPERB!! THIS BOOK IS REAL AND INCREDIBLE!! It is a truly moving bio of a woman finding her own way on her life's path. Everyone who is searching for their true spiritual purpose needs to read this book."

Rachael Comeau

"Great Read! Very Enjoyable! Cracking Open: Adventures of a Reluctant Medium, is a wonderfully written book that made me want to dig more into my own spiritual being and really examine what true purpose awaits me on this Earth."

Eyes Wide Open

CRACKING OPEN

ADVENTURES OF A RELUCTANT MEDIUM

BY

ISABEAU MAXWELL

Cracking Open: Adventures of a Reluctant Medium

---

by Isabeau Maxwell

Published by Intuitive Arts Media LLC Manchester, New Hampshire
IntuitiveArtsMedia.com

All events in this book are true. Some of the names, personal characteristics of individuals, and locations have been changed for privacy reasons.

ISBN: 978-1-7351911-9-5 (paperback)

For Josephine

When you look at me
I am special

When you sing to me
I am at peace

When you hold me
I am priceless

Contents

Part III: Running With the Big Dogs

Acknowledgements

It is with deepest gratitude that I acknowledge and thank:

My boys, Michael and Max—for making me laugh, loving me, and inviting me to be the best person I can be.

Molly Urbanski—for being my life raft. There's a special place in heaven for you, Chica!

Big Dog—for believing in me.

Apple—for your fur therapy and never-ending love.

Dr. Joel Glenn Wixson—for keeping me sane.

Carolyn Taylor Glenn—for allowing me to walk by your side on such a beautiful journey.

Chris Bashaw—for kicking ass and taking names.

Joseph Carringer and Nicole Solatti—for their professionalism and care.

Ed Hubbell—for pushing me out of the nest.

Heather Tacconi—for torturously reading through my first drafts and bringing creativity to my writing.

Every client, every student, and every friend—know that you are honored.

To Mom and all those who brought me struggles and stress, I thank you. I am grateful for all the hurdles you put in front of me. Each provided challenges that fostered strength, compassion, and fortitude, and taught me important lessons about myself.

Introduction

Yes. This book is for you. As you will discover, you are not alone and you certainly are not crazy. There *is* more to this life than is commonly perceived. For some, this book may be an invitation to open up to new possibilities. For others, it will be confirmation that your experiences are valid and real.

Here, I present to you my experience of opening up intuitively—uncensored, raw, and in detail—all the ups and downs that can happen when one stumbles onto their spiritual path. The twisting, roller coaster journey called "opening up psychically" started for me at the age of thirty-one, on the day my grandmother died. That one, pivotal moment changed me from a materialistic, business-driven agnostic to someone who doubted her sanity and reality itself. And I'm excited to say that I ultimately became a reverent lover of life in all its expanded realities—the here, the otherside, and the inbetween.

I invite you inside this journey of mine as I experience hours of frustration, moments of debilitating fear, and times I wondered if the brain I had relied on for so many years had finally put itself out to pasture. Join me as all of this is also met with moments of pure bliss, when life unfolds to demonstrate the spectacular beauty of human potential.

I wrote this book for two reasons. The selfish reason is that I was tired of repeatedly telling the story of how I opened up. The real reason is, when I did tell the story, the person hearing it would often reach out to me in relief, saying things like that happened to them as well but they thought they were crazy. They didn't have anyone to talk to about it. This relief, in turn, allowed them the confidence to share with others what they had experienced as they moved forward on their path. And as a ripple effect, they were able to help others, bringing them out of hiding and into the light as well.

In today's society, the fear of the unknown has built up a wall that has disconnected us from our ancestors and loved ones on the otherside. Imagine, by analogy, going to the store and returning home only to have your child terrified of you because someone told him that people who go to the store never come back. And if they do return, they are haunting you and you should be scared of them. Worse yet, that child will hold their fear in silence because they have been taught that if they see anyone return from the store, they are crazy. They sit in voiceless fear while you, their parent in spirit form, cannot reach them to comfort them. It is time to remember what is real, to eliminate that silence and come together as a whole, from all sources.

We are never meant to be alone. Not in birth, not in pain, not in joy, not in death.

It is now time to elevate the understanding of intuition from a sensationalized spectacle to the truth that this is a normal part of life, something accessible to all. When you read this please know, my abilities are not a gift, they are an expansion of my senses, something everyone has. I have never been a fan of the word gift. I much prefer the word abilities. When one holds on to a sense of specialness, it muddies the flow of intuition. The ability to expand our perceptions to other levels of existence is not unusual. It is a built-in ability that only requires the removal of our personal obstacles. Much of what you will read in this book is exactly that: me removing my mental obstacles and having the courage to keep pressing forward, well, the best I could at the time.

One of my purposes in this lifetime is to empower more and more people to access their own intuitive capabilities. In my many years teaching The SAGE Method, I have witnessed myriad students start with no recognized abilities go on to hone their intuition to levels they would never have believed possible. That simple roadmap allowed them to shed what had been blocking their natural abilities. They see that they just needed to take the first steps to get them opened, amped, and flowing again. More of us can then guide ourselves and contribute to uplifting the collective energy as a whole.

When the masses regain their natural connection to Source, and it becomes a normal part of life once again, societal healing and true community will flourish. We are all truly connected and when we access that connection with our guides and members of our soul group, we have access to a higher perspective that allows us to make more life-supporting decisions. We can now enjoy being conscious, active participants in the creation of our own existence. And that, my friends, is pure fun!

While opening up hasn't always been a walk in the park, awakening to my expanded self has been worth every growing pain and bump along the way. Being a medium is a job I take very seriously. I love my job. I love what being open provides for me. The mediumship channel I have worked hard to hone allows me to do the work my "upstairs" team needs done down here so they can get the bigger picture work done up there. Opening to my abilities has also opened my heart to a new level of compassion. It is a compassion on a soul level that has completely changed my outlook on life and my opinion of others. It allows me to make decisions, not through a pushy, Type-A, human brain, but with confidence, through love.

I invite you, as well, to open to the possibilities that are very real and very much accessible to you. I invite you to say, "I can" to your own intuitive ability to embrace all of life, seen and unseen. I am proud to have you walking with me through this beautiful, interdependent life we have chosen. Cracking Open is just the beginning. You've got this.

Isabeau Maxwell (aka Beau)

Part I

Josephine

1

In the Beginning There Was Fear

I swept the white charcoal pencil across the black page. Grandma had been moved to hospice a few weeks earlier, while I was stuck fidgeting at home a thousand miles away. I filled the time sketching a portrait of her. As I placed the final details in the curls of her hair, the phone rang.

I picked it up to hear the voice of my mother on the other line. She was rushing to the hospice house. She had received word that Grandma wasn't going to last much longer and was frantically driving through traffic to get to her before she died.

"Honey, call them and tell them I'm on my way."

"Alright Mom. Drive safe," I responded, as I hung up the phone.

I was in my bedroom in New Hampshire, half a country away from where I wanted to be—by my grandmother's side, holding her small, plump hands as they squeezed all the blood out of my fingers. It was that special grip she had that reminded me how much she loved me. Words couldn't do justice to what her short little fingers could do. But there she lay in a hospice house in Minnesota, surrounded by a room full of family, all but my mother. My mother's relationship with the family wasn't a good one. Most of them refused to even speak to her—she had done things over the years to alienate them all. Although this family dynamic was often difficult for me, it worked in my favor this time because I was given the task to call the hospice house, and, as a result, one last chance to talk to my grandmother before she passed.

Looking for the number in my phone, I was struck by the realization of what exactly my grandmother had meant to me all these years. I felt incredibly blessed to have had her in my life. She was there through the toughest times, holding my head up and loving me for exactly who I was. I felt my face warm as I imagined her squeezing me with all four-foot ten-inches of her, telling me she was proud of me. She had always been my support, the maternal figure in my life that provided me with a precious, unconditional love no one else could.

Shaking, I dialed my Grandmother's room and counted the rings. With each ring, my heart sunk deeper and deeper into my chest. Two rings. Three rings. Four rings...

"Hello." The voice of my aunt answered.

"Glynda, my mom is on her way," I said.

"Okay, sweetie. I'm going to put the phone to Grandma's ear so you can say goodbye." Her voice was warm and soothing.

I sat silent for a moment as I listened to her broken breath. I was falling and knew the ground was coming up fast. Would I have enough time to say everything I wanted to say? I found myself speechless. I reached with my ears to grab on to any sounds I could pull from the other end of the line. The rattling coming from her throat was a sound I had heard described before but one I had never experienced. A part of me was crushed to hear it, and a part was overwhelmingly grateful. I felt connected to her—one last time—and I started to speak.

"Grandma, I love you. I love you so much. I'm going to miss you so much." I gulped. "You'll be alright. You're going to heaven. You're in good hands. I love you. I love you so much."

In these last moments, all I wanted was for her to be fearless. I knew that I had years to mourn, but she only had moments to be brave.

My aunt pulled the phone away and told me she loved me just before she hung up.

I set the phone down and stared at the clock on my nightstand hoping time would stand still. Hoping that by looking at it I could contain the tears that were quickly building up. The minute clicked over. My chest tightened and tears started to fall. My king-size bed felt huge as I curled up into the six fancy throw pillows to cry. I pictured myself at the store, picking out those pillows, spending a significant amount of time selecting such insignificant things.

After what seemed like a lifetime of crying, I pulled myself together and opened my bedroom door knowing I would have to explain to my young boys why my eyes were swollen and my nose was as bright as their favorite holiday reindeer. I thought about what it would be like to open the door and have the world back to the way it was an hour before. I wanted to pretend the last fifteen minutes didn't happen and life outside my bedroom was normal again. But this was not the case, not on this day. I wiped the sadness from my face and opened the door.

On the couch sat my two boys, Michael and Max. Despite my best attempts to appear content, as soon as they saw me they knew. My husband, Troy, and I had been expecting my grandmother's death and had talked to our children about it days before. Without a moment's hesitation, Max walked away from the television and Michael dropped his colored pencil. They both put aside what was happening in their lives to wrap themselves around me. For the first time in their lives they were strong for someone else. They were strong for me. I was flooded with pride as I knelt down beside them.

"We're sorry Mom," Michael said, holding my head.

"Yeah Mom. We're sorry your Grandma went away," Max added, patting me on the back.

I was overwhelmed. In this moment of pain and loss, here I was immersed in the arms of my sons. I soaked in their love until I was full.

Troy came home within minutes of my calling him.

"So," he paused gently, "I'll take the boys to the store to get some chocolate and wine for tonight and give you some time to be alone."

"Thank you." I paused and looked up at him as if I was a lost child. "What am I supposed to do now?"

"Get yourself on a plane. I'll work things out for the boys," he reassured me as he kissed me on my forehead.

The door shut behind them as they headed out to the store. There I stood in the corner of the living room, frozen, trying to decide if I wanted to curl up on the beige leather couch and cry, or busy myself with travel plans. I paused for a moment, decided not to decide, and instead listened to the silence. Taking in the enormity of the room at that moment, I felt isolated and alone. My security blanket—the woman who was my safe place through a challenging childhood—was now gone. I wanted time to stand still, to hold my position and never have to move again. With my legs locked below me and my mind fogging over, I was startled by a brilliant flash of blue in the center of the room.

My eyes snapped out of their daze and instantly found their way to the small frame of my Grandmother. Standing just ten feet away from me wearing her favorite blue oxford shirt, she beamed a smile so big I could barely see her eyes. Slightly transparent but clearly standing before me, she glowed with a brilliant light that seemed to come from within.

As quickly as she arrived, she was gone, leaving me terrified, shook, and alone once again in my living room. In that flash of a moment I was yanked out of reality as if an earthquake had woken me from a deep sleep. When it was over, warmth began to swell from my center, pouring out to my fingertips and surging through my face. I stumbled backwards and searched for the wall behind me. After fumbling across glass, framework, and molding, my fingertips found their way to the smooth sheetrock, pulling the rest of my body flat against it. Somehow it made me feel safe.

I inhaled deeply, working to get a full breath, and sputtered, "If that's you, don't do that again!"

Silence. Odd silence. A new type of silence I had never experienced before wrapped around me. Distinct, like the smell of a strong odor, the silence was deafening. I stared at the spot where her image had stood just seconds before and battled with myself over the possibility that it could have really been her, the warmth now sneaking out of my body as I became more aware of the room around me. I began to shake uncontrollably, my mind racing violently to rationalize the situation, telling myself that ghosts aren't real. But no matter what words I tried to convince my intellect, the rest of me wanted it to be real. The rest of me, the child in me, wanted that sensation to wrap itself around me again, break this new, uncomfortable silence and take me away from the pain. I slid down the wall landing on my back end as guilt rushed in. If it was truly her, had I just asked her to leave? I let the child take over and wished for one more moment with her.

In a quivering voice, I said out loud to the empty living room, "I'm sorry. I, um... I love you."

2

Heaven, Hell, and the Return Policy

After a horrible night's sleep, the next day came far too quickly. I knew I would be flying home to Minnesota but was unsure of what to pack. Never having lost someone so close to me, I didn't know what one wore for such an occasion. I was still shaken by last night's events and I felt awkward and out of sorts. I struggled with making any sort of decision.

Other than the suitcase, it seemed like a normal day. Max was lying on the bed telling jokes and making hand gestures as he stared at the ceiling. Michael was knee deep in my closet helping me pick out my shoes.

"All right boys, I think that will do for packing," I said, as I shut the suitcase and started to pull the zipper.

"Mom?" Michael asked.

"Yes, baby?" I turned to face him as he sat on the floor of my closet.

"Where is Grandma going?" he asked. "You know, now that she's... well... you know."

I saw Max sit up out of the corner of my eye, as if to pay attention to such an interesting question. "Well," I paused, "I'm not sure."

Figuring truth was the best way to go, I took a moment and collected my thoughts. With two boys on the edge of their seats waiting for my insight, it dawned on me I never really decided myself what I thought about the afterlife. The boys weren't used to church because, well, I simply didn't bring them. I always told them that their relationship with God was personal and they could talk to him anywhere, any day. "Even in the bathroom?" my son would ask. "Even in the bathroom, baby," I would wink.

They didn't have to step through special doors and see the sun through stained glass windows to touch God. I knew He was always with us. I had tried to protect them from the judgment of the church that I had experienced through my own life—the judgments and callousness that were imprinted in my brain from just a couple bad experiences.

The first of these experiences was late in my elementary school career. I had been working diligently to get confirmed in the Methodist Church, going every Wednesday after school to do the self-study program for kids my age. Studious, ambitious, and driven were words used to describe me over and over again. You wouldn't find me chatting in the Sunday School Room or playing ball out back. Instead, I was curled up in the resource room of the church, reading the assigned books, watching the videos, and filling out each workbook with vigor. Week after week, I studied hard and completed the program in record time. A two-year program, I completed it in one. Instead of monthly verbal exams, the Pastor was seeing me every other week as I answered the questions with confidence. I would glow each time with pride at my speedy achievement.

My last visit to the Pastor was my final exam. This was the day I learned that even people of the cloth are human. They are just like you and me—capable of judgment. They have uniforms, duties to perform, and faults. Unbeknownst to me, the Pastor had become frustrated with my pace of learning. When he looked at me he did not see a child. He saw someone who was trying to show him up and belittle the program he had worked so hard to put together.

After the Pastor asked me the last question of my final exam, he stared at me with disgust for what seemed like forever. I froze as his eyes bored into my head. He paced behind his ancient oak desk. He grunted and threw his hands in the air as if he was tossing papers he had just torn up. I could feel the tension in the room escalate. I was confused. I had never seen him act like this before. He was enraged and I was wishing I was anywhere but there.

"You know-it-all little brat," he said in a deep, cruel tone. His fists pressed into the top of his desk. With each word his voice grew louder. "No one finishes this program in this short of time. Who do you think you are?!" He began to pace again as he thought of what to say next.

"I will *always* know more than you," he said, pointing his finger at me. "Never forget it."

I quickly looked down at the worn rug below me, weeping as quietly as I could. All that time I was doing what I thought would make him proud, but I was wrong. To him, I was making a mockery of his Program. I was a threat, not a child.

I went to my Confirmation ceremony the following month and never returned.

Fourteen years later I reluctantly stepped into a church again, this time to baptize my son. The baptism was not my idea. My grandmother was adamant about getting each child blessed in this particular way. Personally, I had a hard time wrapping my head around baptism. The idea that an infant could die on a Tuesday when he was scheduled to be baptized on Wednesday, and end up in hell just because someone scheduled his baptism ceremony one day too late didn't sit well with me. Out of love for my grandmother, however, I booked the ceremony. For financial reasons, we were now living with my mom and dad in a rental house in Raleigh, North Carolina. Having left Minnesota to start anew, my husband was working for the local Coca-Cola Company stocking shelves to support us the best he could. With me not working, we needed to stay with my parents just to financially survive.

I found the denomination most familiar to me and reluctantly signed up as a member of the local Methodist Church. Being in an affluent area, it was a stunningly beautiful church with grand steps, intricate woodwork, and blood-red carpets. One of the first people we met was the Pastor. He asked us what we thought of his church and covered some of the basics about membership in their community. It all seemed straightforward until the last comment. He parted the front of his gown, reached his hand around to the backside of his khaki slacks, and patted his wallet as it rested in his back pocket. "Most importantly, don't forget to support," he said with a wink.

Awkwardly smiling at this odd gesture, I nodded, and my husband and I took turns shaking his hand. We walked away looking quizzically at each other and speaking under our breath.

"Did he really just say that?" I asked Troy out of the corner of my mouth.

"Yep," he responded. "Not very subtle, hey?"

We left that day and returned the next Sunday for the baptism. It was a beautiful day and a beautiful ceremony. All seemed well until six weeks later when we received a bill in the mail from the church. Not for the baptism, but because we said we could donate a certain weekly amount on the application for membership in the church. They billed us for the difference because we couldn't always afford that much.

Less than an hour after I received the bill, I burst into the front doors of the church offices. Two babies in tow, I stormed into the large reception area to find a tiny secretary rigidly clicking away at her typewriter. With Michael sitting comfortably on my left hip, my right hand released the soft grip of the stroller and handed her the bill. I demanded to see the monthly financial report for the church and waited as a reluctant receptionist handed the statements over for my review. I discovered the Pastor not only made more than $60,000 per year (in 1998 dollars) but he received perks, too. He had a car allowance. A house allowance. Even a vacation allowance. Allowance! Man! I hadn't heard that word since I was a kid! I dropped the paperwork slowly and my eyes peered over it to look at the receptionist once more. I carefully calculated what I would say before I spoke.

"The Pastor of this church makes three time what my husband and I do," I stated.

"That may be, my dear, but that doesn't mean you don't give to the very church you're a member of," the receptionist said arrogantly as she tapped her desk with a boney pointer finger, the sound raking in my ears like an antique clock.

"But my husband and I can't even afford to pay our own bills right now," I said.

"Yet you live in this neighborhood," she said, an attempt to be witty and obviously not believing me.

"Yes, as a matter of fact, we do. We live with my parents because we can barely afford diapers!" I was getting more and more angry. "Can the church help me? Can this very church give to those in need? Because if it can, I am in need!" Now it was my finger rapping on her desk.

"It doesn't work that way my dear," she stated, and returned to her work at the typewriter. Click, clack, click, clack, ding.

I left with yet another piece of religious education.

As my children helped me close my suitcase, I reflected on both experiences. I could see how they were designed to help me decipher the difference between spirituality and religion. As a child, I learned judgment was indeed something you could find in the church. As an adult, I learned to see the church as a business, plain and simple. In my heart, I knew there was more to spirituality than judgment or money. I just hadn't found it yet. It was like knowing that in the front of the airplane is the VIP section—you just can't see it. Most people never get out of coach. Myself? Well, I vowed I was going to get out of coach if it was the last thing I did.

This new experience of grief I now faced sparked a desire in me to find the truth. That desire was like a seed, ready to burst open deep inside me, and Grandma's death cracked it open. Yes, my kids were asking me questions. They wanted answers. But now, as I stood there reviewing my half-hearted spiritual path and draping the new pain of losing my grandmother over my shoulders, I needed to know. I needed to know what is on the otherside. I needed to know she was alright.

I took a deep breath before I spoke to my boys. "Okay kiddos. I'm going to do my best to explain this to you but in the end, you have to make your own decisions. Remember, Mommy doesn't have all the answers."

They looked on in silence, waiting for some sort of amazing explanation.

I continued. "There are millions and millions of people in this world and they are from all different types of religions. All religions have a higher power they worship. Some have more than one, and they all have different ideas about what happens to people after they die. The idea you believe in depends on what religion you are."

At this point I knew I had lost them. I smiled and said, "Let's make it easier."

I thought for a minute. I only really understood two of the major religious beliefs on death, so I went with what I knew.

"Anyhow, there are a couple basic ideas out there on what happens to you when you die. One is that you either go to heaven or hell. You both know what hell is, right?"

"Yep," Michael piped in, and Max nodded.

"Okay. So, idea number one is that when you die, depending on how good of a person you were when you were alive, you either go to heaven or hell. Idea number two is that when you die you come back again and again as new people trying to make yourself a better person each time until you finally become the best person you can be," I explained.

The boys took a moment to absorb what I said. Heck, I took a moment to absorb it myself. I had never put it that simply.

"Mom, the first one sounds really silly. I thought God loved everyone. If he loved everyone, then who's in hell? Nobody, right?"

"Well, like I said, it's just a belief."

"But Grandma is a good person. She's in heaven then," Max stated.

Just then, Michael interjected. "Maybe she's in heaven or maybe she's already back here with that return policy thing."

I laughed. I had never heard reincarnation explained as a return policy. I imagined people lining up at the Grand Universe Customer Service counter, complaining about what went wrong and how they wanted a new life that is better than the last one.

"Again," I stressed, "these are just ideas. It's up to you to decide what you believe."

"Well, I believe that Grandma is up there in heaven with stuffed animals that play music," Max said.

Max had a connection with Grandma through stuffed animals. They both loved them so. I choked up at the memory of him sitting on her lap playing with a bear that sang a happy tune.

"I believe," Michael said dramatically, as he stood up on my bed like Superman, "that she will be back, and soooooon."

He paused just then with that look on his face he gets when his brain is working really hard. Max and I waited. Michael was compiling another thought and we knew it never helped to interrupt that process with him.

The thought came together and out his lips. "But why would she come back to try to be a better person if she was already awesome?"

"Well," I thought about this for a second, "even though Grandma was awesome she still had little things to work on."

"Okay," Michael said, "so she's probably just coming back one more time."

"I'll go with you on that one, baby," I confirmed, with all the warmth of my heart.

"One more question then," Michael said. "When do we see her again, you know, when is she back?"

I chuckled at the idea. "She won't come back as Grandma, honey. She'll come back as someone else. Maybe even in a different country all together. Could be a boy or a..."

"Wait," Max interrupted. "So the second idea is the real one? People come back?"

"No, no, that's not what I meant," I explained. "I was just talking more about one particular idea. I wasn't saying that was the idea I believed in."

Then came the inevitable question, "What do you believe, Mom?" Max asked.

"I'm not sure baby." I was honest. "I'm still trying to figure that out for myself."

"Pretty complicated mumbo jumbo," Max said. "Why do people not all think the same? They make it too hard."

"Yep, you've got that one right. There's a lot of people out there that believe their way is the only way," I stated. "You want to know one thing that I do believe?"

They both nodded and focused in tight on my eyes.

"I believe that life is like a big mountain, and heaven or Nirvana or whatever you want to call it is at the top of the mountain. Each person gets to the top; they just start in different places."

I paused for a moment to let them think this over. "If you follow someone else," I started again, "then you will never know if the path you're on is the path that God made for you. The path that is made for you is the one that feels right. For now, all you have to worry about is that at the top of that mountain we will all be together, and we will all be happy."

"Hey!" Max shouted, "Grandma climbed a mountain!" An image popped into my head of my adorable little Grandma reaching the summit and I smiled.

3

Physically and Mentally Flying

I zipped up the last bag and told the boys to go to the kitchen and figure out what they wanted for dinner. I took one deep breath and felt a tiny speck of courage, much more than I had an hour ago. Talking to the boys helped me start processing my thoughts. The innocent conversation between mother and sons got my emotional train back on the tracks toward peace. I knew I would eventually have to come to some conclusion about the afterlife, even if it was just for me to be able to completely let her go. Analysis and complete knowledge of topics always brought me comfort and I knew my grief would be more manageable with deeper understanding.

As I rounded the corner to the kitchen, I noticed Troy sitting at the dining room table along with stacks of cans, boxes, and bread. The boys decided to take me very seriously about picking out dinner and were placing all their options on the table before they made their choice.

"Hey, honey," said Troy. "Ready to go?"

"Nope," I declared like a petulant child, even though my bags were packed.

We finished dinner, loaded the car with my bags, and headed out to the airport. Numbness set in. Having spent the last twenty-four hours crying, this new state of mind gave me a weird sense of calm. I struggled with the vision of my grandmother standing in my living room just the night before. I hadn't told Troy about my experience of seeing her yet, which was unlike me. Instead of talking, I stewed. What did it really mean?

I'm crazy?

It was stress?

My head invented it?

Wait! A memory interrupted my pesky thoughts and stretched around to uncover something long forgotten. I flashed back to the moment when I had seen my great grandmother, many, many years after she had passed away.

I was eight years old, playing with my cousin Molly on my grandmother's living room carpet. I decided to climb the large open staircase in the middle of the house to the upstairs bedroom. What reason I had to go upstairs I still can't recall. As my head bobbed up over the three-foot-tall upstairs banister, I stopped short when I found an older woman sitting at the edge of the bed, rolling a stocking up her leg. She smiled at me, I quickly apologized, and I bolted back down the stairs landing in front of my grandmother.

"There was a woman up there," I said, pointing up toward the top of the stairs.

"Who is up there?" Grandma asked me.

"I don't know. Some old lady getting dressed."

"Ah," said Grandma, "don't worry. That's just my mom." And the three of us went on as if nothing unusual had happened. I didn't get all the answers I wanted about the strange woman at the top of the stairs, but there was a part of me that was content enough to forget.

The memory left as quickly as it came and I was instantly thrown back into the irritating piles of negative thoughts.

What if it was real?

What are people going to think if I tell them?

What if no one believes me?

The battle raged—between logic, my close and dear friend, and faith, my distant cousin who tiptoed through the tulips. If I give in to the idea that my grandmother was really standing in front of me, doesn't that make me a freak? Me, the math major, the scientific, proof-needing, debate winner? I was raised to achieve, to become "worthy." Wouldn't saying I saw a ghost make me one of "the crazy people"?

"Honey?" I spoke quietly.

"You're going to think I am nuts. Heck, I think I am." I started to rattle on aimlessly. "I'm pretty sure it was just my emotions playing tricks on me. I can't be crazy. It's just stress. Dealing with something like this is bound to make someone..."

"Beau," he interrupted me.

"Sorry," I paused. "All right, here it is. I think I saw Grandma last night."

"What?" He seemed thrown.

"I saw Grandma. Right in the living room. Right there. Like right there."

I paused and gathered myself the best I could. "I'm telling you, I think my head is playing serious tricks on me. I don't want to go through this. It's making me feel crazy."

"What would you say if I told you I had a *very* realistic dream last night and she was in it?" he asked quietly.

I stared out my window, "I'm not sure what I would say."

We drove in silence for the next couple miles, negative thoughts echoing in my head again, this time like brokers shouting on the New York Stock Exchange floor. After a few mile markers had passed, I quieted my mind and settled on the easier of the two possible conclusions, that it was indeed the power of our emotions that caused our brains to generate images of her.

Okay, fine. I felt calmer. Letting go of an idea as silly as a ghost manifesting in front of me felt refreshingly safe, like cleaning your house from top to bottom before company arrives.

"You know," I started to speak again, "the whole idea that it was really her is ludicrous. I feel much better getting back to the task at hand. This whole 'someone died and I feel like crap' stuff is enough to deal with without adding crazy talk to it."

"Yeah, you're probably right. I can see how an event like this could play tricks on you. Good idea to regain some focus," he said. "I gotta tell ya though. It was kind of cool how easy it was to recognize her in my dream. She was wearing that blue shirt of hers that I always saw her in. You know, her favorite one."

Blue shirt? Troy's words were already fuzzy in my mind. Did he say blue shirt? I sat motionless. My brain was back to battling itself. I could feel myself split down the middle like a freshly axed piece of wood. One side—the rational side—was doing its best to belittle my experiences and chalk them off as childish and emotional. The other side—the newly awakened, creative side—was jumping with excitement at the possibility she may not be completely gone. I reveled in my creative side because somehow it felt better. She may still be here with me, not lost to the worms, not absent for the remainder of my life. If I could still see her, even possibly hear her, I would be alright, and the pain wouldn't be so deep.

I decided to stay silent for the rest of the drive and shake all the images and thoughts from my mind. I wanted to get back to the comfortable feeling of numb.

My three gallant men walked me to the security gate at the airport, carrying my travel gear for me. As I kissed each of them, I could feel a bit more of the numbness wearing off. It was replaced by a fear of flying. Not for myself, but for them. There was a new heightened awareness of death for me now. Images ran rapidly through my head of my boys getting the news that their mom had died in a fiery plane crash. I shook the thoughts off the best I could, hugged and kissed them with everything I had, and proceeded to my assigned gate.

On the plane I got a window seat and immediately pulled out two magazines I had brought with me. It was a three-hour flight and I was not about to socialize with the person who was sitting beside me. After mixed nuts, a plastic cup of Sprite, and pages of magazine articles, I felt my mind wandering. Thoughts began to come in with a force I was not familiar with, and, oddly, could not stop. Pictures of my grandmother started to flash, moments in time flickering as if my mind had become a movie screen two feet in front of me. I tried to think about something else—anything else—but the visions just kept coming. The images were clearly more than memories. They seemed lifelike, real, and playing outside me. I closed my eyes and embraced the darkness inside my lids, but I knew the visions were still out there, rolling like a film. I gave in. Opening my eyes again, I clenched my fist and allowed myself to fall into the scenes unfolding before me. There she was, my grandmother. I could see her smile. I could see the weave of the cloth in her shirt. I could even smell the fabric softener as I watched her hug me tight. She always used five or six sheets of fabric softener in every load of laundry. There were many nights I crashed at her house, and I would dry off after the next morning's hot shower with a water-resistant towel that was coated in slick fabric softener.

I continued to watch as memories and moments flickered across my mental screen. I watched each of them intently. Soon, however, my numbness began to sink into the background like an unloyal friend. My eyes blurred and tears overflowed in a fashion I wasn't ready for. They were unstoppable. I couldn't keep from watching the visions if I wanted to. I was helpless. In my seat, I could feel someone wrap around me but could not see them. Even more unnerving, I could feel the invisible person's emotions, a cloud of love and protection mixed with sadness and urgency—urgency to stop the visions, as if they knew I had seen all I could handle. The mental screen faded away, reality crept back, and the curtains of my creative mind closed.

I felt a sudden impulse to move. I turned to look at the woman seated next to me and she instantly moved to open a path to the center aisle. Words were not spoken, but she seemed to see my gratitude as she looked into my eyes. I struggled to the rear of the plane, bumping into the sides of seats as I raced to the bathroom. I sighed in relief at the Vacant sign on the door and pushed into the small cabinet. Locking it behind me, I looked into the mirror and gasped for breath between painful, heaving sobs. I pressed my right hand onto the mirror as I braced myself with my left on the tiny sink. The plane was cruising through the air effortlessly, yet I was grabbing onto anything I could to hold myself up. I had never felt so alone.

I hadn't expected this reaction. I am not a crier. I was taught it was better to pull yourself up by your bootstraps because crying is for the weak. Yet, one moment I'm reading about designer doghouses, and the next I could barely stand. I thought of all the people that had passed through my life with stories of death. I thought of all the times I held their hands and said I didn't know how they felt but that I was there for them. I was pissed that I now knew how they felt.

The rest of the flight was like slow movement through warm water. Upon arrival, I schlepped myself through the airport to the baggage return. As I watched piece after piece of luggage creep around the caterpillar-like structure, I grumbled at the idea of putting effort into anything at this point. My mother was coming to bring me to the casino hotel where she was staying. I would have chosen to stay at my cousin Molly's house, but Mom bribed me with a hotel room to myself, her treat. Room service sounded better than socializing.

Dragging my luggage behind me, I headed out the doors to where my mother would pick me up. I found a bench to sit on and took a deep breath, hoping to fill my lungs with something fresh after the long plane ride. Instead all I got was a deep fill of cigarette smoke. "Perfect," I thought. I looked around at the ten or so people huddled around ashtrays built into trashcans, puffing away as if the hours on a plane separated them from a long-lost friend.

One man in particular caught my eye. His hands were shaking, his skin wrinkled and discolored. His cough sounded like a motorboat engine that wouldn't turn over. Each hack an effort to expel the heavy crud that sat in his lungs. I looked at the details of his face and saw something that was straight out of a science fiction film.

He began to morph right before my eyes. I could see him standing there, yet I could also see him somehow fading away. I watched as familiar features came into focus. I saw the cheeks and nose of my grandmother forming in front of me. I had never experienced this type of mind trick before and I wasn't about to stop it. I didn't care what I looked like or who was staring at me. All I cared about was grasping onto another moment with her that was so very real. I refused to let it go, even if it was painful. His face turned from manly and thin to feminine and round. The old smoker's entire image shifted into the body of my seventy-nine-year-old grandmother. I again saw her wearing her favorite blue shirt. She was looking right at me but this time she wasn't smiling. She was coughing and started to hunch over in pain. I felt my heart rip inside my chest.

This new event—this lifelike movie—played out in front of me. I was now seeing her the way I last saw her alive—just weeks before she died. At her bedside, I spent hours talking with her while she was awake and sitting in painful silence as she slept, watching nurses come and go, hour after hour, sticking her with needles, putting medication in her eyes, and cleaning her.

"They think I don't know," Grandma said to me, as she rolled her eyes at the candy dish filled with sugar-free chocolates on the table next to her. "That's a bunch of crap."

"I know Grandma," I said with a smile.

The candy dish reminded me of what was killing her. It was a rebuttal to the purse filled with chocolate Ho-Hos held tightly to her side as she entered the hospital. She knew they wouldn't let her have "her sugar", but she packed it anyway. You could search Grandma's house any day of the week and find candy and sweets hidden anywhere and everywhere. Sugar isn't as "pop culture" a death as cigarettes or vodka, but it still killed her. Standing in the hallway as she lay in the next room, I listened to doctors describe the last stages of diabetes. They explained neuropathy and how it shuts down a person's organs. Grandma was decaying, her body slowly melting from the inside out.

Physically she was failing. Emotionally she was struggling. Spiritually, she was terrified of death. A devout Catholic with a history of breaking the Catholic rules, she never missed a Sunday, but she never honored Lent either. Or rather, she often invented her own rules, saying old people were allowed to do that. And now, there she lay, worried that the broken rules were catching up to her and struggling with the idea that she may not make it to the Big Gates promised to those who are perfect. In all the years she attended her church, not one parishioner visited her in these last hours. Only the priest had come, to ceremoniously absolve her of all her sins. It didn't soothe her fear. There she lay, weak and scared and it tore me apart.

It was this horrible thought that shook me from my trance. The reality of the airport pushed back in and the coughing was once again coming from the old man with horrible skin. I looked around and quickly wiped the tears that soaked my cheeks. My heart was racing, and I was dumfounded by what had just happened to me. Why did I see that? What was the purpose? Why was it so incredibly clear?

A voice I had never heard before went off inside my head. A stranger's voice that was deep, calm, and purposeful. "Your addiction will kill you," it said.

I looked around for the source knowing I wouldn't find one. I looked down at my legs. The biggest they had ever been, I was weighing in at 285 pounds. I needed to distract myself. I decided to call my mother to see if she was running on-time and I opened my purse to find my phone. As I dug through the clutter, the first thing my hand fell upon was a Hershey's bar.

Seconds later, mother's rental car pulled up and she climbed out to greet me. There I sat, candy bar in hand, looking stunned.

"Hellllooooo?" Mom asked as she waived her hand in front of my face. "Anyone in there?"

"Yeah," I said as I looked up. "Sorry, I was lost in thought."

"I understand. This is really hard. Let's get you back to the hotel."

As I got up to leave, I tossed the candy bar into the trashcan. I didn't need it anymore.

The night flew by way too quickly. Before I knew it, the sun was up, and it was time to head to the Church. This was the first time I ever had to attend the funeral of someone I truly loved. I made my way down to the hotel lobby where my best friend from high school, Jessica, picked me up. Jessica had been my closest friend since we were twelve. Driving down the long highway in her green Taurus, I could tell that she wasn't herself.

"You okay?" I asked.

"Huh," she sighed. "Yeah, I'm just trying to keep it together."

We shared many memories of my grandmother. Numerous times Grandma would take Jessica and me to a movie and sing songs during the show just to embarrass us. We would all laugh until we got kicked out. Grandma loved her like a granddaughter too. It made perfect sense. Jessica and I were inseparable. Grandma got two granddaughters for the price of one.

I had written a poem the night before and decided to read it to Jessica to see if she thought it was fitting or not. She had attended more funerals than I had and at this moment I was feeling awkward about speaking.

"I wrote a poem," I said.

"Really? That is so sweet," she said, as she reached over to the passenger side of the car and patted me on the knee. I could feel her genuineness.

"Here it goes." I cleared my throat and took a deep breath. It took strength to read it out loud, but I struggled through it the best I could.

Gumdrops, toads and witty replies
These are the things I'll miss most
Singing songs and unconditional love
These are the things I'll hold close
When I take time to reminisce
I'll picture your devilish grin
And remember the thousands of games of cribbage
Where I would lose and you would win
I will hold my memories close

As I look back and remember when
You would sing to me
"Kiss me once and kiss me twice
and kiss me once again"
I remember the way you would hold me
With your grip so strong
Loving me and not caring
Whether I'm right or I'm wrong
I thank you Grandma and promise
The one thing I'll do
Is pass on to my children
How not to judge and to just be you
I'll do my best to say goodbye
With warmth in my heart and a smile
Saying "See you later alligator
After a while crocodile"

I folded the paper up and wiped the tears from my cheeks. I turned to Jessica for her opinion but stopped short. Tears were falling from her eyes too.

"So," Jessica said, after minutes of silence, "this isn't going to be easy, but you know you'll make it through."

"Yeah. I don't have a choice," I grumbled.

We pulled into the parking lot of the church. We were one of the first to arrive. The numbness came back. It seemed as if pain and numbness were taking turns keeping me balanced so I could do what I had to do to get through the event.

I walked through the heavy, wooden doors and immediately started killing time by greeting family members. I did my best to avoid the grand sanctuary that contained my grandmother's dead body, a body I last saw alive. I was scared to see her in any other fashion.

After a brief period of awkwardly roaming the entryway, I saw my cousin Molly and a sense of comfort came over me. Molly symbolized safety to me. She always took care of me like a big sister would, modeling Grandma in her capacity to love me unconditionally. We hugged, and she immediately pushed her arm through mine as if she was preparing to walk me down the aisle at a wedding. She turned us toward the coffin and I knew where we were headed. She pulled me into the sanctuary and we stood at the back of the sea of pews looking down on the red-carpeted stage where Grandma lay. The coffin was open, but from such a distance I couldn't see her. Of all those attending that day, Molly was the only one who knew how to handle me and what I would need. Putting her own emotions aside she led me off that big scary edge looming in front of me. I was terrified and she knew it. She smiled her nurturing smile, held me tight to her side, and walked me toward the coffin. I felt lost. The ceiling was fifty feet up and the pews were uncountable. It took forever to walk to the edge of the casket.

My eyes focused in on my grandmother's face. I was taken aback by what I saw. The person that lay before me only slightly resembled the woman I held so close to my heart. Instead, it looked more like a suit of skin that she once wore. I gave Molly a puzzled look.

"Yep," she said, "she's not in there."

"She looks silly," I said, "like it's not her."

I couldn't pull my eyes off my grandmother. There was truly a difference between a person's body and spirit. Her body looked like a shell. Someone that used to be. Like something someone takes off when they're done with it. I pictured her pulling the zipper down the back of her body and her soul floating out. A wave of odd physical sensations violently shot through me. It started at my head and raced all the way through to the base of my feet. It was goosebumps. Ice rushing through my veins. Falling off the top of a skyscraper. Surprised, I braced myself on the dark oak that encased my grandmother and centered myself the best I could, brushing it off as anxiety. Before I walked away from the coffin, I made sure to touch her hand very lightly, just enough to feel the cold that had settled into her body. One more piece of proof she was gone.

I gathered myself up and took a seat in the second pew to wait for the service to start. Soon, I found myself surrounded, in long, oak pews, by all those who watched me grow up. I sat next to my grandfather, Poppy. Grandma and Poppy had split a few years earlier. Not because they had fallen out of love, but because they had gone in two different directions in their lives. He was there the day she died, holding her hand and weeping in pain. The love they had was deep and I could feel it as I sat next to him. Person after person rose to speak, all speaking of her incredible ability to love. Here we were, a family of screw-ups. Among the pews sat alcoholics, abusers, and the rest of us who were equally messed up psychologically in some way or another, including myself. Yet everyone was here to honor and give thanks to this incredible woman who could make you feel good about yourself no matter what you did or what road you chose to take. We were better people because of her.

I rose for my turn to speak and felt the knot in my stomach tighten. Standing beside her yet again on the red-carpeted stage, I began to read. Halfway through my poem I could feel my knees start to shake and my throat tighten up. Within moments, Molly was there beside me, holding me and helping me to get through reading this last gift to my grandmother. I started to feel not so alone anymore.

After the service, the family gathered for food and conversation in the church's community room. I selected a wimpy turkey sandwich and piled my plate with my favorite comfort food, cookies. Weaving through the tables, I again felt an unnerving sensation rip through my body, this time coupled with a familiar smell. It smelled like my grandmother. She had a distinct scent that every family member knew. It reminded us of home. As my brain tried to wrap itself around the powerful aroma that appeared to come from nowhere, the physical sensation I had felt earlier wove through my body yet again. This time I didn't need to anchor myself. I felt stronger. I forgot about eating, set my food down on the closest table, and made a direct line toward Molly.

"Molly?" I whispered.

"Yeah, kiddo?" she replied.

"I'm feeling some weird things. I swear I can smell Grandma and I'm having goose bumps, but not regular goose bumps." I could see that nurturing smile slowly come over Molly's face, so I continued. "They're like goosebumps gone crazy, mixed with ice running through me, and to top it off, it feels like I'm falling off a damn cliff, all at once."

"Grandma's here, sweetie," she said, as if it was no big deal.

"What?" I asked, in disbelief.

"She's here." She paused to let me absorb before she continued. "Like I said earlier, she's not in that body anymore. Can't you feel her? She's been talking to me all day. I saw her the day she died standing in the garden at the hospice. Face it, kiddo, she's communicating with you."

"Crap," I thought to myself. This makes it real. Clearly, we are all on the same psycho trip.

"What the heck are you saying? Are you saying that's what the sensations are?" I asked her.

"Yeah," she said, "they're like a rush type thing, right?"

"Yeah," I said with relief.

"That's her," she said. "Come on. Do you really believe she wouldn't be hanging out, nosing around to see what people are saying? She's probably touching everyone. You know she has a big enough heart to do it."

"I'm just having a hard time wrapping my head around it. I know there was talk here and there growing up about Grandma seeing her dead mother, and I know you said you saw things as a child. But I haven't, and I'm not sure what's happening to me. It's one thing to see someone but it's another to feel things. Either way, I think I've lost my damn mind! Did you smell that smell?" I asked her.

"How could you not?" she smiled again and chuckled. "Tell me something. Is there any other smell that you could possibly smell that would identify her so strongly?"

"No. That's for sure."

We laughed, and I felt the sensation yet again. This time it came more gently, with a touch of joy. I was absorbing the validations from my cousin.

For the rest of the gathering I could imagine her floating from person to person, curious to see what they were thinking and doing. I could feel in my heart that she was truly enjoying "her special day."

It didn't take long for me to realize that the more I pictured her the more that amazing feeling came over me, the sensation that would rush through me like water. The pain of her passing was deep, like a dark hole I wanted to crawl out of, and these sensations, which I began to call the "Connection," were helping ease the pain.

Over the next few days the smell came less frequently but the physical sensations remained strong. I let my heart believe it was her and fought the urges to throw out the experiences as nothing more than chance or hallucination. On the plane trip home, during one of those irritating urges to brush off my recent experiences as coincidence, I decided to test out the sensations. Heck, I thought, there was no reason I couldn't talk to her anytime I wanted, right? If it was her and I wasn't crazy, she would hear me and respond.

Thus began two very crazy years in which I teeter-tottered between hope and faith and doubt and fear. The scientist in me needed to test it. I wanted her to prove to me this was real. My grief strengthened my resolve and I wanted it to be real. I needed it to be real. With desperation and determination, I sat on the plane longing for proof like a child at Christmas and closed my eyes to focus on the memory of her face. I began with one question, the question I felt was the most logical. "Grandma, are you there?"

A rush poured through me. Icy tingles raged through my body. I waited for the feeling to subside and asked another question.

"Grandma, can you see me?"

It happened again—the Connection! I took a deep breath and figured I'd shoot for a "no" response and see what happened.

"Grandma, is your name Fred?"

Nothing. I sat and waited. And, nothing. The familiar sound of silence returned. Not only was it nothing, there was a hint of true emptiness to it, like wind whistling through an empty street. So empty, in fact, I felt the urge to ask a "yes" question just so I didn't feel so desperately alone.

"Okay. If it's you, Grandma, can you tell me if I'm flying to New Hampshire?"

The Connection came again, the tears now swelled, rolling down my chin, and I quickly turned my face to the window for a moment to compose myself. I wanted so much to believe. The last lingering issue for me with the Connection was that she was answering questions I already knew the answers to. Can I trick myself out of desperation? Am I creating this "Connection" to avoid the very real fact that my grandmother was gone and I had no one left to watch over me? I needed to stop "playing" and I needed to grieve.

I needed to slow down for a while and think. While I wanted to race forward and cross that "I can communicate with Grandma" finish line like a crazed race car driver, I knew that I needed to give myself space and, most importantly, time.

Still, I returned home from the funeral and my life as I knew it would never be the same. My eyes had been opened and I could no longer live life half awake.

Blowing Up Cars

Autumn rolled on and the school year began once again for my two sons. The boys were homeschooled and at times I found it was difficult to balance my mom hat, my teacher hat, and still find time to be myself. Thus, I signed up for martial arts at a local dojo. The Tai Chi instructor, Chris Bashaw, would turn out to be my first—and most significant—spiritual teacher. I signed up for this class to get physically healthy. Little did I know it would dramatically affect the path I had started to walk.

During my first few weeks with my newly found teacher I was introduced to the idea that people had energy fields. I quickly became intrigued by this something he talked about called Reiki, a healing method from the East. As he spoke, it seemed like an interesting stretch of reality. My naive understanding was that Reiki was a way to heal the body just by waiving your hands over someone. No pills, no doctors, just moving "energy." Through the class I learned all living people have an energetic body. Around and within each person's physical being is energy. There are channels like a subway system—tracks that are the carriers of the trains (energy). When things go wrong physically with a person, the energy has stopped moving, like a train getting stuck on the track. Someone who uses Reiki puts the train back on the track and gets it moving again.

I admit, taking the class was mostly just to prove my grandmother's visits (which were happening more frequently) were real. My secret communication with Grandma was already out of the box as far as "normal" goes, and I figured if I could find the most crackpot idea and prove to myself it's true, then maybe I wasn't crazy after all. It would be a newfound freedom, a license to reexamine all that defined me up to this point. Everything I thought I knew about myself was now up for grabs, to be explored, rediscovered, and discarded if necessary.

After my martial arts class one night I talked to Chris about joining a Reiki class at his personal dojo in the next town over. I downloaded the workbook he emailed me and studied for two weeks before participating.

The night of the class arrived, and I pulled up in front of the dojo. There was a sand and rock garden in the front window, with water fountains and photos of martial artists. I stepped through the front door and felt a cozy, comforting feeling come over me. I instantly felt at home and found a spot on the aged carpet to settle onto. From the moment Chris started to lecture on the history of Reiki, I was captivated. This healing method sounded exotic and foreign. It made me question the techniques of Western medicine. It made me think of the body in a whole new way.

The class progressed and everyone had a chance to ask questions. I was surprised that many of the questions I had written down in preparation for the class were being asked by fellow students. Turns out, I wasn't the only skeptic. You could tell by his responses that Chris had quite a bit of knowledge on that topic and there wasn't much that could throw him. He talked about the different religions of the East and West, about secret societies, and about what it really meant to believe and have faith.

As I listened to his answers, I could feel information start to meld together into a ball that I could almost grasp. I learned many interesting facts that night. I learned that perspective is in the eye of the beholder and that just because I was raised a certain way does not mean all other cultures are wrong. No one person is right or wrong. They are just living their own reality whether they are closed to it or open, which was a completely new idea for me. The statement that stuck with me the most in Chris' class was that each person should listen to new information and ideas, take from it what most resonates with them, and leave the rest. "Take what works and leave the rest," I said to myself. I like it. It was an interesting way to approach being open-minded, and I found myself ignited with excitement and a new longing to learn about the unexplained and the misunderstood. A little bit of my previous hesitation had melted away.

We finished the night with a ceremony called "The Attunement". The Reiki Master, Sensei Chris, performed a ceremony to "attune" each of us to Reiki energy. It is this process that allows us to tap into the energy, channel it, and use it for healing. I had asked to be attuned to both the first and second (of three) levels of Reiki, and my teacher agreed, saying it takes time to develop before a person is ready to attune to the last level. I sat in a chair with my eyes closed as the teacher performed the ceremony. Ten minutes passed with some simple hand gestures and much silence. When it was done, I was asked if I had felt anything, but I had not. A little disappointed, I wrapped up the night, thanked Sensei, collected my books, and headed home.

Two days later I was driving through downtown Portsmouth admiring the different walks of life that frequented the popular city. The boys and I were heading to my favorite Starbucks to get my usual Chai Tea Latte when the lights on the dashboard of my car suddenly became very bright, with a hum that rose and fell with the changing intensity of those lights. This unique light show continued for several seconds, then it was over. I brushed it off as an old car being an old car and parked at a nearby meter. Michael jumped out, popped in a dime, and we went into Starbucks.

Five minutes later the boys and I climbed back into our Trooper and I stuck the key into the ignition. I turned the key. Silence. It was completely dead. I sat puzzled, collecting my thoughts, figuring out my game plan. I turned around to look at my boys, both of whom had cookies in hand, getting smaller by the minute.

Flipping my cell phone open, I called AAA to have them tow the car to our regular mechanic, all the while wondering how big the dollar sign would be on the repair bill this time. They picked it up in no time and the boys and I decided to wait for Troy to rescue us after his shift was done. Troy eventually came and the boys gave him the exciting details of our adventure.

The next afternoon an accumulation of small things led to a sense of frustration. Bizarrely hot for a fall day, I cranked up the air conditioner in our small apartment to the highest it would go, hoping to reduce the sticky effect our leather couch had on my thighs. Before I could walk away, it spit at me and shut down completely, refusing to turn back on regardless of my efforts. Now what? I set up a fan and got out some clippers to shave both of my sweaty boys' heads. I buzzed away at Michael's head. With three quarters complete, the clippers quit. I clicked them on and off, fiddled with the cord, and even banged it on the floor. Nothing worked; they were done. Flustered at an uncooperative day, I cleaned up the mess and plopped down on that adhesive seat we called a couch. Attempting to find inner silence, I instead found outer silence when the fan next to me ground slowly to a stop. There I sat, hot, frustrated, and electronically stumped by three everyday objects. I crashed early that night hoping the next day would bring cooler weather.

A couple days later, I took Troy's F-250 truck to a restaurant to meet some friends for dinner while Troy walked to the repair shop to pick up my newly fixed car. After a relaxing night with wonderful company, my usual craving kicked in and I pulled into yet another Starbucks to get my Chai Tea Latte. As I turned the corner into the parking lot, I witnessed another dashboard light show just like the one in my car a few days earlier. After Starbucks, I climbed back into the beast of a truck and I turned the key and heard nothing. No engine clicks. No hum. Nothing. Another vehicle dead.

I called Troy, who in turn called the towing company to have his truck taken to the same place my car was fixed. He arrived with the boys, trying to smile but clearly frustrated. Troy seemed to grasp the situation before I did.

"Long time no see!" yelled the tow truck guy, as he climbed out to assess our situation.

"Yep. I'm starting to wonder if I should let her drive at all," Troy said jokingly, trying to lighten the mood while the repair bills were adding up in the back of his head.

Standing beside him, I wrapped my hand around Troy's arm, extending a laugh and an empty apology. I expressed how ironic it was that both cars would go within such a short time. Troy, on the other hand, seemed to know.

"Beau," Troy said, as he watched the tow truck pull the F-250 up onto its bed, "don't you wonder why things quit working with you?"

"Haven't thought about it," I responded.

"Listen," he said, smiling as he looked at me out of the corner of his eye, "your chai and your chi both have to go."

"Nice," I said.

"I'm just sayin'," he responded, as his hand slid down my arm and his fingers wove into mine.

"I'll call Ed," I responded, understanding what he was implying. I hadn't thought of it, but it might be more than just a coincidence that so many things in such a short time have decided they don't want to work for me. If anyone could tell me for sure it would be Ed Hubbell, my acupuncturist.

Acupuncture was another one of those things that my inner skeptic wasn't sure of until I tried it for myself. Months earlier, I was suffering from a lower back pain and went to Ed for a treatment. As I look back now, I am glad I took the leap, needles and all. The fact that the needles didn't hurt was almost as remarkable as the fact that they worked. I woke up completely pain-free. Over the next few months I continued to see him on a regular basis with hopes that I could become balanced and peaceful. Experiences with Ed—before the death of my grandmother—were priming me for the journey I was on since she passed away. It's funny how things work out that way without you even aware it's happening.

The night of the busted truck came and went, and I forgot about calling Ed. I was back into my regular routine as a mom when the phone rang. It was Troy.

"Hey, my truck is ready. Do you want to meet me there to pick it up?" he asked.

"Yep," I responded, "meet you there in ten minutes." The auto shop was a quarter of a mile from our apartment, a quick walk for me and the boys. The alternator, the battery, and the starter of my car were all fried and each one needed to be replaced. I crossed my fingers that the truck repair wouldn't be as expensive. Two hits to our wallet in such a short time is not a good thing.

I saw Todd, our repairman, smiling away behind the counter as he fiddled through paperwork. I waited for Troy to arrive and we both headed to the counter to hear the news on the truck, hoping the financial pinch wasn't too painful.

"I'm not quite sure what to make of it, guys," Todd started to explain. "The truck's alternator, starter, and both batteries are toast."

Troy glared at me. I said nothing.

"What did ya do to it?" Todd asked. "Stick an electrical jolt to the starter?"

"These things just happen, right?" I jumped in, before Troy had a chance to say anything.

"Yeah, I guess so," Todd said, "but what I don't get is how the two of you have two cars within a couple days with the same exact thing."

No one said anything. A know-it-all smile started to form on my husband's face.

"You hiding something from me?" Todd said light-heartedly.

"No, I'm just teasing her because she was driving both of them when they broke down," Troy said. "We might have to take her license away."

"Very funny," I said, elbowing Troy in the side.

"Well," Todd continued, "on the surface, it looks like you plugged something into the starter on both vehicles just for the fun of it. But for real, that will be $1,600."

"Ugh," Troy grunted out loud.

Just as guilt started to creep in at the thought this could possibly be my fault, Todd offered up his theory for the breakdowns, increasing my guilt into a full-blown stomachache.

"So, my brother has this weird thing about him, ya know. Don't talk to many people about this, but I got a hunch you should think about this, little lady," he said, as he pointed his finger at me.

"I'm listening," I said.

"All right, here's the deal." Todd leaned over the counter and started to whisper, clearly not wanting anyone to hear what he was about to say. "Ever since he was a small boy, my brother couldn't wear a watch because it would always quit runnin'. He's even known for blowin' lights out when he goes places. All we can figure is he has some type of spooky effect on the electrical stuff around him."

"Is that so?" I asked, amazed an auto mechanic was talking about such voodoo.

"Yep," Todd said. "So, here I am, looking at both of these cars, thinking to myself, hmm... maybe she's got the same situation. Of course, if you do, it's on a much bigger scale and, well, that would suck."

"I'll consider it," I said, smiling as if I was blowing the story off while my stomach was now doing flips.

"You probably should," Troy said, as he signed the bill and put his credit card back into his wallet.

We both drove the quarter mile home and went into the apartment for dinner. Troy stared at me with that knowing stare. I knew what he was getting to.

"I'll call Ed," I said, before Troy could say a word. I walked into the bedroom to crash on my bed as I made the call.

The phone rang three times and I heard a familiar voice say hello.

"Hey, Ed," I said.

"Hey, Beau," Ed responded, "what can I do for you?"

"I'm not sure I understand what's going on, or if anything is going on for that matter. But what I do know is that anything that runs on electricity and spends any amount of time with me ends up not working anymore. I was hoping you could squeeze me into your schedule. You know, just in case there is something to these coincidences," I said.

"Absolutely," Ed responded, with a slight chuckle. "How soon can you come in?"

"Anytime."

"Well, head into the office now and I'll see you shortly."

"See you soon," I said with relief, knowing I always got special treatment from Ed.

In a matter of thirty minutes I wolfed down a quick dinner, jumped in my newly repaired car, and headed to Ed's office.

I always enjoyed seeing Ed. A kindhearted man in his late sixties, Ed has a natural way of supporting his clients, encouraging them, and letting them know it's okay to be themselves. I had been coming to him for treatments for a while and he was now like a father to me. He was a great shoulder to lean on when I was confused, and at this moment, I was confused.

I sat down in his modest treatment room. It was quaint and comfortable, with a welcoming atmosphere you wouldn't find in a western doctor's office. There were countless bottles of Chinese Herbal Powders on an old wooden bookshelf, a dresser that doubled as a desk with incense and sage littered across the top, and beautiful pictures on the walls showing the great outdoors in its finest moments. Ed settled into the chair across from me and leaned in to listen intently to what I felt was a crazy story. He was a man of few words and much wisdom. As I explained in detail, Ed jotted down notes on his yellow notepad. I joked about all the appliances and automobiles that had crossed my path during these last three days. Ed smiled as he quietly contemplated my story. Nervous he'd tell me I was crazy, I sat silent and patient, twiddling my thumbs.

Ed checked my pulse on both wrists and then asked to look at my tongue just like he did every other time. I was always fascinated that by simply looking at someone's tongue, an acupuncturist could determine the source of the trouble for a patient. How odd.

Closing my mouth, I then asked, "What do you think it is? Is it anything at all, or just a coincidence?"

"Give me a minute," Ed replied, as he continued to contemplate what was going on in my strange world.

He stood up and walked around the table in the middle of the room. Coming back to the front of his chair, he put his right hand ten inches in front of my chest as if to say "stop," but he didn't say a word. He slowly and methodically moved his hand through the air as if he was feeling something I could not see. It was almost as if I had an imaginary bubble around me only Ed could feel. "Maybe Ed is trying to feel the energy that Sensei Chris talked about," I thought to myself. He pushed his hand a few inches closer to me and then pulled it back away. He raised it higher and dropped it back again. After a few more seconds of watching this weird display, Ed started to back up as his hand still floated in the air in front of me. Soon he was three feet away with an odd look on his face. He plopped down into the chair across from me, looked me right in the eye, and stared at me with the look of someone who discovered a treasure.

"You are a very powerful healer, my friend," he said.

I was speechless. I sat there trying to absorb what he just said. It was as if someone had walked up to me off the street and told me I was a professional football player even though I had never set foot on a field. Ed relaxed back into his chair, giving me the space I needed. I sat for a few more moments and then started to ask questions.

"What in the world do you mean 'powerful'?" I asked. "I just took a Reiki class a few days ago. Brand new is what you should label me, not powerful."

Ed chuckled. "Some people are born with it. You, Beau, were born with it. Might not have known it, but you were."

"If I was born with it, how come I wasn't aware of it?" I asked, uncomfortable with the label he was giving me.

"Who knows?" His response was short and simple. "But whatever happened, you best be getting started using it."

"Ha," I laughed out loud. "Use it? That's a good one. What in the world do you mean?"

"Lots of people have a natural ability like you. They use it in ways that work best for them. You'll have to take some time and figure out what that way is for you," Ed said.

"Hold up. Does that stuff you're doing with your hand have something to do with the energy stuff Sensei Chris talked about? That chi stuff I learned about in his Reiki class?" I asked.

"Yeah, that's one way to explain it," Ed said.

"And that's what is frying things around me?"

"Yep."

"So what do I do about driving my car?"

"Get a bike." Ed smiled.

"Very funny, doc. Just fix me," I said, half-jokingly.

"This isn't a fixing situation, but we can do some adjusting and balancing. As far as the healing, we'll talk more later," Ed responded with a wink. "Jump up on the table. Let's get you a treatment."

I climbed onto the massage table and settled in for what was always a relaxing experience. As I stared at the ceiling, the one and only psychic I had ever gone to flashed through my head. I had been in North Conway a few months ago with Sensei Chris and some other students when they told me to go see the local psychic. At the time I thought it was a joke, but I went anyway. I'd never sat in front of one of those crystal-ball-holding, gypsy-clothes-wearing voodoo people, and curiosity got the best of me. I was waiting to hear when I would die or if I would move soon. I kept running the words to that old psychic hotline commercial through my head, "Who's the father of the baby?" Ha! I couldn't help but giggle.

When I sat down, I was surprised to find no crystal ball and no wacky clothes. Through the course of the twenty-minute reading, she told me many things, some of which were correct and some of which didn't seem to be. However, one of those "inaccuracies" she put before me was now coming true. She told me I would be a great healer. At the time, my conservative side flashed pictures of medical doctors in my head and I totally blew off what she was saying, fully knowing I would never attend medical school. But now, here I lay, staring at the ceiling while Ed poked me with needles, having one of those eerie moments of recall and feeling like I am in a bad movie. Healer, hey? I wondered where this supposed healing path would take me, if I let it take me anywhere at all.

5

Holy Crap, This Has to Be Real

Saturday and Sunday rolled by as if it was any other weekend. Monday, however, clearly wanted to be different. The morning cast the same light on my face and the sounds of my boys rummaging around their toys was also the same, but my physical body felt odd. I stilled myself under my puffy, rose-covered comforter for a few extra moments trying to figure out what my body was actually doing and why I could feel the sheets but somehow *couldn't* feel the sheets at the same time. I rolled through ideas until my mental Rolodex landed on the work Ed had done on me a few days earlier.

I politely asked my logical side to shut the heck up for a few minutes so I could let the creative side wrap its colorful head around the experience. As I allowed, I found visuals materializing in front of me. I could see myself with a space around me that was filled with a bright white light. The two-inch buffer around my entire being was like a cushion of air that softened my contact with my surroundings. It felt like a funky space suit for my human body. Was this what Ed was reaching out to feel, I wondered? But I had things to do, so I let my feet hit the floor like any other marathon mommy day. As I stepped onto the floor and walked around for a bit on my bare feet, I felt bizarre floating sensations. I hinged in half to look closely at my feet as if it were the first time I realized I had them. I yearned to explore them, to feel every sensation and to watch them being feet, doing feet things like holding me up, padding my bones from the floor, and protecting my ankles from harm. No matter how much I observed my feet, I couldn't wrap my head around this new sensation, that they weren't really touching the floor. When I hit the linoleum of the kitchen floor I could sense the change in temperature, but I could still feel the cushion around me. My logical side was about done with this creative crap and began to push its way back into the driver's seat of my brain. After a few hours I became aware that I was no longer noticing the funky space suit of energy. I wasn't sure if I was adapting to it or just forgetting about it.

By dinnertime, my morning alien experience had my brain reeling enough that I prepared a list of questions for Sensei Chris. It was a class night and if I got there early enough I could pick his brain about the events of the last few days. I kissed my little creatures goodbye, hugged my man, and drove off as fast as I could toward the dojo. I pulled into the dirty lot next to the building and jumped out with all my gear, hoping to be the first in line to talk to him. The place was crowded, chock full of seven-year-olds dreaming of being Jackie Chan. Making my way to the next dojo floor I found Sensei Chris sitting in meditation just off to the left of the mat.

I sat for a moment, then two, then I decided to be the obnoxious student and ask the ridiculous question to someone meditating, "Can I interrupt?"

"Feel free," Sensei said, with a small but comforting smile.

Chris had a way of accepting your flaws, being open about his, and welcoming stupid questions. Well, for beginner students like myself, at least. Thrilled I had captured a moment of his time and inappropriately ignoring the fact that I busted up his moment of Zen, I immediately sat down on the black cushioned mats in front of him.

"I have questions and I'm wondering if I can run them by you?" I asked.

"Feel free," he said again, loving to repeat simple phrases.

"I woke up this morning like I was on a bad acid trip!" I said, "like I have all this space around me that is something but isn't something."

"Bad acid trip." He chuckled as he restated my words, now moving out of the meditation position into a more laid-back seat.

"Yeah, so I went to see Ed. Okay, back up. First my grandmother died, then I took your class, the Reiki class, then I blew stuff up left and right in my house, and then I went to see Ed," I explained.

"Elaborate," he responded, with simplicity and curiosity.

I filled him in on the events of the last few days. I stopped my rant when I noticed one of the other students arrive and set his gear bag down a few feet away from where I was sitting. I looked over at him for a moment to exchange the typical "hey, how are you" type smile.

When I looked back, Sensei Chris looked like the cat that swallowed the canary.

"Man, you're moving fast on your path, aren't you?" he asked me, with his left brow raised.

"Come again?"

"Well, you have a very interesting path in front of you and you seem to be moving relatively quickly down it," he explained. "I have been thinking about your path. I know quite a bit about it. But there is much I can't tell you yet."

I sat for a moment staring at him. He was serious. I couldn't believe it. He was serious. Since when do people, especially a teacher, know things that could be helpful to you and they don't share?

"What do you mean you can't tell me?" I asked intently. "Does this have to do with the Stay Puff marshmallow suit I was sporting this morning?"

"Yes and no."

"Does it have to do with the Reiki, or is it something completely different?"

"Yes," he said, with a chuckle.

I glared at him with as much respect as I could.

"Ok, Mr. Secretive 'I don't want to give a straight answer and I am not telling you what I know, guy', at least point me in a direction to find some understanding," I said, hoping he would snap out of this "wax on wax off" thought process.

"Fair enough," he responded, obviously fine with my pushing. "I have been thinking about putting you into Inner Circle training."

"Go on," I said, more respectfully.

"There are two kinds of students. Look over there," he said as he pointed to the first dojo mat, covered in seven-year-olds.

"Yeah, what about them?" I asked.

"They are commercial students, Outer Circle students," he said. "They come here to learn how to do what they see in the movies. They have no understanding of true energy and how it works."

"Okay. I'm following."

"Then there are the Inner Circle students. They are taught what the Outer students are not."

"This is the Mr. Miyagi stuff ?"

"Kind of," he responded. "Like Mr. Miyagi plus metaphysics and a whole lot of spirituality."

"Okay, so martial arts, spirituality, and metaphysics."

"Yep. And I was asking if you wanted to be a student of the Inner Circle," he said.

"Yes. Many times, yes," I said, jumping at the opportunity, an image of a faster path forming in my head.

"You have to train five days a week. No breaks. You have to tend to the dojo, and you have to welcome new students," he said. "Most of all, you have to be open to what it brings you."

"I'll talk to Troy, but I can't see it being a problem. You've got my interest piqued."

"Great. Then I'll give you more information after class," he said, as he started to stand.

"Wait." I held my hand up, hoping to catch him before he drifted off to the next student needing attention. "One more question."

He paused to look at me again as if he was half-expecting not to get away that easy. I filled him in about the Connection and my grandmother.

"Have you tried pendulum work?" he asked me.

"Pendulu-who?" I stumbled on the word.

"Pendulum work. What you need to do is get a pendulum. Kind of like this one." He pulled a necklace from his bag with a stone hanging from it. "You can use this to ask her questions. Hold it tight to your side. Let it hang about six inches down. You can use any type of pendulum you want. Then, ask your grandmother to answer questions through the pendulum with 'Yes' answers being forward and back and 'No' answers being side to side."

"Hmm..." I responded.

I was absorbing what he was telling me, watching how he held the necklace by the latch with one hand and let it dangle just an inch over the palm of his other. Kind of a funky thing to do, I thought, so I tried it.

"Okay. Hold on. Nope, this isn't going to work. No disrespect, Sensei, but my fingers are moving the pendulum. I'm the one asking the question and, clearly, if I'm holding it, I'm the one answering it."

"Yes, you are answering the question. The trick is to try not to move the pendulum, and allow your subconscious to do the talking. It is the subconscious that spirits use to communicate with us," he explained.

"My subconscious?"

"Yep," he said, as he looked over the dojo floor. "Are you ready for class now?"

No! Are you kidding me? This is just getting good, I thought to myself. But instead I responded, "Yes, Sensei. Sorry for keeping you."

I stepped onto the dojo floor, bowing in respect. I tried to focus intently in class, but I spent most of the time struggling to compartmentalize the thoughts running through my head like groups of trendy cliques in a high school My thoughts were individuals hiding within groups of thoughts all ignoring the other groups of thoughts. I tried futilely to focus on my martial arts classwork, but I kept grasping at the concept of the subconscious instead, thinking about what type of pendulum to buy and imagining what mysterious teachings I would learn in the "Inner Circle". Focus was the last thing I achieved in class that day.

On the ride home my mind continued to race. If there was such a thing as an "Inner Circle", I wanted in. I wanted to prove my hypothesis was true—that my grandmother was appearing to me and manipulating my energy field. If gaining access to the Inner Circle would prove I wasn't crazy, sign me up!

I ran through those last few thoughts of the day before pulling into the parking lot of my huge apartment complex. When it came to my new understanding of the subconscious, I summed up that internal conversation by brilliantly deciding that I needed more information. I made a mental note to head to Barnes and Noble in the next few days to get some more food for thought on the issue.

Finally, what to do about the pendulum? Where do I buy one? As I gnawed on the thought, the idea of buying one felt ridiculous and didn't know why it felt that way. Just then, the image of my grandmother's heavy brass frog popped into my head. She gave it to me a short time before her passing and it was resting safely on top of my dresser back at the apartment. She had given it to me the summer before her death.

It was the last time I had seen her in her home. The house was and always had been the perfect color blue with two massive oak trees in the front yard. These two guardians stood stately at either end of the walkway approaching the house. This was my safe place, the place she lived for my entire life, the place I ran away to when I was young with my pink Barbie suitcase in tow. The family and I had driven cross-country to Minnesota to visit and reminisce. When the time came to say goodbye to her and head back to New England, I discovered I couldn't. It was different than all the other times I had said goodbye. She and I were standing in her kitchen while my husband and two little ones were in the truck parked in the back alley, waiting for me so we could leave. I walked to her and hunched my five-foot-seven frame down to let her wrap her short arms around me. Regardless of her size, she had a way of pulling you so far into a hug that you almost disappeared into her. When I went to let go, I couldn't. I held on tighter and I started to cry. She held even tighter to console me.

"Okay, okay, okay. You're fine," she said.

"I, don't, know, why I'm crying, so much," I said, now sobbing.

"There's no reason to be sad. Shush, shush, shush, my little girl." She patted me on the back gently. "Here, hold on."

She pulled away and headed into her bedroom to grab her maroon cardigan sweater. Returning to the kitchen she shoved it into my arms, but before I could bury myself into her again, she was off. "Hold on, one more thing." She disappeared into her bedroom again, this time returning with a small but heavy brass frog that hinged at the hips, with an opening just big enough to hold one or two items of jewelry.

"Here. Take this too. Take both of them. Come on, it's okay. No more sadness," she said, as she shoved the items into my chest and wrapped herself around me again. I could tell there was something about giving me those items that brought her comfort. But for me, in the moment, I didn't want them. I just wanted her. I wanted to stay in the safety of her arms. I knew something was wrong, I just didn't know what.

I returned home to New Hampshire and a few short months later she was moved out of her house into an assisted living facility. A few weeks after that she was hospitalized, never to return to her home again. Today, I cherish those items. Something deep inside her knew she was leaving and part of me knew it as well, but neither of us were willing to say it.

Now, parked in front of the three-story brick building I called home, I put together the importance of the memory and the pendulum. Her engagement ring was inside, nestled in the brass frog. That ring would be my pendulum.

It was a Wednesday and I was driving down Route 16 to meet my kids at their field trip when I felt it—that familiar sensation, the Connection. I had my new pendulum at the ready. I pulled to the side of the road because it had been over a week since I felt the Connection and I didn't want to ignore it. A sigh of relief came and I started to talk to her.

"Grandma?" I asked. "Is that you?"

A sensation rushed through me again as the ring at the end of the chain swung forward and backward. It was a "yes."

"Alright, lady. I want to know if this stuff is for real. Am I going crazy or are there things out there bigger than science?" I asked.

I felt nothing in response and neither did the pendulum. I laughed at myself, knowing I had given her a two-sided question. I continued. "So, is there something you need me to know?"

I felt another sensation, another swing forward and backward.

"About myself?" Nothing.

"About a family member?"

Another swing came, and I continued using the "twenty questions" format I used to play on long car trips as a kid. One by one, the questions eliminated all other possibilities. I made notes of when the sensations would come and put two and two together until I came up with what I felt was the correct but oddest story. As it turned out, Grandma's message to me was that my mother would be calling me for help with money, but I wasn't the person that would help. A friend of hers would end up assisting her instead. The yes and no process took a good thirty minutes just to get that one story put together. Alright, I thought, this is specific. This is something that will prove to me this entire thing is in my head, manifested by grief.

I spent the rest of the morning and early afternoon at the field trip. When I climbed in my car to head home, I discovered that my mom had left a message on my phone. I called her back and she picked up immediately.

"Hello?" she answered.

"Hey, Ma, got a message from you," I said, as I pulled out of the parking lot and headed down the street.

"Oh, yes, thanks for getting back to me so quickly. You're not going to believe this, but the bank has messed up my account. I am so frustrated," she said.

A sensation ripped through my body as if to say, "Pay attention," but I ignored it and continued the conversation. "What do you mean?"

"Listen, sweetie, I'm in Vegas right now and I can't seem to get access to my account. Something about an incorrect deposit. Long, boring story. Blah, blah, blah. Any chance you can forward me some money? Maybe deposit some into my account for me?" she asked.

Wow, I thought, what are the chances? With the story I received earlier coming to life right in front of me, I wanted desperately to share it with my mother but I knew it wouldn't be well received. Growing up, spirituality was rarely discussed, and ghosts and psychics were not real. Further, my mother was adamant that she was the closest person to Grandma, and my telling her I now speak with Grandma would only end in jealousy and resentment. I was alone with a story that was turning out to be real.

I blankly stared ahead. My fear of being lost on a road to a destination I did not know paralyzed me. But, armed with my grandmother's communication so lovingly and patiently given, I felt my skepticism falter.

I continued the conversation. "Sure, Ma. Just let me know what to do."

"Grab a pen. I'll give you my bank number. Deposit cash so it clears right away," she explained.

She gave me the information and I called Troy to explain what had happened and to make sure we were both on the same page with lending her money. He listened to the story about Grandma and seemed somewhat receptive to it. Although it was disappointing that I couldn't share my story with my mom, I was grateful I could talk openly to Troy. I told him everything, including the part of me not being able to help, and that it would be a friend who would help her instead. Thus, I concluded, my conversation with Grandma was only half right and probably just chance. Troy agreed. I hung up the phone and withdrew the money from my account. As I was driving across town from my bank to her bank with the cash in hand, my phone rang yet again.

"Hello?"

"Hey there. It's Mom," she said, in an even more chipper voice.

"Hey, Ma. I'm almost to your bank," I said, as I turned left into the parking lot.

"Thank you so much, baby. I am so incredibly grateful, but there's been a change of plans," she said. "Lisa has already wired the money to me directly. You don't have to lend me anything. It's already done."

At the end of my mother's sentence, I found a parking spot to settle into, astonished at how the events unfolded. I put the car in park and took a deep breath.

"Cool, Ma," I said. "Just call if you need anything else, alright? Have fun in Vegas."

"Thanks, hon. Love you," she sang.

"Love you too, Ma." I said goodbye and hung up the phone.

I stared at the cars passing by. This was the first time I had received such detailed information from Grandma, and I was stunned at how accurate it was. Looking out the windshield, I noticed how bright the sun was and the number of hawks flying above my car. I was split in half. One half was flying high like the hawks, comforted knowing she was with me. The other half was sitting in a car, trying desperately to stay grounded and on the same road as everyone else.

6

Wearing Mom Jeans and Shaking My Voodoo Rattle

Leaves were now countless shades of red, yellow, and orange, as they always are in the autumn here in New England. People travel from all over the country just to see our foliage. I've always found the word "foliage" to be quite silly, and only choose to use it along with a fantastic English accent.

The boys, who sometimes participate in the game of "English accent" as well, were getting ready early one Wednesday morning for their weekly trip to a homeschoolers' co-op. Since they were not enrolled in public school (or private for that matter) Troy and I spent Monday through Friday expanding their social structure in countless ways, one of which was this co-op for homeschoolers.

A large group of families met every Wednesday. This particular Wednesday felt much like all the others. Little did I know, it would be yet another example of how the attempt to compartmentalize my old life from my new, more bizarre life was pointless. Things were opening up within me and I was beginning to see that I couldn't submerge myself in "alternative practices" (such as communicating with my deceased grandmother and manipulating energy I couldn't see) and then set those things aside like workout clothes so I could go back to the "real world" and dance the cultural dance of America.

A race to pack the lunches, a scurry to make sure the homework from last week was in backpacks, a quick kiss and sniff of the shirts to make sure they didn't make their clothing choice from the dirty laundry basket, and we were off down the freeway for the thirty-mile trip to the co-op. We pulled into the parking lot, jumped out of the car, and collected our gear for the day. Walking to the rear of my SUV I discovered that the fancy tail pipe cover my oldest son had put on over my old, rusted exhaust pipe looked as if it was going to fall to the ground.

"Michael, is that supposed to look like that?" I said, pointing to the loose cover. My son loves cars.

"Nope," he responded. "It's supposed to be on there just like the tail pipe."

"Okay. Well, we'll fix it later," I said, as I grabbed a box full of art supplies.

"Can I just slide it back on now?" Michael asked me.

"Yeah, sure," I said without thinking.

Side note, for those of you like me who don't know anything about cars, the tail pipe is scorching hot after a thirty-minute drive. As a result, the first sound I heard when Michael bent down to wrap all ten fingers around the shiny new tail pipe cover was a distinct sizzle!

I dropped the box I was holding almost as fast as he pulled his hands away from the burning tube and immediately focused on his fingers, wanting desperately to do something—anything—to take away the pain. I took Michael's wrists and pulled his hands gently away from his chest where he had buried them. I used Reiki on his fingers, my hands one or two inches above his, not caring what anyone around me saw. I focused intently on imagining energy from a higher source entering in through the crown of my head and pouring out of my hands into the two smaller hands before me. I was in full Mom mode and my Mom mode doesn't care what others think. I did exactly what Sensei Chris had taught me.

As I held my hands above Michael's, I explained to him I was doing that "Reiki thing" my teacher told me about. Tears rolled down his cheeks and we both watched the tips of his fingers start to bubble, creating blisters on the tips of all but two of them.

"I am so sorry, honey!" I said to Michael.

"It's okay," he said, as he nodded his head forgivingly.

"One more minute and we'll head in to get some Band-Aids and such," I said.

While that minute passed, some of the other parents saw what was happening and helped us carry in the loads of classroom material and lunches and other nameless items I had no interest in anymore. Once downstairs we opened the heavy metal fire door that sectioned off the main area from the tunnel-like hallway that crept to the bathrooms. In the hallway were old pew-style benches lined up along the cold brick walls. As we sat down on a dark and creaky wood bench, one of the mothers arrived carrying a first-aid kit.

"He'll be fine, hon," she said, as she handed me the box.

"I know. I just feel horrible," I responded, still focused on Michael. "I should have known."

"Every mother has their moments where they do something they regret. And furthermore," she said, with a finger now pointing to my face, "many times they didn't know, and it was simply a mistake. We can't be perfect."

"Oh, don't feel too bad," added another mother, who was standing by. "I once sat on my daughter by accident when she was two years old and broke her arm! Try explaining that one to the doc!"

I smiled and started to chuckle. It was a welcome relief from the desire to cry. In that moment I reflected on how cool it was that moms could come together like this. No judgment. No disgust. Just support, just moms.

I finished bandaging up his last few fingers, watching the smile come over his face as the realization sank in that he wouldn't be able to hold a pencil.

"I can't do schoolwork now, you know. My fingers won't let me," Michael said.

"I know, cutie pie." I winked at him, my panic starting to subside.

There were eight Band-Aids covering the now dime-sized blisters that swelled up like white balloons on the tips of his fingers. We headed off to officially start our day in co-op. With Michael in the lead, we walked back through the underground tunnels to the brighter area known as "the classrooms" as I listened to Michael tell his war-wound bragging stories to his friends.

When the sun was setting and the entire family (including Troy) had reconvened back at the apartment, I told Troy what happened, and he volunteered for medical duty that night and the following morning. Before sending Michael to bed, Troy changed the eight bandages, putting gobs of pharmaceutical cream on each of them to avoid infection. We tucked him in, kissed him goodnight, and I went to bed thinking nothing more about the Reiki I had done until the next morning.

"Beau?" Troy called, with a subtle sense of urgency as the sun was working its way up in the sky. "I think you should come see this."

I slithered out of bed to see what was so important. There was Troy sitting on a kitchen chair, looking confused with Michael in front of him. I walked toward the two of them and leaned over to examine more closely what Troy had discovered under the bandages. There, for all eyes to see, were all ten of Michael's fingers, blister free. Not a sign or even an inkling there was ever a burn.

"Is that normal?"

"I don't think so," I said, now looking closer at Michael's little hands.

"Hmmm." Troy examined the fingertips again.

"Well, I did do Reiki on him right after it happened," I told Troy. "Maybe that did it, or maybe some burns just heal that quickly?"

"I don't know. I guess it could be," Troy said. He turned to Michael and said, "It looks like you are burn free."

"Yeah, so grab a pencil!" I added with a wink. "Grrr," Michael grumbled.

I arrived at the dojo that evening and told Sensei about Michael's fingers. He worked as a nurse by day and he asked a few nurse-type questions that seemed like he was eliminating any of the obvious possibilities. When I was done answering his Western Medical questions, he sighed and nodded his head.

"What?" I said, now used to having to pull information out of him.

"Well, it looks like the Reiki did it," he stated, tilting his head just slightly like a dog that is curious. "Perhaps you need to be doing more of it."

"I just did it because it was the first thing I could think of."

He laughed. "Of course it was the first thing you thought of. That's because it's the natural thing to do. You are getting more in touch with who you are, less the American bullshit."

"Oh...," I mumbled.

"So, what are you going to do with it? Sit on your ass and wait for your immediate family to need help, or are you going to go out there and offer your services to the rest of mankind?" he asked.

I stared at him intently for a moment before responding. "Is there a closet I can do the work in?"

"Very funny!" he said, with a broad smile. "Well, if you're not interested in doing it now, good luck with that. Spirit has an interesting way of changing our lives even if we don't want them changed."

With that he walked away, again looking a little bit like Mr. Miyagi.

I absorbed what he said and filed it in the back of my head, labeled "Too Woo-Woo for Me." Surprisingly, and somehow not surprisingly, that file was growing larger each day.

Later, I met with Ed again for my weekly needle fest. I sat in the tiny waiting room scanning the magazines as I waited for my appointment to begin.

"Hey, it's my favorite girl!" Ed called out, as he opened the door to his office.

"Hey, Ed. Can I run something by you that was out of the ordinary this week?" I asked, as I climbed up on the massage table, letting my bare feet dangle toward the Persian rug.

"Out of the ordinary is always welcome," he said with a smile, as he grabbed his yellow notebook.

"So, I think I might have used Reiki. Well, I know I used it, but the cool thing is it worked, I think," I started to explain.

"What do you mean, 'you think?'"

I told Ed the same story I told Chris. Ed busted out in a smile and a chuckle.

"You, my dear friend, are going to be so amazing."

"Um, Ed? That's not advice. That's something else."

"I know, but listen to me. You need to get out there. You need to share your abilities with the world."

"Abilities?" I asked.

"What do you think we've been talking about these last couple months?" he questioned back.

"Okay, I know you said that I'm supposed to be a healer or something, but what the heck am I really supposed to do? That's not me. I'm not a healer. Do you want me to get a witch's dress while I'm at it?" I said, in my typical cocky-defensive mode.

"You are too much, Beau. Stick out your tongue," he demanded as usual. "One of these days you're going to realize what you're capable of."

I didn't respond. I couldn't. My tongue was still out.

"All set," Ed said. "Don't worry anymore about what is to come. Go ahead and lie back. Let's get started."

"One more thing. Well, because you know how talented I am at beating a dead horse, what really am I supposed to do?" I asked Ed.

Ed looked at me for a minute, most likely picking up the hesitation in my voice, like I was a child leaving home too young. "It will all be what it's supposed to be. I am fortunate to be able to witness your opening."

"Ed?" I said more than asked. He knew the serious and silly combination in my voice.

"At least take the first step and come to the retreat at the end of this month. There will be plenty of people that are in the same place you're at and you could use a few days of focusing on your abilities and your spirituality," Ed said.

"It could be like a spa vacation?" I asked.

"Yeah, something like that." Ed smiled.

7

A Weekend in the Woods with Woo-Woos

Envisioning bathtubs overlooking a beautiful vista, I decided to take Ed's advice and attend the retreat. It helped that Sensei Chris strongly urged me to attend. So the boys, Troy, and I headed north to drop me off for my three-day weekend at Lake Ossipee.

The drive was beautiful. Split between my fear of the unknown and my excitement to prove I'm not crazy, I looked out the car window to stare at the trees, and something happened. They were not just trees to me. They seemed to have a personality, a voice. What was even more frightening is that they were staring back at me. They looked through my fear and straight into my soul, as if to say, "Welcome back".

We drove almost two hours and pulled into a large camp littered with wooden shells of buildings. It was clearly more of an "outdoor" retreat than I expected. Hotel accommodations these were not, and the spa weekend image slipped away quickly. Each building was wired with purpose. One was for dining, one for sleeping, and one for gathering. There were walking trails darting here and there with quaint hand-painted signs marking their final destinations.

"Hey, Ma, it looks like we're dropping *you* off at summer camp!" Michael said.

"Yeah, it kind of looks that way," I said, as I continued to take in my surroundings. I may have been uncomfortable with the scene when we first pulled in but after stepping out of the truck and looking around for a moment, I became more excited, and I did sort of feel like a kid at camp again.

"Hey Ed!" Troy said, as he spotted him walking toward us. Ed was working at the event as a Qigong instructor.

"Hey, Troy. Hey, you guys." Ed wrapped both of his hands around Troy's outstretched hand.

"They're dropping me off. Sending me away. Having 'Boy Time,'" I said sarcastically.

"Very good. Very good. Well, I'm glad you came. Elizabeth will let you know where to put your stuff. Good to see you all again," Ed said, just before he headed back to the crowd of participants and practitioners.

I kissed the boys, wished them a ton of fun while I was gone, grabbed my gear, and went to find my room. Elizabeth was the go-to person. I had met with her previously and found her relatively quickly. Elizabeth was a Shamanic Practitioner, among a variety of other healing modalities. She hugged me, took a step back, and exclaimed that it was a good thing I was here. She said she could feel how badly I needed it and she was excited for me. Having heard about my grandmother's passing, Elizabeth also expressed her condolences while we walked toward one of the larger buildings.

"You are going to be staying with me in the ladies' bunks. We're on the second floor, right up here," she said, as she climbed the stairs ahead of me.

"Okay, so do I just pick any bed?" I looked across the massive room. There were twenty single beds lined up like an old hospital, with small wooden shelves next to each, so I grabbed the first empty bed I could find and looked around for the bathroom. I found it—a college-dorm-style bathroom with four shower stalls and a row of five sinks. It was all clean enough, but still, it was official. I was at camp.

The first event was a community dinner. Everyone was there and the food was very different from what I was used to—this food was "healthy." I sat down and introduced myself to a few of the people. Some I had met before, like Nicole and Joseph. Nicole was the amazing cook who was responsible for making healthy food taste fantastic, and Joseph was a friend of Ed. Everyone there seemed peaceful and excited to be participating in the weekend.

After dinner we had "free time," but that was the last thing I needed. I wanted structure. I needed to be led by the nose down the rabbit hole, not left to wander the woods finding my "inner child." I wanted a guru, an all-knowing sage, my own personal answer-giver and sign interpreter. Much like the rest of the guests here, I was seeking enlightenment outside myself.

When I couldn't find peace among my personal belongings at the bunk, I decided to head out to explore the lake. Walking down the short path, I looked at the trees that lined the way. They seemed to be the same "human" trees I saw on the ride up. They led me to a short beach—not expansive by any means—that somehow played to its beauty more than a huge commercial-style beach would. I pulled my coat in tighter as the night came on. It was getting chilly.

Ed and Joseph were building a fire pit, stacking wood and clearing it out for tomorrow's events. Happy to hear life around me, I walked toward their voices. I took the opportunity to chat with Ed.

"Hey, Ed, I have a question for you," I said, as I climbed the small hill to where they were working.

"Go for it, kiddo."

"How is it that you have such faith in this alternative stuff?"

"Well," Ed paused to think for a moment, "I didn't always have the faith that I have now. It took some lessons and some amazing experiences to really plant me on the ground where I stand today."

"Like what?" I asked curiously.

"Like two separate experiences of white, blinding light that flashes before you. The type of light that changes the way you think about life and stops you from ever looking backwards again."

I sat for a moment thinking about what he said. I must have sat too long because he walked over to me, put his hand on my shoulder, and said simply, "Faith is there. You just have to welcome it in."

The words sank deep and anchored themselves into my being, to a place I could get to them later when I was ready. I thanked Ed, stepped back, and continued my wandering. I pondered what he said, the path beneath my feet, my path through life. There was so much to absorb in so little time. How is it that I could have gone from a complete non-believer to someone who just couldn't seem to stop searching for the next amazing intuitive experience?

I returned to my bunk, settled in for the night, and woke up the next day excited about the scheduled events. I spent blissful time on the beach with the other students as Ed taught us Qigong, the Chinese practice of manipulating energy for life balance. I laughed over lunch with everyone else as a variety of stories flew from table to table, but "easygoing" took a back seat when it was time to focus on my path once again.

Afternoon settled in and I went to the Gathering Hall to participate in a meditation session with a didgeridoo. I had never heard a didgeridoo played live before, and thought it would be cool to experience. I watched as retreat participants rolled in one by one, getting comfortable on the floor in the formation of a slumber-party-like circle, so I decided it best to fit in as I slid off the couch I was sitting on and lay down between two other students.

Joseph, the didgeridoo player, arrived. He was a well-known sound-healing therapist that had an amazingly centered feeling about him. He sat with the group and talked about the history and capabilities of what he lovingly referred to as "The Didge." I relaxed, and listened intently to all the information he was giving us—until he said, "Okay everyone, go ahead and get comfortable for your Journey." I jerked up automatically and wondered if I should raise my hand and say something—like I already knew I was not capable of Journeying.

Months earlier I had found my way to a Journeywork class in Rochester that used Native American drums. I quickly learned the only mystical meditation journey I would go on was one directly to frustration. I would lie there, eyes closed, waiting for my personal Journey to start—and it never did. Even though I had a fantastic Shamanic teacher leading the sessions, I had so many visual blocks I just couldn't see the Journey. Time and time again I tried, only to see nothing. I would lie there with my eyes closed, focusing on the beat of the drum, wondering if seeing purple blobs was the actual vision or just light pouring through my eyelids. The others in the class were all telling stories of visions of soaring over waterfalls, experiences of having deep communication with magical animals, blah, blah, blah. Me? I had nothing. Just blackness sprinkled with self-doubt and frustration. After six months of purple blobs, I gave up.

Today, however, was different. Amazing. I still can't recall exactly when during Joseph's workshop the Journey started for me that afternoon, just that it did. And, when it did, it was unexpected, powerful, and incredibly beautiful. Of all the stories I had heard others tell regarding their own Journeys, I found my own personal experience to be breathtaking in comparison. I couldn't believe the sense of freedom, and the vibrant colors and textures I experienced just by listening to the echoing hum of the didgeridoo.

This mental adventure began in a meadow standing next to a massive and beautiful tree. I felt the dark rich soil beneath my bare feet. Behind me flowed a deep blue, twisting river. I lifted my hand to connect with the texture of the massive tree's bark, each chunk floating above the next, shimmering with a depth I instinctively knew I wouldn't understand until I felt it. With this simple touch I felt as if the worst experiences in my life, the ones that caused me to curl up in bed at night and pour mascara-filled tears into my pillow, were easily released from their stubborn position at the core of my being into the powerful trunk. I began to feel lighter, more passionate, and unable to fight away the smile that was now plastered across my face.

When I felt the tree absorb my non-verbal gratitude, I turned to walk toward the river, and settled in on the ground just a few feet away. I watched as the surface of the water flowed to the right and then to the left, switching directions like ballroom dancers. I stretched my bare foot toward the water, my toes curiously yearning to touch the ripples. I dipped one just slightly into the river. Wet and cool, I felt the chill of the water surge through my entire foot. My independent toe felt like a tourist standing still in the center of Grand Central Station. As I watched the water struggle to make up its mind which direction to travel, I felt compelled to understand the complexity of what I was seeing, like the water's flow was reflecting the core of who I am as a person. It was my own personal river and my own personal metaphor, but it didn't last terribly long. The sun on the back of my neck was soon replaced by shade pouring over me, matching the cool of my toe.

Sensing someone standing behind me, I turned to see who the weather-changer was and found a massive set of furry knees, each at least two feet around. My eyes trailed up the legs to the tremendous chest of a moose standing over me. A small part of my brain jumped to warn me that I should be afraid while the larger part told the smaller part to get a grip. Curiosity won out over fear. Leaning back to take in more of this massive creature, I heard an immense and powerfully deep voice say, "Get up."

"Wha, wha, what?" I stammered. Wide-eyed and excited, I stumbled back.

"Get up," the massive moose said again without moving his lips.

"Cool!" I said with a chuckle in the back of my throat. He rolled his eyes at me and turned to walk away. "Wait!" I shouted, now noticing that my lips were also not moving.

He turned his colossal head back to look at me, this time with more patience in his eyes.

"Okay, whatever, yeah, whatever you want, just tell me," I rambled, way too excited at the entire experience. "I'm listening. Really listening. I mean, this is too much. Did you see the tree? And the water, do you think that's fish causing the water to move that way? I'm kind of afraid to put my foot in too deep, you know, well, because fish sometimes like toes."

"Are you done?" he interrupted.

"Ah, yeah," I said, trying to shut myself up quickly.

I fell in behind him as he lumbered off in the opposite direction of the tree, picking up my speed every now and then to equal his pace. My eyes focused in on the fur of this massive beast. Everything in me wanted to touch it. I reached my hand out, then hesitated a few inches away from his hind leg.

"Go ahead, if you feel you need to," he said.

I yanked my hand back, startled at his statement. "How did you know I was going to touch you?"

"Aren't you sweet?" he chuckled. "You're very predictable, and I've known you for such a very long time."

"Ah, um," I had to think for a second. "You've known me for a long time? Now I'm confused."

"No need to be. It's just the way it is. It's simple," he responded.

"Simple. Isn't that how life's supposed to be?" I asked, somewhat proud of my Zen-like question.

"Nope."

I paused, waiting for him to elaborate. He kept walking.

"And?" I gave in.

"And what?"

"Nope. AND," I tried to coax him into more dialogue.

"Life isn't supposed to be simple. My response can be simple. Life can't," he said.

"Witty," I replied to his comment in my head.

"Thanks," he said.

"Oh, you heard that?" I asked, surprised and a little ticked that my every thought was clearly on a bulletin board in this twilight zone.

"Yes, I hear everything you think," he explained, as he slowed to a stop and turned his broad neck to face me. "Please don't think your mind isn't safe with me, because it is. Be done with worrying what others think. Be done with hiding your true self from the world. You can't hide from me, and you can't be shamed by me."

I stood silent in thought and word, staring into the glossy eyes that felt as if they held my soul. I was safe. I could feel it. I reached out one more time to touch him, this time he stretched his neck slightly as if to say, "Go ahead." My hand settled on the long, muscular neck, and slid gracefully down to his foreleg. His hair, both soft and hard at the same time, tickled under my fingers. It made me feel young again, very young. Connected to him I was untouchable. I was uncorrupted. I leaned in to nestle my face into his massive shoulder as he stepped into me as well, welcoming me. I sat there for a wonderful eternity, saying thank you, thank you, thank you.

"Make sure to come back again," he said, as his nose wrapped around my back, securely holding me to his side.

"I will. I promise," I said, as my ears started to pick up on the faint sound of the didgeridoo in the background, a sound that pulled me away from the moose, the river, and the tree.

When it was over, it took everything in me to pull myself out of this strange new Spirit world and back to this one. I opened my eyes and was flooded with emotion. I had returned to my body, and all the experiences I had on my Journey were now speeding through me trying to catch up. Tears fell quickly and without warning. I excused myself out the side door of the Gathering Hall for some privacy while the tears soaked my shirt. I found my way down to the beach, sobbing by the time I got there.

When my feet reached the edge of the water, I looked down and found a stunning rock, pink with white marbling, resting in the sand. I bent down to pick it up and was shocked by its warmth on such a cold day. As I touched it, I heard my Grandmother's voice. All four-foot-ten of her was now standing off to my right.

"You're alright, I am here now," she said.

Eyes wide, I stared at her for what felt like eternity. I held my gaze, not wanting the moment to end. I stood there in silence. When the tears slowed down and the time felt right, I turned my eyes away and walked back to the main house, beaming with excitement over what I had just experienced. I had finally seen her again. Halfway back, I peeked over my shoulder at her and there she was, still smiling at me. From that moment on, whenever I needed her, I would look for her and she would be there.

The next morning, the camp was abuzz with people walking, talking, doing Qigong. I scanned the crowd for Joseph the didge player from yesterday. He was across the way near some barren trees talking to Nicole. I made a beeline toward them, wanting to process what had happened yesterday.

"Joseph," I said. "Can I chat with you?"

"Yeah, what's up?" he asked.

"I've tried to Journey like a bazillion times in the past and failed. Well, my teacher said I didn't fail, but I never did see anything, so my Type A personality decided I failed," I rambled. "Anyway, I went to your didge journey and actually went on an amazing trip! I hope I didn't insult you by leaving early. Something happened, man. Something weird. When I sat up, it was like eight years' worth of tears started streaming down my face and I couldn't stop them."

"That has been known to happen from time to time. You have to let it all out, which I hope you did."

"I think so," I said, reflecting for a moment. "Yeah, I think I did."

"Cool," he said. Joseph not only used the word cool, he actually was cool. Over six feet tall, slim and muscular, his hair was tied back into a ponytail at the base of his neck. He fit perfectly into my stereotype of the bohemian/rave man.

"So, I'm wondering if you do other groups or private sessions."

Elizabeth, standing nearby, perked her ears up.

"Yeah, I do private sessions," he said. "It's called Didge Therapy. I think it would be incredible for you to do an individual appointment."

We decided to connect after the weekend to set a time, and parted ways with a warm hug.

Elizabeth stepped up as I turned to leave.

"Beau!" she exclaimed, throwing her arms around me in a snake-like vice grip.

"Hey, Elizabeth," I said, as I stiffened beneath her embrace.

"So listen, I was standing there and I started to get *a message from Spirit!*" she said, as she pointed to the sky. This was beginning to look like a bad movie scene, even to me. "I'm hearing from my *higher source* that you need an energetic treatment with me, and, hold on, it's coming to me, I can see an image, Ah, yes! And with Joseph!"

"What?" I asked in the same tone I would say "pass me the popcorn".

"An energetic treatment! You need to be balanced and... and... healed," she explained. "I can do that. I'm a Shaman, you know. I would treat you energetically and Joseph can come along and play the didgeridoo."

I told her I would think about it as I tried to make my escape. Elizabeth wouldn't have it. Her "higher source" was clearly not done with me just yet. "Well, yes. Think about it, but another message is coming through. Spirit tells me you don't have a drum." Her hand was on my shoulder, no doubt to keep me from running away.

"Huh?" I asked in a dumbfounded voice. I most certainly did have a drum. I picked one up months ago for my first Journeywork class, I thought to myself.

"*Spirit* tells me you don't have a drum. I'm having a drum-making class coming up this Thursday at my house. It's only $95 per person. It is clear that *Spirit* wants you to come."

Spirit certainly seemed to send Elizabeth an awful lot of messages, and it was exactly then that I received a message of my own. Not everyone who says they speak to Spirit really does.

"Elizabeth," I said, taking her hands from my shoulders and holding them firmly in front of me, "I already have a drum."

I walked away, stunned and hurt and confused. Did she lie to me? Was it her imagination? I couldn't understand. I vowed then and there, I would never give people advice on how to live their lives—and *certainly* not take money from them for it—until I knew I was giving them something real. If I was going to do this at all, I was going to do it well. With Grandma by my side, I was going to do it right.

8

The Road to Success is Paved with Poop

I returned from the retreat in the woods and started to really accept my spirituality as a permanent fixture in my life. As I walked through the apartment, I asked myself what "the gift" was in all this craziness—everything I had lost to get here. As soon as I asked, I knew. The gift was the woman standing to my right, my grandmother. Even more so, the gift was being opened to a depth of life I had never known, and the joy that comes from living in the moment, seeing what is right in front of me instead of constantly looking forward. For the first time I didn't care what would happen to me a month from now, two weeks from now, or even a minute from now. I only cared about being in this moment, with her. Getting here was painful at times as I furiously flailed my arms and legs trying to stay afloat. It felt so strange to me now, the path that led me here.

My mind drifted back to the summer before my grandmother's passing. We had just purchased my dream home, a 2,600 square foot, one-level, old theater built in the early 1900s. It was originally built for a well-to-do (and clearly bored) female aristocrat and her son. It was one of three buildings on a large parcel of land in Rochester, New Hampshire, that had been divided up by the current owner. He had experienced a slew of bad times, including a neck snap from falling off his horse, and a business and personal bankruptcy. When my real estate agent first opened the large double doors, I fell in love. The interior walls were all wrapped in deep mahogany wood, planks that climbed twenty feet high to ceilings speckled with skylights. There were nine rooms falling to the right and left of one grand hallway, six feet in width, that split the entire house in two. To the immediate right was a kitchen that was clearly an afterthought. I didn't care because, well, I don't cook. Up ahead, beautifully centered in the home, was the main room. It was twenty-five by thirty-five feet in size and it held a quaint stage that rose one foot above the rest of the floor. Next to the stage was a door that led into a gorgeous thirty-foot-wide, semi-circular sunroom reaching out into the front yard. All around, the windows extended from my waist to the ceiling. I spent many nights in there, staring at the stars, leaning against the cool stone of the fireplace behind me.

I never did use that fireplace. Why? I don't know. I guess I didn't appreciate it. I was excited to live there, thrilled to spend time renovating and picking out colors for the bathroom, but I never stopped to breathe. I never slowed down to take in what I had, and when I tried, I was pushed in a different direction.

Then, my husband's business had its first bad financial year. I needed to do something to get us a second income stream to save my dream home. I turned my focus from renovating the old theater to opening a business. Unstoppable, driven from birth, "more" was the only solution. Thus, the Holistic Spa and Fitness Center was born. Ironic but true, I opened the Spa, not for the love of owning a spa (or to help people, for that matter), but simply for the money. Nothing more.

Exactly one month later, I found myself standing in the middle of thirty employees and 4,000 square feet of spa in full swing. Six more months, however, and I was seeing signs that the business should close down. They were little at first and I wasn't yet able to read them, or even notice them. The first sign showed up when one of the yoga instructors came running to the front desk about a brown and black bird that mysteriously got into the yoga room. Bizarre, I thought. In order for a bird to get into the yoga room it would have to push open the front doors, turn left, turn right, meander down a long hallway and then take yet one more left into the windowless room. Regardless of its journey, it was there, and quickly rescued by three employees, a box, and a broom.

"That's a bad sign, you know," said Chris Bashaw, the Tai Chi instructor (who would later become my Sensei). Chris said this in a very matter-of-fact way, as if he were commenting on the weather. The first time he and I met was the day I hired him. I heard through the grapevine that he was a great Tai Chi instructor and I figured Tai Chi was a fashionable thing to offer. I learned in those first few months that Chris had a way of speaking that was always tender, but still dared you to ignore him. For some reason, when he spoke, I listened. Willing or not.

"Bad sign?" I asked.

"Yeah. I don't know exactly what it means, just that it's probably not good." He turned toward his classroom and left, knowing this was as much information as my reality-based, society-driven brain could handle.

Now alone at the front desk, I Googled "black bird omen." I found pages of sites that lured me to click on them and read into the doom. I picked some random page and read until I reached the words, "Stop what it is you are trying to achieve." I stopped, all right. I was being stupid, and playtime was over. I shut down the screen and turned back to the accounting task I had been working on before this nonsense started.

A few weeks after that feathered visitor, I was at the front desk with one of the personal trainers, Allison, talking about the dwindling public interest in spas and fitness centers. Well, mine, at least. It had been two weeks to the day with not a single soul walking through the front door. I was puzzled by this drop-in foot traffic. Inside my building sat a beautiful fitness center and it was September, the month in New England that chills people just enough to get them to take their fitness indoors. This was the second bad omen.

"What am I going to do?" I asked Allison. "I have to do something."

"Too bad we don't have a monkey suit. Someone could dance on the side of the road with a big sign," she joked.

"Ah, we may not have a monkey suit, but we have other things," I said, as I slowly turned to face Allison.

"Oh no, don't look at me." She saw the gears grinding in my head.

"Come on. No one will know it's you!"

"And how exactly can you promise that one to me?" she asked.

A bathrobe, a towel-wrapped turban, and one green facial mask later, Allison was on the street holding a sign that said, "Save 20% on all Spa Treatments Today."

Sign or no sign, and irrespective of her attire, it didn't bring people through the doors. I left the office that day completely discouraged. That feeling stayed with me for several days, until a disaster at home shook me out of my concern for my precious new business. I arrived around dinnertime to let the dogs out for a while only to find they were already having plenty of fun inside the huge house, traipsing through an inch of water mixed with human feces and urine. My septic system had blown up. It plunged its way up through the shower, filled my bathroom from wall to wall, crept out into the hallway, and covered the entire floor. If the smell wasn't bad enough, letting the dogs roam free had made it worse. I looked through my bedroom door and saw the crusty brown paw prints scattered over my king-size, spiced-pumpkin-colored, quilted bedspread. I dropped to my knees in the entryway of my dream home, the only spot left not covered in fecal matter, completely defeated. This was the third sign, and the third strike. I was out. I called Troy in tears.

"I can't do it anymore, I can't do this," I sobbed.

"Do what? What's going on and why do you sound like the world is over?" he asked.

"I sound that way because it is! I don't have what it takes to keep going, Troy. The house, oh my God, the house."

"What happened to the house?" Troy said, now clearly understanding this wasn't a random call from me to simply vent.

"The septic blew up. All over the place. The floors, everywhere."

"Shit," Troy said.

"Yep. Exactly."

The next day was a Saturday. We spent it cleaning up that which we previously thought we had flushed down the toilet for good. As Troy and a way-too-kind neighbor tackled the inside, I met with the septic man in the front yard. He agreed to come out on a weekend for emergency purposes (and for a little more money). Dressed in a blue T-shirt that read, "If I'm not on your shit list, I should be," he stood over the septic opening, pumping out what he could. He held a huge plastic tube that extended off the back of his scary-smelling truck. I could only imagine the gag mask on the guy that had the job of cleaning out that... receptacle.

"So what do you think about the septic tank," I asked with dread.

He pulled his eyes away from the immaculately decorated house across the street and back to my tank-o-crap. "I think you should call your insurance agent and maybe a plumber as well."

"Yeah, that sounds like a good idea." I looked over to the edge of the property to see the neighbors staring out their window at me. I wondered how much it would cost to install a fence. "Who stores their shit in their front yard anyway? Doesn't everyone have city sewer?"

"You're funny, lady." He started to pull the tube up from the mouth of the septic tank. Figuring this was a good time to leave, I walked away quickly, sick to my stomach over the entire thing.

A few days later we discovered via the hired plumber that the septic tank had been added on to another, older, ancient septic tank that was buried deep below a hundred-year-old tree. Instead of removing the old tank, they just extended a pipe further out into the yard and attached another tank, hoping the first tank would magically disappear. Discussions with the previous owner, my insurance agent, and God all failed. Troy and I were stuck with a backhoe rental and thousands of dollars' worth of repairs. With no income from the Spa and no way to pay the huge repair bills for the house, Troy and I had to make some big decisions.

The very next week, after a long Wednesday at the Spa, I walked out to my car, looking to escape. As I opened the door of the SUV Troy came up behind me.

"Hey honey," I said, as I turned to him.

"So, what do you have planned tonight?" He finished the short walk to my side and leaned against my car.

"Not much," I said. "I'll take in a movie and then head home."

"What are you gonna watch?"

"Not sure. I'll see when I get there. I should be in time to catch something," I heard myself say. I wanted to sound "normal," like nothing was going on, but my voice was different somehow. My voice was unique, and one that I had never heard before. It was as if I was on automatic pilot, doing my absolute best to act nonchalant, easygoing. I wanted to convince Troy I was fine so he wouldn't stop me from leaving. So he wouldn't ruin my plans. I knew I was lying to him. I knew I wasn't going to the movies. I knew I was heading out so I could have the space I needed to figure out how to kill myself.

"Cool," Troy responded. "Just call me later when you know what time you're going to be home.

"Will do, sweetie," I said, flawlessly.

I got into my car and drove. Every moment that passed seemed to fade away like it didn't exist. I parked a few miles away in a busy shopping center. The glow of a red and white sign on top of the building hurt my eyes when I stared into it. Memories of my life were gone as if they had been locked away in a closet that I now didn't even know existed. I had forgotten I was married. Forgotten I was a mother of two amazing boys. Forgotten all the things I had once enjoyed. The only thoughts left running through my head were mechanical and fixated on one thing. I'm done.

I considered a gun, but knew I couldn't get my hands on one on such short notice. An image of a bridge flashed in front of me. Drive off it? Jump off it? I was debating which to choose like I was picking between a cherry-filled or chocolate-glazed doughnut. There was no emotion left. The emptiness was oppressive and at the same time so very welcome. I stared straight ahead as I waited for my mind to give me another instruction, like a robot waiting for its next command.

Unaware of the time that had passed, my plotting stare was broken by a mother and two children walking just a few feet in front of my SUV. The mother stopped to adjust the heavy bags she was carrying. I stared as if I was watching through a one-way mirror in a laboratory. One boy reached up to grab a bag that was slipping, taking it off her hands and lightening her load. Just then, a flood of reality came pouring in and filled up the empty spaces created by the depression in my head. I could feel the sensations of emotion and knowledge wash over me, headed up by the images of my two beautiful boys. I was a mother. It was this simple act, played out a few feet away, that snapped me back into reality. I was a mother. I can't kill myself. I just can't.

Thinking more clearly, I started to shake. Now aware of the disconnect I had just experienced, I was scared. Scared of what I was going to do and horrified that it could have happened. I picked up the phone and called Molly.

"Molly? Where are you?"

"Hey Chica! I'm in New York, shopping with the girls," she said in a chipper voice.

I paused for a second. I said the words that very few have ever heard me speak. "I'm not okay."

"Alright. Hold on, don't go anywhere, Mindy, move. I need to get outside." I could hear her talking to her girlfriends, clearly and urgently trying to get to a place where she could hear me. She had picked up on the seriousness of the situation. "I'm here. I'm right here. What's going on?"

"I'm not okay. I'm just, not." I didn't know what else to say. A tear was sneaking out.

"Talk to me, sweetie. Where are you?" An image of Molly jumping out of an ambulance to save me passed through my head.

"I'm in some parking lot. I don't know where I am. I want to do things, bad things," I said, disgusted at myself as the words poured out of my mouth.

"Honey. Sweetie, what type of things?"

"I, well, I, I was just trying to figure out how to hurt myself. Molly." A knot solidified in my throat and tears started to pour. "I don't know what to do. Why am I thinking this way?"

"You need to go to the emergency room," she said.

There was a pause. "Do you hear me?!"

"Why would I go there?" I asked innocently.

"Because they need to help you. Do you understand? I want you to go there right now. Do you know how to get there?"

"I don't understand." The surreal numbness started to leave me.

"Let me put it this way. If you don't go to the emergency room right now, I will call your mother and have her come find you."

With those words, reality rushed over me. It was a backhand to my numbness, sending clarity to my head. The threat of my mom coming for me made me sit up, pay attention, and follow any orders Molly was giving. The last thing I wanted in this fragile state was to deal with my mother.

"Okay, I'm listening. I'll go. I'll go now."

"That's more like it," she said. "I'm going to stay on the phone with you until you get there, okay?"

"Okay," I said, now sobbing as I felt her compassion wrap itself around me. Molly was one of the few that I could fall on.

As I drove, she kept me together by explaining to me who to talk to and what to say. She expressed the importance of being honest with them and told me they would know what to do. Never having experienced anything of this sort, I was grateful to have Molly's instructions.

I arrived, hung up the phone with Molly, and walked through the front doors of the emergency room. With each mile driven, each step taken, I felt the familiar worry of what people would think creep back into my consciousness. I had spent my lifetime putting on a good show to impress everyone. It was expected of me. Now I was forced into the position of telling a perfect stranger I was thinking of suicide—that I had failed to juggle all that life had thrown at me and all that I had taken on.

"Can I help you?" asked a perky nurse, sitting at a gray, semi-cubicle desk that held an archaic computer.

"I'm not sure," I said, as I sat down in the dull office chair on the opposite side of her desk.

"Well, what seems to be the problem?" she asked, with routine in her voice.

"I, um, my cousin told me to come in." I found the courage to take my eyes off the floor and connect them with hers. "She said, well, I told her that I was thinking bad things."

"Okay," she said calmly. I saw the subtle gesture of her left hand just below her desk waving to a police officer standing in the background chatting with another nurse. He saw the sign and slowly walked toward her and our conversation. "What types of bad things?"

"Bad things that I might do to myself."

Before I finished the sentence, she stood up and moved outside her cubicle. She approached me like I was a wounded tiger, carefully sliding up to my side and wrapping her arm through mine. She immediately walked forward with me in tow, gently pulling in the direction of a heavy wooden door. I let her pull me with ease anywhere she felt I needed to go. I had surrendered to whatever would happen.

I was brought to an isolated room that was completely empty except for one bed and one stool. In the only exit stood the six-foot-two police officer facing the busy hallway outside as if he was trying to give me as much privacy as he possibly could. I climbed onto the shiny metal gurney and settled into the light blue sheet that covered the thick mattress. Lying on my right side, I located a speck of black on the white wall and focused in on it. My mind went blank as my eyes glazed over.

"I am so very sorry it took so long for me to get here." I heard a female voice in the doorway.

I pulled myself out of the haze I was in and turned to see a beautiful woman with long dark hair, sporting an oxford shirt and brown khaki pants. She was strikingly different from the rest of the hospital staff I had seen.

"I really apologize," she said to me, making herself comfortable on the stool as I stared at her with confusion.

"You shouldn't apologize," I said. "I've only been here for five minutes."

She leaned back slightly on her stool and tipped her head slowly to the left. "No, you have been here longer than five minutes. You've been here for four hours."

"Four hours?" I started to wonder if I was still out of it.

"Yep. Did you sleep?"

"Um, no. I don't think so."

"Okay. Let's talk for a bit to see what's happening." She was very matter of fact. "I am Dr. Harrison and I am the hospital's psychologist on staff tonight. I want to talk to you a little bit to see where you're at and what happened. Let's start with the events tonight. Can you describe what happened before you came into the hospital?"

I looked in her eyes while I searched for an explanation in my own head. "I really don't know what to tell you. I have never thought of suicide before. My friends will tell you I'm too driven to stop and even think about killing myself. Hell, I'm too selfish to want to kill myself," I said as I started to smile. I welcomed the light feeling as it warmed my body.

"Okay. So, do you think you were going to kill yourself?"

"Not sure, exactly," I paused. "I guess so, but I gotta tell you, that was really weird."

"What was really weird?"

"The whole thing. Whew. Wow." I pulled my hair back from my face and sat upright in the bed. "Damn. Hmmm."

"Care to elaborate so I can get an idea of where you are?"

"Oh, yeah. Sure," I said. "It's just weird, that's all. One minute I'm fine. Well, fine for the most part. I was taking on a lot. Oh my God, yeah. That's it. I was taking on too much. That was stupid."

"Slow down. Try to elaborate a little bit on what was stupid in your mind and what you were taking on."

"Funny thing, doc. I don't want to elaborate. I just want to be done."

"Be done as in suicide?" she asked.

"No," I answered. "That's the cool thing! Be done with that crap, the business, the money, the chasing of the stupid American dream. I'm sick of chasing this stupid pipe dream." A smile now landed on my face, so big the corners of my eyes started to wrinkle.

"Okay. I hear what you're saying," the doc said. "You took on too much. Sounds like you were overwhelmed. Have you been in this situation before?"

"Does a racehorse have trophies!?" I asked her, still smiling.

"Is that a yes?" she said, starting to smile herself.

"Damn right it's a yes. Top of my class, salon-beautiful hair, fake nails, achieve, achieve, achieve. I'm done. Wow I'm free."

"Sounds to me like you're having an epiphany," the doctor commented.

"Not sure if it's an epiphany, doc," I said, as I stared at my hands. I could feel the tiny details of my fingers, details that I had never felt before. The memory of my feeling suicidal seemed so distant now. "Not sure what it is at all. Just thinking two things. First, how the heck do I lose four hours lying here, and second, how soon can I start a new life?"

We talked for a while, I can't recall for how long or about what. The conversation was gentle, comforting, and eventually wound down.

"Professional opinion or not, I think you are going to be alright," the doc said.

I didn't respond. I just smiled. I listened while she repeated to me the typical protocol of information and helped me with my paperwork.

"I'm outta here!" I said, as she was walking out the door.

She turned to look at me again. "I think you're going to do great."

I rested at home on the couch for a few days, babysat by my faithful Cocker Spaniel, Apple. After making some life-changing decisions with Troy, I returned to the Spa to make the announcement. "We're going out of business!"

When the spa had originally opened, I had no grasp of what it meant for something to be truly holistic. All my business-savvy self knew was that it was the up-and-coming trend. As the year ended, this so-called "holistic" business had closed its doors. Bankruptcy, foreclosure, and weeks of getting to personally know the local repo man, I had let go of it all. There I sat, looking over the bloody remains of the paperwork.

So that was my "path." That was "staying afloat." When I look back on those up-and-down times now, maybe they were more like cliffs. I fell off each one, one after the other, with no turning-back option between them. They, and my grandmother's passing, brought me to that retreat so I could start my life over, building my new world as I went.

9

I Thought This Would Be the Epilogue

It had not been a banner year for me. I lost my business. I lost my house. I lost the closest thing to a real mother I had.

I made it through to the other side of all that with a change in perspective. All I had *really* lost were material things—things I wanted but didn't really need. Even Grandma. As deeply and powerfully as I loved her, her passing was inevitable. With what the diabetes was doing to her, perhaps her passing was even necessary. As it turned out, all that was gone were the parts that stopped working. Her body had reached its limits, but her spirit carried on, and carried me on too.

After the retreat Grandma became a regular part of the household. Just ask Troy. He was always the skeptic—he still is, even now—but he shared in the experiences with me.

"Hey Troy, check this out." I held up the pink, marbled, arrow-shaped rock I had found at the retreat.

"Ah, yes. Very interesting, a rock."

"It's not just a rock, Troy. You have to look at it." The two of us stood in our bedroom getting ready to settle in for the night. I held the rock up in one hand to show Troy as I reached for a box of Angel Cards with my other.

The cards were a gift from the weekend retreat, and I was excited to try them out. I had never heard of Angel cards before, only Tarot.

They work about the same, but "Angel" sounded much less dark and foreboding. The box was blue, with the picture of a particularly beautiful angel dressed in a pink gown with pale, marble-like shading throughout. Her wings stretched out to the corners. The colors reminded me of the stone, so I placed it on top of the box. It matched as if it was carved specifically for that set of Angel cards. I took it as a sign and couldn't wait to share my discovery with Troy.

"Look," I said as I lined the rock up with the angel on the cover. I stretched my arms so he could see what I was doing.

"What am I looking at?" he said, with a heavy dose of nonchalant.

"This is the rock Grandma gave me. See? It matches the box of cards I got as a gift from the retreat."

"Yeah, right. What a bunch of crap," Troy said.

All of a sudden, Troy's body lurched toward the bed and he tumbled.

"Ow!" He broke his fall by catching his left hand on the bed and his right on the wall. Troy shouted, looking stunned. "Dude! What the hell?"

"What happened? Are you okay?" I asked.

"Yeah, ummm." Troy hesitated, looked around quickly, and walked out of the room.

I turned to my right to look for Grandma. I was getting used to seeing her there when I needed her, and, sure enough, there she was. I asked her what was going on. No response. She just gave me a sneaky smirk and a giggle. I knew I was safe. Troy, not so much.

"Troy, seriously. What happened?" I followed him down the hall, insisting on knowing what his experience was about.

"Someone kicked me!" Troy spun around to look me in the eyes intently. "In the head!"

I covered my mouth trying to muffle the laughter. It was definitely her; she had struck him as surely as she would have had she been physically there. Troy shook his head side to side, harrumphed, and walked down the hallway again. I stepped back into the bedroom, still holding the rock and Angel cards in my hands. I sat down on the edge of the bed and delicately placed the rock once again on the cover of the box, lining it up neatly with the angel.

"Thank you, Grandma. I love the cards," I whispered.

Grandma seemed like she had moved right in, and I was loving it. I was seeing her more clearly, and more often. Other things started happening too.

The day of my Didge Therapy session with Joseph arrived. He rapped on my door promptly at 11:00 a.m., didge in one hand, fold-up cot in the other. For the thirty minutes he played he was constantly moving around. It seemed one moment he'd be inches away from my head, and the next he'd be feet away from my toes.

The vibes shook me and held me, all at the same time. I imagined tiny pieces of myself breaking away, then reassembling, like my cells were doing some kind of a weird waltz. Eyes closed, I sank into another journey.

It started just like at the retreat, with my feet landing on soft ground and the feeling of sunlight pouring around me. I saw the familiar visions of my great tree and my beloved moose and flickers of color and movement of water. I approached the river that cut through the middle of my vision. I slipped. I felt like I was being pulled in, feet first, deeper and deeper until I was no longer able to see the light from the surface. Just as I began to think about being scared, I landed. On my butt.

Sitting upright like a toddler with his legs pointing straight out in front of him, I felt cold cement on the palms of my hands as they pressed into the floor below me. I looked down to see familiar deep maroon paint all around. I eagerly looked up to find myself sitting on the floor of my grandmother's basement. Shelves were full of boxes of Christmas decorations, cabinets hung randomly around the room, and plywood covered the sides of the simple stairs that lead up to the kitchen. I could smell the damp must of a Minnesota basement. I was there. There was no doubt in my mind, I was there. The sensations I was feeling now were stronger than my previous journey. They were more real. I walked over to the root cellar, where

I used to sit as a child when I wanted to be invisible. I touched the brick along the sides and was thrilled to feel the old paint crumble under my fingers.

I kept saying over and over, "I'm here, I'm really here."

I turned toward the stairs and walked as quickly as I could. Grandma was at the top of the stairs, I just knew it. This was her house, and I was here. She would be here too. My pace picked up to just short of a run.

As my foot hit the first step, I froze. I watched the stairs in front of me get swallowed up by the room itself. It was as if the basement was swallowing itself from the inside out. Then, it was over.

Next thing I knew I was back in the room with Joseph. He ended the session by playing at the base of my head, skillfully drifting the sound of the didgeridoo into a background of silence. I lay there for a moment. Tears ran down the sides of my face, pooling in my ears. There was no release of energy, no need to "let go" of anything. Instead I wanted to hold on. I wanted to go back. I was angry that I was that close to my grandmother only to have that part of the experience taken away.

"You alright?" Joseph asked, once I had sat up and wiped the wet from my face.

"Yeah. I just don't know what to do with all of this," I said. "I am communicating with my grandmother, that's clear. How I'm doing it and what's happening is not as clear."

"Communicating?"

"Yeah," I sighed. Joseph was only the fifth person I had shared my secret with.

"Do explain," Joseph said.

"I see her sometimes, and I talk to her. I actually hear her voice. And now, while you were playing, I was in her basement! I didn't expect it. I was just there, like really there!" There was a hint of frustration in my voice.

"Well, if you want to pursue it, just let me know. I'll see what I can do to help you out," he said with a warm smile. "Be well, my friend."

I thanked him as I walked him to the front door. After he left, I slumped into the leather couch in the center of the room and stared at the boys playing with their toys, listening to their imaginary worlds unfolding before me. I thought about what imagination meant and how it could possibly be connected to intuition, and how crucial it was to separate the two. It had been a long time since I had used my imagination and here I was having a surreal experience of my grandmother's basement while my body was miles away on a cot in my spare bedroom. Intuition—I was now comfortable with saying it—was starting to feel like someone else's imagination played out in front of me, unfolding like an interactive movie.

"I was there too." I heard Grandma whisper in my ear. The Connection ran down my spine.

"So I was really at your house and not here?" I asked her, speaking out loud into thin air.

"Hee hee," she giggled in response.

My boys were oblivious to my conversation. Or perhaps they chose not to hear it. Like Troy, maybe they weren't sure of what exactly I was going through, or what exactly they should or would (or could) do about it even if they knew. There were no direct answers to be had or given. Regardless, things kept happening.

A few weeks later, I headed out to the store to find a warm winter coat for myself. I had gone through the previous brutal winter with a substandard jacket I tried pretending was a warm coat. This winter I committed myself to splurge on a brand-new winter coat, one I would really like. At the store, I walked up and down immense islands of coats, taking my time sliding hangers one by one to get a glimpse of the coat that hung on each. I eventually selected two. One was a fitted tweed coat that was flattering to my figure but not terribly warm. The other was stitched in such a way that it was comparable to a huge, green cocoon, one that would give birth to a butterfly with a twenty-foot wingspan. It was made of down, and the bottom of the coat hovered close to my ankles. The top, a hood, wrapped itself neatly around my head. Wearing the green monster and holding the tweed coat in my left hand, I stared into the mirror positioned on the end of the long rack of coats.

"I wish you were here," I whispered to Grandma. Even that whisper was done in my head so as to not look insane. *"You always helped me buy my coats. I don't know which one to pick. I just want to be warm this year."*

I didn't bother turning to my right to try and see her in her spirit form. It wouldn't have helped or comforted me. I didn't want an image of her in spirit form. I wanted her. I wanted her short, plump fingers shoving coats in my arms saying, "Keep trying them on. We'll find one you like eventually." I started to feel emotions rise up inside as I went over in my mind all the times she would take me shopping for clothes, and the last Christmas gift I received from her, a beautiful, black, dress shirt with cream colored paisleys scattered amongst the stitches.

"I wish you were here," I said again to myself, as a tear rolled down my face.

Great, I thought, I'm standing here looking like a giant lime-colored, crying caterpillar.

"That one looks great on you!" said a small but loud salesclerk. As I spun around, I noticed she was no taller than five feet with gray hair and delicate features. "It brings out the color of your eyes."

"Thank you," I said as the woman began to walk away, and I fumbled to make sure my cheeks were dry.

"Well, I guess that does it then." I hung the tweed coat back up on the rack. "At least I'll be warm," I teased myself and started to walk in the opposite direction of the tiny salesclerk. I made it six aisles away when I heard someone say, "Young lady!!" I heard the bark come from behind me. It was her again. I whipped around in my new green cocoon, shocked and startled.

"Yeah?"

"You're going straight to the shoe department to buy yourself some boots... AREN'T YOU?" she said crisply, as she pointed to my bare toes conspicuously poking out of a pair of sandals.

"Um, yes. Ah, yep," I stuttered, stunned that I was getting yelled at by a stranger.

"That's good," she said. "It's important for you to be warm."

And with that she was off to resume her regular work duties, walking briskly away. I watched her for a second and heard the giggle come from my right again. I knew in some weird way the salesclerk was her—my Grandma. I didn't know how. I just knew.

Part II

Who Are You?

10

The Grocery Store or the Twilight Zone?

A few months passed. The holiday season came and went with many conversations between Grandma and me, including a tear-filled one about Christmas, her absolutely favorite holiday. I had spent many a Christmas at Grandma's house singing carols and hanging tinsel on the tree. This was the first year I didn't get to watch her light up with excitement. But there was a trade-off. What I lacked of her in the physical world, I gained in the spiritual world. Our relationship was different now but nonetheless fantastic. As our conversations grew in frequency and clarity, so did my trust. I could hear her words as clearly as if she were three inches tall and sitting on my right shoulder. It was bizarre at times, to walk through life with a built-in friend by my side, never to be alone again. She honored my successes and scolded me when I needed scolding, just as she had always done. I was comforted to know she was there. That is, until the "others" showed up.

I went into my bedroom one evening and sat on the floor in front of my new meditation table. The table was sparsely decorated with the pink and marble stone, the Angel cards, my handmade pendulum, and an old candle I had dug out of the bottom of a kitchen cabinet. I picked up the pendulum and held it over my palm as I had done time and time again.

"Grandma, are you there?" I asked the pendulum.

It swung "No." I froze. With the hairs on my arms now standing at attention, I realized someone other than Grandma had answered. I set the pendulum down, stood up slowly, and quickly left the room.

"Troy," I half whispered, half shouted.

"What?" he responded, imitating my tone.

"I think I just talked to someone else."

"What do you mean, 'someone else'?" Troy asked.

I explained to him what just happened. "I'm freaked out. Do you realize what this means?"

"Clearly, I don't," he said, with one eyebrow raised. "It means someone else is in the bedroom!" I said, still trying to whisper as if that someone might hear me. "In the bedroom. My bedroom, your bedroom, our bedroom. They're there, waiting for me to come back in."

"How do you know they're waiting for you? Are you the special one to talk to? Ooohhh," Troy joked.

"Not funny, smart-ass," I said, standing a little taller now. "Okay, I'll go back in there, but what if something happens?"

"Isn't that the hope?" he smirked.

I put my hand up in a "talk to the hand" flourish and walked back toward the bedroom. I stopped at the door and took a deep breath before going in, running the words "it's fine" through my head over and over with the hope I would quickly believe it.

Sitting in front of my meditation table but far enough away so my back could safely press against the end of my bed, I picked up the pendulum again.

"Okay, who's there?" I asked. I shook my head, remembering I needed to focus on yes and no questions. *"Um, okay, is someone there?"*

The pendulum swung firmly, from the tips of my fingers to the base of my wrist, as if it was insisting I hear the word "yes."

"Do I know you?"

"No," it responded.

"Do I know someone you know?"

"Yes," it swung again.

"Is it a family member?"

The pendulum slowed its forward and back swing and then shifted slowly, but quick enough for me to see that it was changing its course. "No."

"A friend?"

"Yes."

Okay. I didn't have a huge list of friends. I named them one by one until it landed on my friend, Lynn.

"So it's Lynn?"

The pendulum continued to swing "yes," but with more intensity.

"Are you female?"

"Yes."

"Are you her mom?" I asked with fear, knowing her mom was alive and a yes answer might mean otherwise.

"No."

I took a deep breath. *"Her grandmother?"*

"Yes," it said, and then stopped dead, right in the middle of a swing as if she had left.

"Are you still there?" I asked, with hope and confidence building.

The pendulum didn't budge.

"Anyone?"

Nothing. Not even an itty-bitty swing, and there was that odd silence I had felt a few times before. Was this what it was like to not have any spirits around you?

A few months later I finally got up the courage to start treating people with Reiki. My class with Chris taught me we all have seven chakras—energy centers—that lined up in the body from a person's knees to the top of his or her head. I would hang my handmade pendulum over each of the seven chakras and was able to see if that particular energy center was flowing or not by the amount of movement in the pendulum, giving me an idea of what areas needed help. Through time, I discovered I could feel the difference in chakras that were not flowing and ones that were open. It was like running your hands over rough stone versus polished granite.

Lynn was my first "victim" because she was such a close friend. She agreed to let me practice on her, so we met at my house one afternoon. With the connection to her grandmother still rattling around my head, I told Lynn to climb onto the massage table for her treatment. I pulled out my pendulum and held it over each of her chakras. When I got to her throat, I found a really interesting blockage of energy, one that caused my throat to feel as if it was closing. I didn't remember learning about feeling someone else's pain in class, but I went with it.

"Are you having trouble swallowing right now?" I asked her.

"Yeah, I am," she said.

I gulped hard and continued, "I'm concerned with the chakra that has to do with your throat."

"I'll make note of that," she said, smiling.

I kept working on her energetically for a while and then asked her to turn over so I could work on her back. Having done so, I held my hands a few inches above her back and could feel where the energy shifted and where it seemed stuck. Homing in on the stuck area, I began to see a figure standing on the other side of the table. It went from invisible to semi-transparent in just a few seconds. It made my heart stop and I couldn't breathe. Regardless, I kept my hands over Lynn. I raised my eyes to focus in on the apparition more closely. It was a woman, tall and slender, with gray hair. I could just make out her features.

"*Who are you?*" I said in my head. She stood silent, smiling at me.

"*Who are you?*" I asked again, consciously trying to remain calm and keep working on Lynn.

No response. The woman simply looked down at Lynn as her smile shifted. It wasn't a smile you would give to a stranger; it was one you would give to someone very close to your heart. I figured it was for a grandchild, for Lynn.

"*What are you doing here?*" I asked, still silently.

She raised her eyes to mine and said nothing. She began to fade. In my mind I could see what looked like a movie. It began at a beach. Waves were crashing in and out as the wind was blowing just enough to make its presence known. I saw Lynn standing ten feet away from where the water landed, in front of a grown man whose very presence made me feel uncomfortable. He was intimidating, almost six feet tall with a husky build. More disturbing, and yet fitting his personality, was his scarred face, speckled with a history of acne and warts. I turned my attention back to the Lynn in this vision to see that she was also uncomfortable with him standing there, but she was not moving. She was like a deer in headlights, locked in place.

Behind me I sensed another individual and turned around to see who it was. It was a young woman, possibly seventeen years old, sitting on a rock wall at the edge of the beach where the sand ends and the parking lot begins.

"Come with me, Lynn!" she shouted, loud enough for Lynn to hear but with a sense of serenity in her voice. "Lynn, I am your babysitter. Come with me, not with him." I looked back toward Lynn just in time to see her eyes turn away from the man to look at the young woman. I felt relief inside me, like the young woman was saving her from something. At the same time, I saw the relief on Lynn's face as she started to walk toward me. When she was close enough for me to touch her, I realized she was not looking at me, but through me. Passing me by as if I wasn't even there. I was simply an observer, like Scrooge with his three ghosts. I turned to follow her as she walked past. Lynn reached her hand out to the young woman and I watched the two of them walk hand-in-hand down the beach and fade into the distance. The movie in my head then faded out to nothing and I was once again staring out the window to my backyard.

"Lynn?" I asked.

"Yes?" she responded, somewhat muffled by the headrest cradling her face.

"Can I tell you some information coming through?" I asked with a calm tone in my voice.

"Sure," she said, "that's why we're doing this, right?"

"Yep." I proceeded to tell her about the vision, giving her as many details as I could. I waited for a response, but she remained silent in her head-rest, her body still stretched out on the table.

"Lynn? You still there?"

"Yeah." She sniffed back the tears that were coming.

"Oh, hon, what's wrong? What did I say?" I asked, now fearing I had hurt more than I had helped.

"No, no, it's okay. It's just something I haven't dealt with yet," she said, clearly knowing more about what the vision meant than I did.

"Do you want to talk about it?" I asked, as she sat up.

"Yeah, it's fine. It's just that when I was young my mom hired a babysitter. It was a boy just a few years older than me. He had these growths on his face, kind of like how you described the man in your vision. I think the babysitter my mom hired is the man you saw but grown up now. When he was younger he watched me, and, well, did things to me. You know what I'm talking about, right?" she asked.

I nodded silently, not knowing what to say.

"I think the image you saw might mean I'm supposed to deal with what happened, finally. I guess I've been putting it off," Lynn said.

I focused deeply on Lynn and what she had told me, and we talked about it for a while. I hoped it would distract me from the fact that I had just communicated with someone else's grandmother, received a vision from her, and had had the courage to tell it to Lynn. We ended the session and hugged our goodbyes. That afternoon gave us both quite a lot to think about, and work through.

Weeks went by and it was just another morning. I went through my daily list. Feed kids? Check. Help with schoolwork? Check. Take them to see their friends? Check. When Troy pulled in, I was free to go—to the grocery store, that is. What a glamorous life, I thought to myself.

I headed to the store dressed appropriately for a grocery trip, in an aging T-shirt and baseball cap. After collecting cheese, milk, et cetera, I took a left down the cracker aisle. There were three other people there, all female, picking up cupboard necessities. One was noticeably older than the other two, smaller in width and height, and strangely lacking in "life."

I turned to stare at the countless boxes, trying to decide between saltines and oyster crackers. The more I stared, the more difficult it was to focus on them. They blurred in front of me like they were falling into the background. I looked away for a moment trying to figure out why I couldn't focus. I turned my head back to the older woman and saw she was staring at me. She had a sad look on her face, as if this world just wasn't fair. For a split second I felt a jolt of pain jump through my heart. A moment later she looked away, but I just couldn't stop staring at her. I began to see a male's hand, opaque and thin, wrap itself around her tiny shoulder. The hand was connected to a slender arm, a sweater vest, and a full form. I stood frozen as I watched the man, who I could only guess to be her husband, materialize in front of me. It was as if I was getting a sneak peek behind the curtains, at what happens behind the scenes. He smiled at me, which should have been soothing, but instead I was frightened. I pulled my eyes off him to get my bearings on the grocery aisle only to find where once three people stood, there were now eight!

My eyes shot from one to the next and then back again. Five of the eight stared at me like they could see through my soul. Three of the eight were still shopping as if nothing was wrong. I reacted the only way I knew how. I forced my eyes to the floor and centered them on my toes. Panic rose inside me and slowly wrapped itself around my heart and lungs making it difficult to breathe. Without removing my eyes from the floor, I let go of my shopping cart. My hands ached as I opened my white-knuckled grip. I stealthily slid my purse out of the cart, clutched it to my chest, and quietly slipped out of the store. My half-full grocery cart flitted through my mind for a split second only to be forced out by images of dead people. I imagined them zombie-like, in shredded clothes, and dragging one foot behind them as they pursued me. Once securely locked inside my car, I glanced around for them, certain they'd be attacking at any moment.

"You sure were cute the way you scuttled out of there," a voice said to my right. I snapped my head around and found Grandma sitting in the passenger seat.

"You would've run too if it was you!" my mind shouted at her. Seconds passed, and we just stared at each other. Finally, she smiled, and I realized how idiotic my last comment was.

"What the hell was that?" I asked.

She gave me a smirk that I almost didn't trust.

"Are you going to explain or do I get to fumble my way through it?"

Her smirk became more sympathetic. "If you can see me and hear me, there's no reason you can't see everything that's around me," she said. "I'm not alone, you know."

I was stunned. I didn't know what I expected Grandma to say, but it wasn't *that*. *"But I* can *see what's around you,"* I whimpered.

"No, you can't. You think you can, but you can't. Until recently, I was the only one you could see. Soon, you will see us all."

It took a minute to sink in. "*Check, please*?" I whined light-heartedly, deeply hoping what she was saying wasn't true. Being scared enough to speed-walk out of a grocery store was enough for me. How did she expect me to handle seeing dead people *everywhere*?!

"Quit your whining," she said, as she stared out windshield at a new dad trying to figure out how to buckle his baby in his car. "Anyone who has crossed can participate in this world, and those who are stuck have no choice—they're still here. You should know this by now, sweetie, so suck it up a little."

"*Okay*," I whispered in defeat, as I now stared at the awkward dad too. For a second I thought I saw a faint shimmer of light behind him, as if someone was whispering in his ear how to do it right. My jaw started to drop and I turned back to Grandma, but she was already gone.

11

Family Choices

It had been a year and a half since I said goodbye to my grandmother on the phone. In those eighteen months my life was completely turned upside down. It seemed as if every day there would be another amazing new experience, shifting my attitude more and more from "confused and hesitant" to "eager."

I had another out-of-body experience, this time while driving to class. There were no words to express the intensity of what happened. All my senses were on board from the minute I landed on Grandma's front lawn. I could feel the wet grass under my feet. Inside her home I could smell the dark wood that filled the interior as I walked into the kitchen. In the living room I saw the small television resting near the back wall, the tall, crank-out windows, and the red brick fireplace that filled an entire corner of the room. I was there, that's all there was to it. I remember feeling amazed that I was really, truly there.

As I stood next to her armchair looking out the back windows, I remembered how she would line us kids up for what was famously known as the "Butt Shot" every Christmas when she told us Santa was in the backyard, snapping a photo as we all turned around to look. As that warm memory faded, my attention came back to the "now" with me still standing in her living room. I could sense she was in the house. It felt as if she was standing right behind me and the excitement of seeing her "face to face" rushed through me again.

As I began to turn around, I felt a small, plump hand press into my back sharply, as if to shove me. I lost my balance, one foot letting go of the soft carpet below, and instantly found myself back in the driver's seat of my car. I stared out the windshield at the two lanes ahead, each with cars traveling in different directions. I sat still for a moment as the scenery continued to pass me by, stunned and panicked by what had just happened.

I snuggled into bed that night, excited to share my recent metaphysical adventure with Troy. Unfortunately, I made the bad call of telling him the out-of-body experience happened while I was driving.

"Driving?!" Troy was quickly interested in what I was telling him. "What do you mean, 'driving'? It's one thing to be doing voodoo. It's another to do it behind the wheel!"

"That's not the point," I said, frustrated. "Now I have to start all over again. So, I was driving to class and I wanted to talk to Grandma. Well, I kind of did and then I didn't. She was there and then she was gone. So I pulled over, took the chain with the ring on it off my neck, and held it in my right hand. Or maybe it was the left. Hmm."

"How long is this going to take?" Troy teased. He already knew that sooner or later everybody spaces-out while driving, so that wasn't as much of an issue as he pretended.

"Funny," I said, and then sat there for another minute staring at both hands, trying to remember which hand I held it in. "I can't remember which hand. I'm really struggling with my memory, dude!"

"Dude yourself!" Troy laughed. "So, you forgot what hand it was in. Can't you continue the story without the details?"

"Um, yeah," I said, wrapping my arm around him. "Okay. So, I put the necklace with her ring in one hand and then, well, um."

"Then what?" he asked, now rolling over to face me.

"Then, I don't remember," I said. "I know it happened, but I don't remember *what* happened." I took a minute to think of how to describe it.

"Seriously Troy, I don't remember. This has been happening a lot lately and it's really freaking me out. This out-of-body experience thing I'm telling you about just happened today. There's no reason I should have forgotten it," I said.

Troy stared at me silently, so I started again, "I really think this is a problem. And I'm rambling more lately. I can't finish my sentences and sometimes I can't even find easy words when I need them." I rolled back onto my pillow with a huff. "I can't find the right words. My speech is messed up and now I have these amazing experiences that I can't seem to remember after I have them."

"Well, are you forgetting everything?" he asked.

"No. I'm just forgetting the cool stuff ," I sighed.

"Okay. You're remembering to feed the kids?" he smiled.

"Yes," I said, smiling, too.

"Then don't worry about it."

Troy reached to put his arm around me, but I slipped out of his arm and reached for my journal. As I looked through the pages of what I had written just hours before, the entire experience came flooding back to me, details and all. As long as I write the experiences down when they are fresh, it seemed, I could retain the moment on paper instead of in my mind.

The next morning the four of us drove to the small town of North Conway. Only an hour and a half away, it was one of our favorite mini-vacations and the spot where I had received my first psychic reading. We walked along the main street, popping in and out of the small shops. North Conway is busy and quaint at the same time. It's surrounded by mountains and beautiful scenery—in the middle of nowhere—yet you could still get a fabulous Chai Tea.

We stepped into one of those touristy-type stores, filled with moose souvenirs and corny T-shirts. As the boys wandered off to find the perfect shirt to beg for, I felt the old sensation of chills up and down my spine. It had been months since Grandma used the Connection—she didn't need to anymore; she was simply there and the excitement stopped me in my tracks. Clear visuals and full sentences made the attention-getting Connection unnecessary, yet here I was, in a tiny store in North Conway, feeling it again.

"Is that you?" I asked her out loud, not caring who would overhear.

The Connection ran through me again. I went outside because it was noisy in the store and I wanted to focus.

"Grandma?" I said in my head, as I paced back and forth in the parking lot.

Nothing. No sensations at all. I felt my chest tighten and I wanted to cry. I searched the lot quickly for her, and there she was, just off to my right smiling and pointing to the front doors of the store. Without hesitation, I rushed back inside and stood frozen in the spot where I had earlier felt the Connection, and there it was again. It made my heart leap. The feeling was like smelling chocolate chip cookies baking. It just made you feel at home. I turned to look at her and her smile broadened.

"What is it?" I asked, with excited impatience. *"What is it you want me to know?"*

Grandma pointed to her ear, and then the ceiling. I stopped the racing in my mind so I could focus on listening. I heard a beautiful but eerie song playing over the speakers in the store. I couldn't recall ever hearing it before, so I listened more intently, trying to catch words or phrases. When I had a few sentences in my head I looked back at Grandma, and she nodded her head as if to say that was all.

Later that night after we returned home, I went upstairs to our home office to search for the song on the computer. Just as I was entering the words into a search engine, I felt the Connection again. I squeezed my shoulders up to snuggle into the sensation and I turned to Grandma to ask her what she wanted. She flashed an image of my father in front of my face.

"But he walked away from me four years ago," I said to her, puzzled.

"I know," I heard her say as she pointed to the computer screen. "Type."

I turned back to the computer and entered the lyrics of the song I heard in the store. I hit the enter key and countless links appeared for this one particular song, so I downloaded it. As I waited, I glanced back at Grandma, who was nodding in approval. I pushed play and listened to the song's haunting message. It didn't matter who the song was originally written about, every word matched exactly how I felt, exactly what I would have said if I had one more chance to speak to my dad.

My father was alive. He just decided to step out of my life. Our life. My whole family. The "disconnect" started five years earlier when my parents and I lived side by side in North Carolina. Each morning I would walk the thirty feet over to my parent's house, Michael and Max in tow, to find out what was happening that day. Then, one day, everything changed.

"Sit down," my mother demanded, as soon as I came through the front door.

She was sitting at the small kitchen table wrapping her hands around a coffee mug as steam floated toward her face. She was young when she had me, but now she was in her early fifties, well-manicured, and very much in charge. Our two households ran like clockwork all because of her. Everyone knew their place and their days were predictable. But today was different, I could feel it as I stepped in through the door. She wasn't bustling around. She wasn't cleaning or working or sewing or anything you would typically catch her doing in the morning hours. Instead, she was sitting there, looking very serious.

"Sweetie, right now I need a friend." She emphasized the word "friend," then paused dramatically. "Not a daughter."

I sent the boys into the living room to play to with their grandpa and I sat down across from her. I could see the seriousness simmering up from inside her, her eyes staring off into the distance. My mother was always very dramatic. That is her signature. It is a particular brand of drama that pulls at your heartstrings and makes you feel obligated to give her whatever she asks.

"What's wrong, Mom?" I asked.

"I have fallen in love with someone new." I sat silent and still for several minutes.

"What?" I finally said, with the air that was left in my lungs.

"Listen, sweetheart, it's complicated. I've been unhappy for a while. I didn't want to burden you, but," she let out a sigh, "I've been seeing people on the side. Other men."

The pain that was settling in as I listened to her speak now rushed out of my body, leaving me completely numb. This could not be my mother sitting across from me.

"Mom, I don't get it." I hoped that if it didn't make sense it couldn't be real. "How many other men?"

"How many doesn't matter."

I sat silently as my thoughts shifted to my dad—my stepdad, I mean. He was the only dad I had ever known. He adopted me when I was five and told me he'd love me forever. He was a tall man with kind brown eyes and a scruffy beard that always poked you when he wrapped his arms around you. There he sat, in the next room, on the overstuffed designer couch with two small children climbing on his lap. Did he know? He had to. I didn't want to believe Mom could hurt him like that.

"What about dad?" I asked, to be sure.

"He doesn't know. But in a way, he's had warnings. I told him if he didn't make me happy, I'd go elsewhere."

Disgusted by her sloppy ultimatum to my dad, I spoke again. "So you haven't actually told him?"

"Not yet, but I will in time. I just need to figure out what it is I want to do. There's one man in New Hampshire that I just absolutely cannot be without," she explained.

"His name?"

"Dave. Oh honey, you'll love him. He is so wonderful to me. I feel new again." She twittered as she spoke.

There it was. A name and a moment that would change me forever. Over the next month or two my mom had moved partially out, dramatically floating back and forth between Dave and my dad. Witnessing the pain it caused each day, I found myself growing further from my mother and closer to my dad.

My boys had spent every day of their lives with my dad. Some days he would just check in, others he would play with them for hours, but every day he saw them. Now, desperate to start a new life and never wanting to deal with her again, he wanted nothing to do with his grandsons. In a last-ditch effort, I explained to him that I couldn't keep up a family relationship with him if he didn't want one with my kids. He agreed, and quickly walked out the door.

That was four years ago, and now here I sat listening to a song that perfectly spoke of my pain. Through the tears, I asked Grandma why she gave me the song.

"So you could start to heal. It's about time, honey," was all she said.

"*Not so sure I want to feel the Connection now,*" I tried to joke, as tears slipped down my cheeks.

She pulled in closer to comfort me. "I will only use the Connection when I really need you to listen. You no longer need it to know that I'm here, because I am. Always."

And the song played on, while Grandma gently rocked me in her spiritual arms.

12

Getting My Glide On

Healing became the theme of the moment. I was tasked with healing the wounds caused by my father when my old acupuncturist, Ed, decided to start a free healing clinic in town. I had never intuitively read for a stranger, but I got on board and told him I would be there anyhow, working by his side with whatever he needed.

I arrived on opening day to find that it was being held in a meticulously beautiful yoga studio located directly above the Portsmouth Health Food Store. Owned by two gentle and kind yoga teachers, the studio consisted of two rooms. The first was a waiting room with two small changing closets, a couple chairs, a counter that served as an information-type desk, and a long bench that typically protected a dozen pairs of sandals and one or two pairs of tennis shoes below it. Above the bench floated a string of Buddhist prayer flags and a row of beautiful photos of perfect bodies in a variety of yoga poses. Opposite the bench was a set of French doors that opened into a large carpeted room that was softly lit and had beautiful Buddhist artwork hanging on the walls. In the center sat a large bowl that contained sand and candles. It was there I found Ed, down on one knee, lighting the candles in preparation for the event. I could see his focus and wondered if he was saying a prayer while he lit them.

"Ed?"

"Yeah?" He stood up slowly, clearly struggling from knee problems.

"Do you say a prayer or something when you light the candles?"

"Why do you ask?" answering my question with another question.

"It's just when I watched you light those, I felt like something should be said. I don't know, like taking a moment of silence or something like that.

"Yep, you're right. There should be," Ed responded with a grin. "Before you do any work on anyone, or anything for that matter, you should always say a prayer."

"What prayer, exactly?"

"The prayer is your prayer. You'll have to figure that one out for yourself," he said. "Just let it come to you."

I turned to the bowl that sat on the floor with the intention of saying a prayer. When my brain quit giggling at how stupid it felt to pray to a candle, it went blank. "*Fine!*" I thought. "*Okay, here's a prayer. I'm here to help people. Help me to help them to help me to help them.*" I sat for another moment wondering if that was too simple, as if there were higher powers on the otherside sucking on cigars and sitting in recliners, laughing at me.

People began to arrive, took seats, and—one by one—created that familiar circular sitting pattern I've come to recognize in "alternative" gatherings. At first, I wasn't a fan of the circle format. I always liked the structure of theater seating because it let me avoid eye-to-eye contact with the other participants. But, seeing how it made for a more meaningful event, I eventually warmed up to the idea of the circle. As the clock reached 7 p.m. I was pleased to see a perfect balance of twelve people, six were healers and six were looking to be healed. I sat in between two of the healers and listened as Ed stood up and spoke.

"Welcome all to the first day of our new Free Community Healing Clinic. I'm very excited to be here and I am thankful you have come. We are small now, but the goal is to grow the clinic and be able to help more and more people," he said. "It looks like we have six people here for treatment. Let's take a minute and let the practitioners introduce themselves." He flourished his hand as if to introduce the woman sitting to his right.

"Um, well, my name is Sarah and I work with Chi Kung and moving energy," she said.

"Hey, all," said the next practitioner in turn. She had a beautiful Scottish accent. "My name is Michelle and I use stones in my healing work. I am a Reiki practitioner, along with some other stuff."

Panic set in. I didn't realize people would be going around saying what they did and announcing who they were. I didn't know what I was even capable of doing, let alone naming it. As it got closer and closer to my turn, I tried to think quickly. "Psychic medium?" No, what if spirits didn't show up? What if I was *wrong*?! I saw imaginary images in my head of trying to read for one of the clients and telling them what I saw, only to find out I was totally off base. I imagined the embarrassment I would feel if a fellow healer stood there and watched me make a fool of myself. I tried to remind myself that each time I had used my intuition up to this point I was pretty accurate and that I should be fine, but it didn't help. I bounced between doubt, panic, and terror, while I waited for the last person to introduce herself before it was my turn.

"Thank you. I guess it's my turn," said a familiar woman sitting just to my left, nodding at Michelle confidently. "My name is Rondi and I also work with energy, but I work with the body in such a way that it speaks to me, giving me messages as to what it needs."

Rondi stopped speaking and turned her head to me as if to say it was my turn.

I spoke with as much confidence as I could muster. "Hi. My name is Isabeau. You can call me Beau for short. It's a heck of a lot easier than Isabeau. Otherwise you'll want to call me Isabelle, which would be fine. But that's not the point. It's just easier." I paused and scolded myself silently for babbling. I took a deep breath and continued. "Um, anyway, I work with energy and sometimes communicate with spiritual stuff."

The next breath I took was one I could grab onto deeply, and I looked to my right to happily pass the introduction process off to the next person.

When the introductions were over, the clients began talking about what problems ailed them and why they came to the clinic. Almost as if they were being called, the five other practitioners got up and started to work on different people around the room. I sat still for the first few minutes, looking around hoping I could connect with a spirit clear enough to give me the confidence to speak up, or at least tell me who the heck I was supposed to work with. I turned my head slowly from one corner of the room to the other until I was drawn to one quiet and timid woman. She was older, maybe in her late fifties, and behind her stood a female spirit. I sighed with relief. She stood semi-transparent behind the quiet woman, leaving space where another spirit would possibly stand as if to tell me that she was not her mother, but a grandmother or great grandmother.

Despite her position, the female spirit was clearly angry. I looked around for a more congenial spirit, not a bent-out-of-shape grandmother, but didn't see anyone else. I looked at my own grandmother who nodded with encouragement toward the female spirit as if to say it wasn't going to get any clearer. I took a deep breath and pulled myself over to settle in next to the client.

"Can I sit with you for a moment?"

"Sure," she said, with one of the kindest smiles I had seen in a while.

"I'm Beau," I introduced myself, and reached my hand out to shake hers. She reached for my hand and told me her name was Betty.

"Hi Betty." I pulled myself into a cross-legged position on the floor just a few feet in front of her. I sat quietly for a few moments trying to connect with the female spirit. "I feel like you have a grandmother with you who has passed away," I said, as Betty nodded yes. "I am also feeling like your mother is still here, still living. Is that how it is? I mean, is that right?"

"Yes," she said quietly, as if polite to her was to say very little.

I continued to look toward the grandmother, who had been waiting to start the information rolling, until I was completely on board and ready. I gave her a very tiny nod, and she quickly began to flash the image of her granddaughter being abused by someone. I couldn't see who was abusing her, but it appeared as if it was happening now, in the present. In the vision, I was facing Betty, and I could see the fear on her face. From behind me, a female's voice screamed at her brutally. I watched as Betty in the vision flinched backwards, and the woman lunged past me to attack her. Startled, I closed my eyes and opened them again, forcing myself out of the vision. Breathing heavily, I looked at Betty again sitting on the carpeted floor in front of me, smiling as if to say she was listening. The spirit of her grandmother was still standing behind her, still very much outraged at the abuse.

I thought about the experience. I felt strongly that it was happening currently in Betty's life and it was by the hands of another woman. I asked the grandmother if the client was gay. She shook her head no. I asked her to show me who the abuser was. Another flash in front of me. A vision, of a mother shaking a baby. A mother that was supposed to love her daughter but instead lashed out at her viciously, abusing her for over fifty years. The images stopped, the intensity of the situation sank in, and I mentally withdrew from the entire thing.

I looked at this graying woman in her fifties, Betty, and wondered how likely it could be she would still be taking that amount of abuse from her mother. What if I was completely wrong? Accusing this woman's mother of abusing her was relatively high up there on my personal taboos. I watched an imaginary news anchor in my head say, "And in today's news, a thirty-three-year-old woman accused the mother of a fifty-eight-year-old stranger of..."

I wasn't brave enough to step out on that ledge. Instead, I excused myself, walked over to Rondi, and asked for help. I had met her before the clinic and, other than Ed, she was the only one there I felt comfortable leaning on. She graciously agreed.

I pointed over to where Betty sat, and I lied. I told Rondi the messages that had come through weren't clear. "Can you see what you pick up?" I asked her.

"Sure hon. Let's see what's happening," she said, as we both walked over to sit next to the client.

Rondi was wonderful and sat down between me and Betty as if to take the lead. I was thankful and she felt it. She asked me about the information I received and then passed it on to Betty with caring and tender words. The woman was receptive and admitted that her mother was relentlessly abusive to her on a daily basis and had been her whole life. She also felt it must have been her grandmother who was coming through because her grandmother cared for her immensely. I was amazed. There I was, timidly hiding behind Rondi, looking on at this woman in astonishment that what had come through was accurate.

Rondi continued to work with the woman, talking to her about her situation and doing energy work with her to help her through the struggle. As she tended to Betty, she would flash me a warm smile as if to say, "See? You had it right, and there was nothing to be afraid of."

I left the clinic that night feeling disappointed in myself, and frustrated that I wasn't prepared to say such strong things to a person. I kicked myself for second-guessing what I saw, and for letting my insecurities get in the way of helping someone in need.

The clinic met again two weeks later, and this time Rondi didn't attend. Further, Ed was busy treating people in the group, so I had no one I felt I could fall back on. I did it anyhow. I forced myself to talk to people, reading the messages that were coming in and passing them along regardless of what I thought. I read for two people that night.

The first was a short, dark-haired woman in her mid-forties and her accent told me she was originally from somewhere other than America. She said she was from Russia and that she had come to the clinic because she was suffering from severe pains in many different places. I started doing Reiki on her, hoping a spirit would show up and start chatting with me.

I was right. Just a few short minutes after I started, messages began to come through. I reintroduced myself to her, this time as a psychic medium.

"Have you ever had a reading?" I asked her. She shook her head no.

"Is it okay if I relay some information that is coming through?"

"Why not?" she responded, shrugging her shoulders. I saw a small elderly woman with a cane, very petite.

I then flashed to a cabin, describing it in detail—where the kitchen was located and items that sat on the counters. The tiny female spirit kept banging a cane on a big silver pot on the stove, yelling rather emphatically, "Eat the soup! Eat the soup!" When the first vision faded another jumped in, a huge city surrounded by water. I told the client how I saw her leaving the country and now living in the city. By the end of the reading I had come to understand that the old woman in the visions was her grandmother and the food she had been eating in the city was different from what she was eating in the country, and that she needed to look at that closely for her health. Then another spirit came in, also a female, but not a loved one. There's a different "pull" to the person that a loved one gives—it could be seductive, authoritative, or even like they are in cahoots together—but this spirit didn't feel that way. More of a "push" than a pull. I asked her if she was a guide. She nodded and began to show me images. I told the woman I was reading for that her guide was there and that she was talking about how she was connected to her through mirrors. As soon as I passed the information on, the guide was gone and the reading had ended.

The Russian woman shook my hand, said it all puzzled her, and left. I felt as if what I said to her made no sense at all. Regardless, after the first clinic I had made myself a promise to just pass along whatever came through, so that's what I did. I checked my ego, pulled myself up by my bootstraps, and kept that promise. I looked around for the next person I could help, trying to forget the obvious failure of the reading I had just completed.

The next person was sitting just a few feet away. I was already on the floor so I simply crawled over. He was a younger man in his early twenties, sporty-looking build, and trendy clothing. He said he was only looking for energy balance, so I made myself comfortable by his head and proceeded to give him a Reiki treatment. After a few minutes a male spirit appeared, tall and slender with graying hair. Barely visible, he kept saying "Kate" over and over again and, as I did in the first clinic, I fell backwards in my courage. I figured the odds of getting a name right was way too risky, so I looked away from the male spirit and focused on my Reiki. He would have none of it. The spirit moved directly in front of me, just inches from my face. My heart started to pound as I stared into his eyes—they were glossy, sunken, and full of frustration.

"Get over yourself!" the spirit growled at me. "Just tell him!"

I took a deep breath and did the only thing I could. With my eyes still locked on the spirit, I asked the client, "Do you know anyone by the name of Kate?" and watched as the male spirit backed away from my face.

"Yeah," he said. "Actually, two people named Kate."

Two is better than none, I thought to myself. "Are either of them significant to you?"

"I guess both of them are."

Back to the drawing board, I thought. I looked up at the male spirit for guidance and after he crossed his arms and smirked as if to say "I told you so" he showed me a young girl wearing many different dresses.

"Does one of them wear dresses and the other doesn't?" I asked.

"Yeah, Katherine wears dresses but Kate doesn't."

"Okay, so the messages I'm getting are about Katherine."

"What do you mean, messages?"

I hadn't fully introduced myself, so I explained briefly, "I get messages from passed loved ones and guides and this is what is coming through."

"Oh. Alright," he said. "I'm open."

I was relieved at his easy acceptance and once again felt as if my worrying about what others thought was way out of proportion. I made a mental note to quit worrying.

I continued, "So what does this Katherine mean to you?"

"She's a friend, but I've liked her for a long time and I just can't get the courage up to tell her how I feel," he said. "I'm worried she won't like me and I'll ruin the friendship."

I paused for a moment to watch the next vision play out in front of me, now trusting the male spirit. I saw the client and Katherine eating lunch in a coffee shop.

"Are you going to be seeing her soon?" I asked.

"Yeah. We're going to lunch tomorrow."

"At a coffee shop?"

"Yeah. How did you know?"

"Like I said, it's just the messages I'm getting," I explained. "I see you in the coffee shop telling her how you feel. But I see you posing it as a question first which would give you a way out and help you retain the friendship in case her answer was no. Kind of like asking her what her take is on friends dating. Does that make sense?"

He nodded.

Next, I saw a vision of the young man with a creeping black substance starting at his throat and radiating through his entire body. I asked the spirit how to stop it and he played a scene of the young man speaking his mind to Katherine while the black substance dissipated.

"If you don't tell her how you feel, the emotions will continue to stay inside you and do harm," I interpreted. "It will be as if it's eating you up inside."

"That makes sense," he said. "That's what I'm feeling now."

"Okay, so you'll talk to her tomorrow?"

"Yeah."

"Good," I said, as I got up to leave. "It was nice to meet you."

"Thank you," he said.

I took the thank you and held it close to my heart. Up to this point I had read for a handful of friends and people I knew over the summer, but this young man was only my third stranger and I could already feel a natural flow to it, like I was stepping into the work I was meant to do. My confidence, which was clearly coming and going whenever it darn well felt like it, was back. For now.

A few weeks later (my third clinic), the Russian woman showed up again and quickly pulled me aside before the event began.

"I have to talk to you tonight," she said urgently.

"Okay," I hesitated, "we'll connect later."

She nodded and smiled as Ed pulled the people into the circle to get started. I was perplexed as to why she would want to talk to me if the information I had given her earlier didn't make sense, but I told her I would.

The clinic started and I wasn't quite ready to hear the critique from the Russian woman. I decided to first work energetically on two children that had come in with their mom. When I finished doing Reiki on the kids, I felt more relaxed and I quietly moved over to the Russian woman while she was being worked on by another practitioner. I smiled at the healer and could feel her warm support instantly but was still nervous about what the woman might want to tell me.

"How are you doing?" I asked, as I turned to the Russian woman.

"I am good. I wanted to talk to you," she said. "Everything you said last time was right. I have talked to my mom and everything was exactly how you said it. The city, the cottage, the soup. Everything!"

I could tell she was excited. I was too. Now my confidence was back in full force and I had proved to myself again that I shouldn't worry so much about whether or not the information makes sense.

"Good. I'm glad you got something out of it," I said to her.

"Yes, and I've been eating my mother's soup more. I feel better and I know the older woman in my reading is my grandmother. But please tell me, who is the other spirit? Do I know her? Now I really want to know."

I sat quietly for a moment, looking away from the woman so I could focus on who might be around her energetically. I felt myself tap into her energy field, like settling in to listen to the lyrics of a song, and this time it was a lot clearer than before. I quickly got an image and some messages that floated in front of me. My newfound confidence was clearly making a difference.

"I'm seeing a spirit guide and she is very light, almost like a Tinkerbell-type of spirit. Whoever she is, she's saying she came into your life at a particular time."

I paused for a moment to gather more information and the Russian woman sat patiently waiting for me to speak. I saw an image of the woman as a child. I figured she had to be about eleven or twelve.

"Your guide," I told her, "I think she came into your life when you were eleven or twelve. I see you then with a heavy darkness and depression. Your guide is showing me that she is light because you were so heavy with an emotional burden at that time. She is trying to lighten your energy because what you went through when you were that age was extremely hard."

"My father died when I was eleven," the Russian woman confirmed.

"I am so sorry," I said. "Well, the guide is here to help you through that. But since the guide is still here, that tells me that you still haven't gotten over it in some fashion. I mean, I understand that you can never completely get over the loss of a loved one like that, but there is something more, right?"

She nodded her head yes, so I continued. "She is showing me images of you looking into the mirror. You see aspects of your dad in the mirror. Do you share a lot of facial features with him?"

She nodded. "My father and I look very alike."

"I see you in the mirror crying, but I can't seem to put the information together. I'm sorry."

Just then I felt a bizarre new experience. A huge rush of dark, dark pain and sadness, emotions that clearly weren't mine, surged through me. The feeling gripped me like doom. My first reaction was to pull back from the reading, like I had been bitten and needed to run. On the surface I managed to hold back tears. Inside, however, the next few moments were quite difficult for me. I had never felt anything of this intensity during a reading and, not wanting to quit on this woman sitting in front of me, I struggled with what to do.

I looked to my right and pleaded with Grandma to help me through the reading without the pain that was bearing down on me. I felt something inside me split, a part of me step forward to do the work and another part of me, the more tender, self-analytical part, step back as if to be only a witness.

I went on with the reading, the shift helping me to manage the darkness as I went. The worker part that stepped forward seemed as if it knew what to say, when to say it, and how to say it. The witness part, needing to protect itself, simply sat and waited, suspended in time until it was over. It felt like I found some kind of "disconnect" switch inside me for when the empathies get too deep.

"You're afraid of dying like your father did," I continued, speaking with one breath so I could catch the next.

"Yes," she admitted. I could see her hands start to shake just slightly. "I am so very afraid of getting cancer. That's what he had. I'm afraid of every disease. When I learn about a new disease, I feel like I get it. I know it's in my head, but I'm afraid."

The part of me that had stepped forward reached further out and grabbed onto more information coming in, information that was lining up in front of me like breadcrumbs leading me to where I needed to go.

I began to speak, unaware of the next word, just doing it moment to moment. "I believe that fear of death can cause fear in general, heartache, and even physical pain at times. Your fear of death is crippling you."

She nodded again.

"Search out people to listen to and books to read on the topic of death and the afterlife—many of them, not just one. Educate yourself on death and formulate your own opinions on what you believe happens when you die. That will help you find peace with death and take this grip of fear away from you."

"I don't like to read. It can be difficult for me. Can I talk to you about death?" she asked.

"Absolutely," I said. "With the work I do, I've learned to not hold a fear of death, but you have to talk to more than just me. Take from many people and use what works for you. Find audiobooks that you can listen to."

"I will. Thank you," she said, as she reached her hands out to grab mine. I welcomed the touch and held her hands until she was ready to let go.

I said my goodbyes and that I would see her at the next session. We could take more time to talk if she needed to. As I got up to leave, I felt the two pieces of myself—the worker and the witness—reconnect, and shed any remnants of the reading.

Before I could walk away, another healer (who had been listening to the conversation) asked if I could take a moment to speak with her. I said yes and followed her to a corner of the room where we could have more privacy. To my surprise, she wanted me to give her a reading on something that had been blocking her for quite some time. Seeing what I had done with the Russian woman, she felt I might be able do the same for her. I agreed to help as much as I could. Her guides came through for her and, filled with a rush of gratitude for my peer who had so much faith in me, we ended the session and the evening.

As we all were walking out the back door to our cars, the practitioner I had read for called out to me from across the parking lot.

"Hey Beau!" she shouted.

"Yeah?" I shouted back.

"I have a direction now!" she said, smiling.

I smiled back at her and waved. That was the sign. That was the icing on the cake for me that night. It was my first taste of purpose. It was the first moment that I felt like I was gliding on my path instead of climbing it. I started to see how it was my job to help give people direction in their lives, and I had direction now too.

13

They

My confidence in my abilities grew and I began to revert to my old pre-dead-people comfort zone—"everything's a business." Everyone I had met so far in the alternative world was treating it like a business, so I figured I should too. I needed a business plan. I thought about all the people I had met these past few months and the one who stood out the most was Joseph, the cool didgeman. He extended an offer to help just a few months earlier so I took him up on his offer and he invited me to his office.

"Hey Beau!" Nicole said, as she opened the door with her right hand while holding back a gorgeous hundred-pound, purebred German Rottweiler with her left.

"Hey, Nicole," I said, taking a moment to say hi to the dog, too.

"Ugh, he is such a handful," she said. "His name is Kodiak."

"Hey there," said Joseph, as he walked toward Nicole and me. "So where are we going to start?"

"At the beginning?" I said jokingly, scratching Kodiak behind his ears.

"Good place to start." He led me further into the lofted space. "How about a title? What do you call yourself?" I sat down on a futon that rested on the edge of a room lined with singing bowls, flags, and didgeridoos.

"A medium, I think."

"Medium? Hmm. Tell me about what you're doing." He offered me some tea and poured himself some as well.

"Um, well, I'm talking to people. Dead ones, to be more specific."

"Yeah. Dead ones," he said without missing a beat. "Tell me about them."

I looked up to see the seriousness in his face. He wasn't laughing and he didn't hesitate. A sense of worth came over me and I shifted to a more serious position. "Well, it started with my Grandma, but over the last few months I've moved on to reading for friends. And now I've read for a handful of strangers at Ed's new clinic."

"Yeah, I heard about Ed's clinic. I'm thinking about participating if I can fit it into my schedule."

I told Joseph about my Reiki work and the spirits that inevitably show up with information. After listening to me rant for a few minutes, he stated, "That sounds like a medium to me. Maybe there's a better word for it?" He headed toward the computer to search through terms on the internet. "Tell me more. Do you see things, feel things, hear things?"

"Not sure."

"Explain how you're not sure."

"Well, at the clinic I've had rushes of emotions along with the things that I see with my eyes," I explained.

"Can you see things when your eyes are closed?"

"Nope."

Joseph asked me to explain the rushes of emotions, so I thought for a moment. I didn't know how to explain it.

"Give it some time. It'll come soon enough," he said. "For now, we'll work on the marketing. Actually, I'll work on that. *You* need to get out there as much as you can. Every day, if possible."

It was refreshing to be around someone who treated me like what was going on was perfectly natural. My circle of support was growing and it made a massive difference in my life to not feel alone.

The remainder of the visit was extremely helpful. Joseph had talent in the marketing field. He laid out business cards, titles, and the beginning of a website. He sent me home with a few assignments, including a reading for a close friend of his, and doing scheduled readings at a metaphysical shop a few towns over. I thanked him as I left, knowing that what he was bringing to the table was more than I could have done for myself. One week later was my first "professional day" at Crescent Moon Herbals.

An old workshop now turned into a metaphysical store, it sat just a few feet away from the main house where Mary, the owner, lived. Located in the tickle weeds of a small town in Maine, it was perfectly nestled in the middle of fences, flowers, and tractors.

I was nervous, so Troy drove me to the shop. He was being supportive and, well, that's how he supports. We arrived at the store with just enough time for me to set up my table, compose myself, and chat for a bit with Mary. I had met her once before when I was tagging along on a class Sensei Chris taught there. I looked at my Reiki table (a massage table) and took a moment to gauge what was left for space in the room. It was a large area at the back of the shop with almost five feet of space remaining on each side. My so-called workbench was tiny compared to the space around it. I walked around it one last time performing a pre-reading ritual of protection, burning a sage smudge stick as I went. Ed told me to do that during one of my acupuncture treatments with him, I never asked why.

Waiting for my first client (Mary herself), I turned to my right to talk to Grandma one more time. *"Alright lady, here I am; people scheduled to see me and having to read on demand. Just where you want me. Oh, and nervous as heck too. So, I need your help to calm my nerves. Tell me this is the right thing to do."*

I paused for a second with my eyes closed, waiting for my Connection with her. The sensation washed over me and did exactly what I hoped it would do—calm me. *"Alright."* I looked around the room. *"Here we go then."*

A few minutes and a ton of deep breathing exercises later, Mary came in for her reading. We continued our earlier small talk while I grabbed my deck of Angel cards. I used them as a distraction by spreading them out on the table in front of the client. I found they were a great way to divert those I read for from "staring at the medium." Even when reading for friends, that problem existed. I found there was always that quirky time in the beginning when I would sit in silence trying to get a clear image or vision to follow while the client would also sit in silence, staring at me. I was distracted by that awkward moment, squirming while the client leered at me like they were leaning over the bear enclosure at the zoo waiting for it to move.

"Okay, Beau," Mary said. "Where do you want me?"

I rolled a smile across my face to hide the nerves inside. "Let me do a five-minute card reading for you first and then I'll have you get comfortable on the table."

I asked Mary to shuffle the deck to get her energy on them, then drew a few cards and spread them out. I found they sometimes gave me insights as to what the spirits might be talking about when I met them. They would lie out in a theme-like spread for the meeting, but nothing more than that. If I wanted more information I always had to look away from the cards and speak to the people on the otherside directly. I stared at those cards for a long time before Mary finally spoke.

"What?" she said anxiously. "What do you see?"

"I'm just putting some thoughts together," I responded, and then paused. "It looks here like you're giving too much and not putting enough back into yourself."

I kept looking at the cards, trying not to look up. I didn't like being so vague. It sounded like something you'd expect from a five-dollar street psychic. I kept focusing on the cards, trying not to read Mary's facial reactions so they didn't sway my thought process.

"Also, there's a physical connection lacking. It could be a number of things," I said. "Why don't you climb on the table and we'll get started? You can lie face up or down, whichever is more comfortable. Do you have any physical ailments right now that we can work on?"

"None that I know of," she responded, as she climbed up and positioned herself comfortably, nestling her head in the nook designed for that.

It wasn't long before spirits and guides started to arrive. I could see two people, both unfamiliar to me, slowly take shape. I did my protection statement again and happily sent gratitude to the two that showed up to assist me.

The Reiki part began as it always did for me. I scanned Mary's body, starting at her feet and moving to her head. I focused on the first of the two strangers in the room.

This spirit had a powerful but positive presence. It was a female energy, older and a little bit bossy.

"Okay, Mary. I have two spirits. One is a loved one, female, and one is a guide, male. The loved one is pushing the guide back and telling him that he needs to wait his turn."

Mary chuckled, and I continued. "She is shorter and not the frail type. She is showing me a cane that she used toward the end of her life. She is talking about religion. She wants you to know that she gets it now and it's alright. Also, she is showing you in a large field by yourself and says that is where you need to be."

The information was coming through quickly and I didn't have time to think. "Now she is showing me a box. It's very pretty decorated with pink decorations. It has a lock on it and it's filled with papers but the papers aren't real papers. They're symbolic, your childhood dreams. She says you've done two of the dreams already but there are many, many more here in the box that you need to take out and do. Also, she is showing me a clock and saying that you don't feel like you have enough time to fit it all in."

I paused for a moment. "How are you doing, Mary?"

"I'm great," she responded. "That makes total sense."

"*Really?*" I thought to myself. "Okay, so do you have any questions for her?" I asked out loud.

"Actually, that's my mom, and not really. I get the picture with what she's saying," Mary responded.

"Okay, so do you want me to ask any questions?" I asked again, surprised that there wasn't more dialogue between us.

"No. You can chat with the man if you want. I'd like to know who he is," she said.

I settled in once more to what was happening in front of me. The woman smiled a huge smile as if to say, "Thank you" and then faded into the background. Where she once stood now appeared a very tall, thin man. I wordlessly asked the spirit who he was and awaited his answer.

"I have the spirit guide here now. He is a very tall man, slender also." I paused as I stared at the interesting image in front of me. "He looks a lot like Abe Lincoln. Ha! That's cool."

"Abe, hey?" Mary asked.

"Yep. And he's telling me it's all about the pennies. He's saying to look for the pennies," I explained.

There was a moment or two of silence between us because when the Abe look-alike finished his statement he was gone. I searched for anyone or anything else, but there was nothing. I told Mary to take her time getting up while I went to fetch my smudge stick to clear the room out again. It was kind of like an eraser to a blackboard, removing the remaining energy from the reading.

Mary sat up and immediately started to give me feedback. "That was really, really cool, Beau! It all made sense!"

Mary went on to tell me she had been finding pennies in the most unusual places the last three days and that she had been doing some prayers with "abundance work." I wasn't sure what she meant by that, but it didn't really matter to me in that moment.

Mary then told me about a reading she had the week before that came through with a similar message. "She told me my mom had a box that was locked with papers in it, just like you did. I thought she was totally off, but then today you repeated exactly what she said almost word for word." She paused for a moment before she spoke again. "Obviously, I'm supposed to do something with this box."

Mary gave me a big hug and headed out front just in time to send the next person back to see me. Over the next few hours, with each person I read for, the readings became increasingly clear.

The next sitter's grandmother came through so strongly the client was sobbing by the time her reading was finished. Her grandmother showed me exactly how she died, what she looked like during life, her personality, and an image of herself walking back and forth in front of her granddaughter's couch hoping she could be seen. The sitter wanted to know when she would get past the pain of her death, and her grandmother laid out two calendars in front of me and took the second one away fast, meaning somewhere between one and two years. In addition to her grandmother, she had a very powerful spirit guide that explained how the sitter had lost one of her strongest attributes along the way—her sense of humor. The client agreed and expressed that it was something she was consciously trying to regain. After the reading the client told me she was excited to hear the messages, most of which resonated strongly with her.

The third sitter was a healer herself, so I fell back into anxiousness all over again. Thankfully, I connected with her spirit guide almost instantly. He was a very powerful Native American who showed me the place she would be moving to. He described it very well, even the time it took to drive there. I told her about the fire pits, that it was sacred land, that she had already planted herbs on it, and how the land was the key to unlocking a great spiritual growth for her. After the reading she complimented me, hugged me, and said the information I shared about her new place was accurate—even the herbs she had planted.

The fourth and final client of the day came in and I could tell this was not going to be as easy as the others. In her late 40s, she sat perfectly upright in an almost antagonistic posture. There was only one spirit that came through for her—a young, perky, female guide that spoke very clearly to me. She told me a man had broken the sitter's heart and abused her in her late twenties. I could see a black goopy substance that remained in the center of her body where the man symbolically placed it in her heart. I explained to her what I believed the goop was—the negativity and burden he left her with—and expressed that although there were times she believed she had gotten rid of it, it always came back. She nodded. The spirit then directed me to tell the client there was a bridge she needed to go to. She said she knew exactly what bridge her guide was talking about.

I continued asking the guide questions and listened while she told me there was something significant about the color green in the client's religion that would play a healing role in getting rid of this goop. I tried to get more details but the guide told me not to bother trying to figure it out. She said the client had a different religion than I did and it would be too difficult for her to explain it to me. I told this to the client and she grinned broadly, nodded excitedly, and said she absolutely knew what it was. The guide gave me a small nod and faded away.

I gave that last client some alone time to collect herself. I went out to the main area of the store where Mary was working and told her how I felt so much more confident about the readings now that I had done them, and how grateful I was to have been able to test myself like this at a professional store. When the last client came out and headed toward the door, she stopped to tell me she was really impressed. She said I was dead on, and that I would be a great success at this type of work.

As Troy drove me home, I stared out the window and talked to Grandma about the events of the night.

"Yeah, yeah. You did great," she said, with a slight blow-off about her. "But that was practice. That wasn't the real work." Puzzled, I leaned back a little deeper into my seat to get comfortable. We had an hour drive before we'd be home.

"What do you mean, that wasn't the real work? Isn't that what you want me to do?"

She looked intently in my eyes. "Yep, that's what they want you to do, but that was easy. It's the other ones that will be more difficult."

"The 'other ones?' You mean other readings? Like these weren't hard?!" I said, almost off ended, before it sank in that the day's readings weren't all that difficult.

"Yep. The ones like the Healing Clinic are what they want you to focus on," she said. "Those are the tough ones, the emotional ones, the ones they know you can handle. Oh sweetie, I am so proud of you."

As I sat there wrapped up in her praise, the word "they" came into my head and stuck there like a brightly colored pushpin. I had heard her use it twice now.

"What do you mean 'they?'"

"They. You know. Them," she said, like a politician trying to sidestep a question.

"Excuse me? I don't know who 'they' are," I snapped. *"I thought it was you that wanted me to do this work?"*

"I do, honey. I do," she said. "But I'm just here to support you. 'They' are the ones that want you to do the work."

We went back and forth like that for several minutes but Grandma just wouldn't give me more details.

"You'll know more later," she said. "You know I would never let anything happen to you."

"*Yes, I know,*" I said, as she winked at me. Her wink sent me back, remembering all the times growing up that I landed safely at her house and in her arms.

The road passed along for a few more minutes as I digested the idea that she wasn't alone in wanting me to do this. I felt her hand reach out to mine and squeeze it just slightly. It felt so real. My heart skipped and I held perfectly still so as to not ruin the moment.

"Is this where you get mystical and mysterious and fade into the background?"

"Fading, fading." she said, as she visually dimmed away to nothing.

"I love you."

For the rest of the ride home—and in many quiet moments after—I would continue to wonder who "they" were.

14

So This is What a Gunshot Feels Like

The next time I worked at Ed's Healing Clinic I had enough confidence to introduce myself as a psychic medium. As I walked around the space I felt more focused and purposeful, and wondered if this purposeful atmosphere was coming from "them."

I looked at each of the clients one by one and felt pulled toward only one, a young woman in her early twenties. She sported a trendy hairstyle, classy punk clothing, and tattoos and piercings that speckled her body. As she snuggled comfortably into a yoga chair on the floor, I approached her and asked if she wanted a reading. I felt confident enough to simply sit in front of her and relay any messages that would come through. She agreed and I took a seat, settling in face to face. It felt natural to read this way, both of us resting our backs on ergonomically built chairs that still allowed us to sit on the ground.

"My name is Beau. How are you?" I asked, as I reached out to shake her hand.

"Hi. My name is Carrie," she said, taking my hand in hers and shaking it gently.

"If it's alright with you I'd like to just sit silently and see who comes through to talk to you." As I spent a few moments stumbling through an explanation of how my intuition worked, two things happened. My inner critic put a mental sticky note on the left side of my brain to remind me to get my pre-reading speech in order, and she started to cry.

"I'm so sorry. What did I say?" I asked, stopping my rambling mid-sentence to comfort her.

"It's not what you said, it's just that," she paused. "I just lost someone really close to me a few days ago and I was wondering if they'd show up."

I sat silent for a while. Before this moment, it was always "my grandfather who died five years ago," or someone they couldn't identify at all. Carrie was wondering about someone who had *just* passed. It drove the point home for me; was I really doing this? *Can* I really do this? What kind of emotions would I stir trying to connect with someone whose death was so immediately "present?"

"I can do my best," I said, as I tapped my hand gently on her shin in the most comforting way I could manage. "I can sit and see who comes through."

"Okay," she whispered, as she started to pull herself together.

The pressure I began to put on myself was immense. What if I couldn't see the person she'd lost? Were they even available? I made another mental note to ask someone about how the otherside works.

"I just need to sit for a minute to really, really focus," I said, trying my best to act like I had done this before, fully knowing that my metaphorical training wheels were just now coming off.

She nodded and the mental chatter in my head started to take off. *"Don't start worrying now! You have to just go with it. Don't care about the outcome, just relax!"*

After what felt like forever trying to quiet my mind, a young man gradually appeared at her left side. He was down on one knee, as if to speak to me face to face. I stared at him for a while, watching as his gaze shifted slowly from me toward Carrie. When his eyes finally settled on her they lit up like she was the only person in the world.

"Did you lose a person who is male?"

"Yes," she responded quickly. I could sense she was working hard to be silent, to let me focus, in hopes I could succeed.

"A young man?"

"Yes."

"I'm sitting here looking at a young man, but, hold on," I said, as I started to see other images circle around him. I saw two numbers, a two and a four, floating in midair as if I was watching a Sesame Street skit. "Was he around twenty-four years old?"

"Yes," she gasped.

I could see him smile with a sense of relief, knowing she knew it was him. He reached out to stroke the side of her cheek and then gently ran his hand toward her ear as if to tuck away any loose strands.

"Were the two of you closer than friends?"

She nodded silently, tiny edges of her mouth starting to rise in a smile.

"Okay, I think I'm connecting with him," I said, taking a deep breath. A sigh of relief escaped me. "He seems to have an interesting personality."

"You could say that," she said, as her smile grew larger.

"He seems colorful in some way." He reached his hand out toward Carrie, pointing at her shoulder. I could have thought he was simply pointing at her but somehow I knew he was referring to her tattoos. "I think he's talking about tattoos."

"Yes. He had them," she confirmed.

"Tattoos," I said again, as I watched him move his hands back to himself in such a way that I knew he wanted me to elaborate on them. I saw flashes of a tattoo studio and countless sketches.

"I think he drew tattoos as well," I added.

"Yes, that was his job. He worked at a tattoo shop," she said, now leaning toward me as if to absorb anything that might come out of my mouth.

I kept looking at him, staring intently at his face. I watched as his eyes dropped from mine to the floor beneath him. Just then I felt heavy emotions rush in. I knew they were his and I felt myself "shift" as I had done a few times before. The witness—my vulnerable part—retreated, while the worker in me stepped forward.

Then, I heard the gunshot. The witness in me watched in horror as the worker now had a bullet tearing through her skull. I looked at him with a look of terror in my eyes. He looked back, apologetic. Somehow, I knew he had intentionally waited for me to split before he delivered that next piece of information, like it was the compassionate thing to do.

"What? What is it?" Carrie said, now frightened at my expression.

"Nothing," I said, quickly trying to return to a calm appearance. "Nothing. Well, it's alright. I'm just feeling something, that's all."

"Is he okay?!" she asked intently.

"Yes. Yes, he is perfectly fine." He continued to look on at me apologetically. "It's just that he's talking to me about a gunshot, um, I think to the head."

Her hands now pressed on her lips and her eyes flowed over. "Yes, that's how he died." She could barely get the words out.

He spoke of how he felt for her. How he wished she didn't have to go through the pain of his leaving. How thankful he was to have found her before he left. The conversation went on for a while between Carrie and her lost love with me sitting there like an interpreter.

Eventually his words slowed, the feelings started to fade, and I could sense a disconnect happening. He didn't leave, he just "disconnected." He didn't fade, only the intensity did. This was an entirely new experience for me. I could still see him standing there, even as I got up to leave.

"Thank you," I heard him say to me.

"*You're welcome,*" I said back to him in my mind.

I moved away from Carrie for the next person. I looked back one more time to see him crouched down on his knees, gently resting his forehead on her shoulder.

15

Help

With new eyes I now saw this ability Grandma opened up in me as a part of myself. It slowly became more natural for me to see and talk to those on the otherside. While I still marveled at every accurate piece of information, often running home to share it with Troy, anticipation and excitement slowly gave way to comfort and ease. And then, as soon as comfort and ease began to take root, "Their" plan for me started to unfold. One serious event after another.

One such event involved my friend Donna. We had been confidants for a number of years, sharing everything except one key piece of information—Donna was an alcoholic. The day she confessed her secret to me was the day she could no longer keep it together. For six months I tended to her; she was a friend I squeezed into my to-do list when I hoped no one was looking. Cleaning her apartment, checking her into the emergency room each time she reached her incapacitated limit, and doing her laundry were all responsibilities I took on for her, regardless of the pressure it put on me, my husband, my family. Her job gone and her license lost to a DWI, I was someone she called when she needed a ride to her therapist. The last time I drove her there, however, I realized I could do no more. She asked me to stay by her side through her appointment. I sat just a foot away and listened to her argue for an hour with the therapist over all her reasons for not checking into a rehab center. She didn't have the money. She didn't like how the treatment programs were run. And, mostly, she looked down on the level of company her fellow patients would be. As the irritating debate continued, I saw a male spirit come into form behind Donna. It was her father. I had met him before, during a previous reading for her, and I recognized him by both his appearance and the sadness in his eyes. He looked at me and said just one thing. "If she doesn't get help, she will die in ninety days."

I left that session arguing with her even more than her therapist had, letting my fear of losing her blossom into full-fledged anger. It went nowhere so I pulled up to the now familiar emergency room doors of the hospital instead of driving her home. "Until you check into a rehab program, I can't help you anymore," I said, as I looked into her drooping eyes.

"You have to drive me home! I am not going in there again," she yelled at me, as she swayed slightly in her seat. I turned to stare at the steering wheel, too tired to keep looking her in the face. "This is where I am dropping you off. I'm not bringing you home drunk. If you really want to go home, you'll have to find a different way."

"Aaahhh!" she screamed even louder.

"Bring me home NOW, Beau!"

"No, I love you, get out," I said, as I pointed to the red glowing sign over the automatic doors.

"You do this, and we are no longer friends!" Her fingers gripped my dashboard. "I am serious, Beau! You don't understand. You've never been in my shoes, and you don't know what you're doing. Drive me home!"

"You're going to die if you don't get help! Do you hear me?!" I yelled at my steering wheel. "Your dad, he told me."

"How dare you," she said in a quieter tone, staring at me as if I had slapped her.

I started to cry, quietly at first and then harder. With nothing left to say, she got out of the car. I drove away that day promising myself I would not help her or speak to her again until she made a real step toward getting sober.

Three months passed and I let Donna fade from my mind while I focused more on my intuitive path. Then, in an instant, she snapped back into my life. I was leaving a local movie theater and was crossing the street to the parking lot. It was cold and damp, so I pulled my coat in just a bit tighter to my body and looked both ways before crossing the street. Before I could step off the curb, the parking lot in front of me faded away and was replaced by a life-sized image of Donna lying face down in a ditch, dead.

As quickly as it appeared, the vision faded, and the parking lot came back into view. I stood frozen at what I had just witnessed, racing my eyes around the parking lot looking for something to ground me back into reality. I spotted my car and bolted for it.

"What was that?" I asked Grandma, as I climbed into the driver's seat and slammed the door.

She looked at me from the passenger seat, "It's Donna. You need to help her."

"Is she dead?"

"Not yet," she said, as she faded away.

"Wait! Come back here!" I shouted to Grandma as I felt myself panic.

I looked around and found nothing but a cold, empty car. I turned the key and did the only thing I could think of. I drove to Donna's apartment complex hoping I could find her. When I arrived I pounded on her front door. No answer. I peeked through the sliding glass doors and scanned for any motion. There was none. I spun around and searched for her car thinking she may have been stupid enough to drive, license or not. There it was, parked where it was always parked. Finally, I jumped back into my car and followed the vision as best I could, slowing down each time I came across a ditch. With no more help, no further advice, I was running out of things to try. It was time to give up. Should I call the police? What would I say? I picked up my cell phone. It rang while I was holding it, Donna's name on the caller ID.

"Where are you?!" I demanded as soon as I picked up her call.

"I'm... I'm...," she said in a feeble voice. "I... I need you."

"Donna! Look around. Tell me where you are."

>Click<

I stared at the road ahead, taking a second to let the reality of the moment sink in. I took one deep breath, turned my car around, and continued to search for her.

"Okay, I tried to do this myself because you are nowhere to be found, but now I really need your help. Where are you?" I yelled at the empty passenger seat next to me as tears now streamed down my face and sobs rolled through my gut. Images of Donna's dad replaying through my head, his three-month warning sinking into me like a Dear John letter.

"Please! Someone help me find her."

"Take a left up ahead," a voice echoed in the back of my mind. It didn't sound like Grandma's voice but I didn't care. It was a direction I gratefully followed.

I turned, and then felt a "pull" in my gut like a cord that was wrapped around my waist, tugging. I drove past a gas station and watched as the populated road turned to wilderness. When I felt the tugging sensation ease up, I slowed the car. A tiny flash of white flickered off to the left. I turned my head to it and saw Donna slumped down in the ditch, leaning against the base of a tree. I slammed on the brakes and pulled to the side of the road. Three giant leaps down into the ditch and I was by her side. There were incoherent noises coming from her mouth. Once all ninety pounds of a deathly cold Donna was loaded in my car, I was off to the emergency room. Again.

I parked directly in front of the large glass doors and ran in for help. I grabbed the sleeve of a six-foot-tall male nurse and pulled him toward the door as I told him how I had found her on the side of the road, passed out and drunk. He took a look at Donna, felt her icy neck for a pulse, lifted her into a wheelchair, and rolled her directly past the waiting room and into the back area.

"I need some information from you, please." I was startled by another nurse, who was also standing in the entryway.

"Me?" I asked.

"Yes, you. This way," she responded, as she motioned for me to follow her.

I was feeling stunned by what had unfolded. I watched the nurse walk away from me and round into the office chair behind the front counter. I knew the questions would soon begin. She would want details on how I found her and I wasn't sure what I would say. I looked back at my car parked in front of the doors and mentally started to plan my escape. After a few seconds of plotting, I turned back again to the nurse and did as she had asked. I walked up to her desk.

"Her name is Donna Walters," I said, with both hands now gripping the front counter. I looked over my shoulder at the exit door again. "I have to move my car."

As I walked quickly away, I could hear the nurse behind me, calling out for me to stop. Each step I took was one more step away from potential embarrassment. I climbed into the driver's seat of my car, felt the safety of silence, and took one deep breath as I turned the key in the ignition and headed home.

For the first time, I felt the enormous weight of responsibility that came with my ability to see and talk to spirits. Donna's father had warned me of her death and I had a choice to act on the information or leave it alone. That time, I chose to act.

16

and Regret

"Ah, Beau, you there?"

"Huh?" I said. "Sorry. I can't focus."

Troy stood up from the couch to head to the kitchen. "Yeah, I've noticed."

"It's not on purpose. I promise. I'm annoying, I know. It's just that I'm really struggling with focusing. People talk and I'm there at first, but then it just becomes like the teacher in Charlie Brown, you know? Whah, whahh, wuahh."

Over the last few months I had begun to feel "the pull" more and more. I would be focused in a conversation or task and then a fog would settle around me and invite me to think about something else, someone else, or somewhere else. At first I chalked it up to a late onset of an attention span disorder. Then I decided to monitor when and where it happened—and more importantly, why it was happening.

One week later we were in the air and on our way to Disney World, a trip that my family and I would make every few years. The three-hour airplane ride was almost too much for me to take. I couldn't put my finger on any particular cause, but this time flying felt different. I was more aware of how unnatural it was for humans to be flying. The metal body of the airplane was encapsulating me, making me feel like a sardine. If that wasn't enough, the massive guy sitting to my left fought for space with me, squeezing me into a seat that didn't quite fit to begin with. And to top it off, I clearly felt irritation hidden behind the forced smiles on the flight attendants' faces. I closed my eyes and squirmed in my seat to find comfort.

"Open your eyes," I heard Grandma say.

"But this makes me feel better," I responded in my head.

"It's not helping you. You need to look."

I leaned my head back, opened my eyes, and focused in on the call button for the flight attendant. Next to it were a few small fans and a couple other buttons that I didn't care about. *"What? There's nothing here but buttons."*

"Feel around you."

I was confused. *"I thought you wanted to show me something."*

"I do. But not with your eyes."

"Ugh! 'Open your eyes' she says, so I do. 'Don't look with your eyes' she says. What the heck?"

"Stop it. You're being a brat." Her voice deepened just a hint.

"Well, lady, come on. I'm squeezed into this sardine bucket, feeling eighteen different forms of anxiety, all of which I'm sure aren't mine. I can't really label it claustrophobia, but it feels really weird and now you want me to see something but not with my eyes?" I rambled through my thoughts. *"Can't I just get to Disney World?"*

"Are you done?" she said sharply.

"Yes. Sorry."

I sat quietly for a moment staring at the call button above me. It was red with a worn-down image of a stick figure flight attendant pasted on it.

"Just listen."

I perked up my ears and listened to Troy playing cards with the boys, to the woman in front of me complaining about the way a convention center was set up, and to the man behind me and to my left mumbling and flipping the pages of something I'm sure he was trying to read. Slowly, and almost without knowing it, that familiar foggy daze started to settle in, and the inside of the airplane began to fade away. The sounds closest to me became muffled and new sounds entered my head. I heard a dull whistling of air and the low hum of an engine. The sounds pressed their way into me and invited me to go further. The call button that was once dirty red had blurred and dissolved. One more blink and I was looking at silvery metal, pieced together with copious rivets. I was outside the airplane, below it and just under the wing. I turned to my right to see Grandma floating in air just under the main body of the plane.

"What are you doing out here?"

"The real question is, my dear," she winked, "has it sunk in yet that *you're* out here?"

I blinked, panicked, and was pounded back into my original seat and my original awareness, annoying sounds and all.

I looked around frantically for Grandma, spotting her sitting in the seat just in front of Troy. *"What the heck?!"*

"Neat, hey?" she asked me, with a huge grin on her face. "Now do it again."

"Um, yeah. Don't know how I did it the first time."

She nodded her head slightly, enough to say I knew more than I wanted to admit. "Just relax. Let the distraction take you."

I nodded back, thankful she took my sarcasm with patience. I leaned back in my seat and stared at the call button again, trying to retrace my actions to get the same result. I felt the force of my mind pushing to allow me to fade out of the plane. Every push, every thought, every idea got me nowhere.

"I don't think I can do it again," I said to her.

"That's because you're trying. You're not the driver, you know. You're the passenger," she explained. "I want to show you something and all I need you to do is say okay. Just breathe."

I nodded again, hoping the big man next to me simply thought I was adjusting my head. I decided to take a few deep breaths and focus only on the in and out of the air through my lungs. Finally, after more breaths than I wanted to count, I felt everyone around me fade away and the floating sensation start to work its way back into my core.

Just as the excited words *"I did it!"* rolled through my head, I was slammed back into the reality of sitting in a cramped airplane yet again.

"Yeah, you did it," Grandma said. "And you lost it."

"Grrr."

"Try again."

I tried again. I focused on my breathing just as I had a few minutes ago and found myself fading much more quickly this time. Reality around me fell away and I was once again under the wing of the plane.

I looked at Grandma with a curious expression on my face. She was under the body of the plane, floating in the same spot as she had the first time. "It's okay to be excited now that you did it. You're really here."

"Okay. In that case... cool!" I said, with enthusiastic nervousness.

I turned and let my eyes follow the metal to the front of the plane. It was a strange view for me, one I had never seen before. There was no front of the plane, just metal fading into nothing as the nose curved up toward the front.

I turned back to Grandma to ask her the only question on my mind, *"What is happening to me?"*

"The distraction, sweetie, isn't a distraction. It's an invitation to let go of the agreed upon reality," she explained. "Focus is just something people say when they don't want to really see."

"I actually understand that, which I think is the weirdest part of what's happening right now," I said.

She smiled back at me. "I just wanted to let you know that I am holding the plane, you know, making you safe on your flight."

"Ah, thanks," I said, confused. *"It's kind of strange, though, since you were so scared to fly when you were alive."*

"Two things, sweetheart," she said. "First, it's hard to be scared of dying when you're already dead. Second, yes, I was terrified to fly. Why do you think I'm holding up this damn thing?"

My eyes naturally closed as the laughter rolled over me. When I opened them I was back in the cabin, smells, noises, and all.

"Grandma?"

"Yeah?"

"Why aren't we outside anymore?"

"Well, I just wanted to tell you I was watching over your flight. You know, so you wouldn't be scared."

I didn't respond. I was too excited to even tell Troy.

Or not.

"Troy," I said, as I leaned over the aisle to him. He leaned back, listening. "Grandma is watching over us."

"Um, okay. And?"

"And nothing. That's it. I was just excited to tell you."

"But she's scared to fly."

I chuckled at the image I had seen earlier. "I know, right? How weird. I guess she lost that fear."

Troy leaned back in his seat to continue his card game with the boys, as if what I was saying lacked interest. A few minutes later a familiar smell filled the air, that sweet, unique smell of Grandma. I breathed it in deeply to soak up the comfort.

"Beau!" Troy said with urgency, from across the aisle.

"Yeah?" I leaned in toward him.

"Do you smell that?"

I nodded with a big smile on my face.

"That's her!" he said, eyes wide with shock.

I nodded again, this time fighting back the tears. He smelled her too.

Finally, Disney. The happiest place on earth. At the end of our third day there, Troy led the way onto the shuttle bus that took tired tourists back to their hotels. We settled into the fourth and fifth benches where I sat next to the window, exhausted, waiting patiently for the rest of the bus to fill up. Troy took the aisle seat while the boys sat in front of us.

"Are you happy now?!" yelled a grandmother at her ten-year-old grandson as they walked down the aisle, stopping next to Troy. All seats were full, and standing was their only choice.

The boy nodded his head as he sniffed back the tears that had been pouring down his face.

The grandmother bent down to growl in the boy's left ear, loud enough that we could hear. "I don't know why you always need to call your mother!" The boy simply looked straight ahead, trying not to move.

I looked at Troy and we both rolled our eyes at the situation. Disney is a slice of heaven, if you can ignore the occasional dysfunctional family.

"We had a pretty good day," Troy started to speak, "I like the fact that..." his voice fading into the background as the fog in my mind started to creep in.

After I lost the sound of Troy's voice, I lost the sound of the rest of the bus too. I was too tired to fight it, and, remembering what Grandma had said about focus, I let myself fall into it. Replacing the sounds of the bus, the chatter, the kids playing, and the nasty grandmother, was a new sound. It was the sound of a little boy, isolated and alone, in a room large enough to create an echo.

"If I'm quiet then it doesn't hurt as bad," I heard the boy say to me.

I looked straight ahead to what should have been the back of my son's head but instead I saw the ten-year-old boy from the bus crying. His unhappiness was not news to me. What happened next, however, was. The grandmother entered the vision, walked up to the boy, and grabbed the back of his neck with her hand. She squeezed and shook him as her eyes lit up with rage. I gasped at the sight, and it brought me back to the reality of the crowded bus. I looked over at the boy, still standing in the center aisle, quietly staring at the floor below him.

I grabbed onto Troy's arm tightly and leaned into his ear to whisper. "I just saw a vision of that grandmother grabbing the back of that boy's neck and hurting him!"

Troy leaned back and smiled as if to say I was overreacting.

"I'm serious."

"I know you are," Troy responded, as his look shifted to one that said, "What the hell do you want me to do about it?"

I stared ahead but from the corner of my eye I saw the ten-year-old boy start to fidget. He had worn a hooded sweatshirt that was now, in a crowded bus, too hot to keep on. As he pulled at the sweatshirt's sleeves, his neck revealed four bruises, three on one side and one on the other. They were the perfect fit for a hand.

"Troy!" I said, with force under my breath as I slugged him in the arm.

"Huh?" he said, as he looked at me.

My eyes shot back and forth from Troy to the boy, begging my husband to look at the ten-year-old. He saw what I saw.

"I am sorry, honey," he said. "The bus ride is almost over. Hang in there."

I sat still, feeling the tires turn slower and slower as they pulled into the next stop. "Why would they show me something like that? I don't want to see things like that," I said, with sad frustration.

We went back to the hotel room and I struggled with how to handle the situation. Feeling lost and alone, I buried the memory of the vision and uncomfortably chose to be present with my family for the remainder of our vacation.

The Pull, it seemed, could feel like a blessing or a curse.

Whenever I think back to that day, I imagine what I would do now if presented with a similar situation. My intuition alerted me to someone in peril and it was even confirmed in the physical. Then, I was afraid—or embarrassed—to get involved. Now, I walk a fine but clear line between respecting others' privacy and stepping up to serve those before me. After all, it's not about me.

17

Mama Told Me Not to Go

"Passed by an office that was for rent today," Troy threw out at me randomly one day, after he came home from work.

"Why would you get an office?" I responded.

"I'm talking about an office for you," Troy said. "That's what you said your Grandma wanted you to do, right?"

"Fine. You get the office and I'll step up to the plate. Promise," I said, as I heard the very quiet words of "good job" come from my right.

I hoped he wouldn't follow through, but he did. And in less than three weeks I was in my new office doing readings. The building itself left something to be desired. After climbing the split entry stairs, I found myself standing in a 1970s waiting room for what was once a medical building. Renovations were clearly done only when something fell apart, thus the dark wood and musty carpet remained, well, dark and musty. My office was one of seven, all lined up one after another on the second floor.

Troy sealed the deal by installing beautiful new carpeting. Unfortunately, due to his work schedule he had to install it at ten o'clock at night. As he did, I stood in the long hallway of the empty building and watched as a male spirit manifested twenty or so feet in front of me. He came through transparent, but clear enough for me to see his dirty, blue-collar clothing and an intimidating look on his face. His stare captured me and I felt trapped in my body as he came closer and closer, my heart beating faster and faster.

Now just inches away from my face, I felt my stomach flip as he began to speak. "This is *my* building, understand?!"

"Ah, yeah," I said, thinking how I could get him the heck away from me.

"Beau?" I heard Troy say, from inside the room. "Who are you talking to?"

"Um, a really creepy spirit," I answered. The stranger laughed a grinding laugh that rasped through my body. If his intent was to scare me, it was working fabulously.

"I think he's upset that we're putting new carpet in," I called out to Troy.

"Why should I care? He's dead," Troy said, as he stretched one corner of the carpet under a heating unit, clearly not affected by the spirit's presence.

With Troy's comment the male pulled back from me, standing a few feet away looking at Troy. He was stunned, as if he was reminded this was not a dream. He really was dead, and Troy's comment snapped him back to reality.

"I know you're dead, but this is my new office and I'm just trying to make it look nice, that's all. You should be happy with that, not pissed off and all cranky," I said aloud to the stunned spirit.

My fear was subsiding, which probably had something to do with the fact that he was no longer two inches from my face and his energy no longer mixed with mine. He turned to look at me again, this time with defeat in his eyes.

"Okay, don't feel bad," I said. "I'm sorry. I just mean that I'm trying to make it nice. You don't have to get all up in my face about it."

"But it's my building," he said again. This time it was different. This time I could hear heartbreak in his voice.

"The building is important to you?" I asked him and watched him nod to confirm.

"Just respect my building," the man said, as he turned to walk back down the hallway.

"Will do," I said, happy to have my personal space back. The man walked to the end of the hallway and took a left into the waiting room. I was struck by the curious behavior of not fading away to nothing like the other spirits had done, like taking a left around a corner was a better exit for him, an exit that reminded me he would always be there.

The carpet was installed and all that was left to do was to bring over the furniture, which was currently piled up in my living room at home. But before I would move in and start doing readings, I decided it would be smart to get a better grasp on what it meant to really do this work professionally. I signed up for another event at Crescent Moon Herbals. This time it was a group reading being done by a well-known medium named Joanne.

Part of me was going out of curiosity, the need to see someone else with my ability in action, someone who was established and knew what she was doing. I wanted to see how she handled the crowd, and if she was one hundred percent accurate or if she faltered from time to time. The other part of me was drowning in doubt (yet again) over my own abilities. Sick of the struggle, I went to see if a stranger would tell me I had no reason to doubt.

I parked the car along the edge of Mary's manicured lawn and Grandma came through before I had a chance to even open my door.

"Tell me again why you're coming to this," she said, as she looked straight through me.

"You know why. You know everything about me. Why would you ask?!" I said in frustration.

"I'm asking so you'll consider it one more time before you go in."

"Are you telling me I shouldn't be here?"

She chuckled, "No, you should go. Go on in, if that's what you think you need."

"I do need it, otherwise I wouldn't be here."

She winked at me and spoke sarcastically. "Yeah, because comparisons work great for you, don't they?"

I glared back at her.

"Why would you set yourself up like this? To compare yourself? This, this, all this," she said, as she waved her hands around as if to point out everything in life. "This isn't about comparisons. This is about being true to you."

"Can I go in?" I asked, wanting to watch Joanne more than I wanted to take Grandma's advice.

"Yeah, honey," she said with a sigh. "Let's go."

I checked in at the front counter and made my way back to the familiar room where the event was taking place. There were a handful of people sitting in chairs lined up row by row, but Joanne was nowhere in sight. I counted fourteen people—not everyone was going to get a reading in the next two hours. I found an empty spot in the middle row that was perfect for me, secluded enough to feel safe but not too far away from where Joanne would stand. I looked around the room wondering what each person's reason was for coming to such an event. Chances were good, I thought, I was the only other medium secretly watching and taking mental notes. One minute after seven, Joanne came into the room.

You could tell she had been meditating, centering herself, focusing in on what she was about to do. My first professional observation of the night—meditate before a group reading. She began by talking about mediumship in general and what she does compared to other psychics and mediums. I found her to be very down to earth and not overly rehearsed. My next professional observation—relax.

Fifteen minutes into the presentation, Joanne started to tune into people on the otherside. I liked how she presented them and how they fell into line with a guest each time. Once someone raised his hand to say the spirit she was communicating with was for them, Joanne really honed in to the spirit, hardly looking at the living person sitting to her side. She pulled out detail after detail. I was impressed. I was excited that I was lucky enough to witness a true medium at work, to see how she works with her abilities. I sat back and finally felt at ease because I had gotten what I came for. Turning to Grandma, I smiled and she smiled back.

The night went on, and with only twenty minutes left in the event a thought hit me. Joanne had just enough time to do one more reading. Wouldn't it be cool if Grandma would talk to her? Looking to my right, I smiled at Grandma. Quietly, in my head so as to not interrupt, I sparked a conversation with her.

"Pssst."

She turned to look at me with that knowing look across her face. She was the same transparency as she always was, but this time she had a particularly strong glow about her.

"Go talk to her."

"Why?"

"Come on, Grandma," I responded like a whiny ten-year-old. *"Here I sit, with inside access to my loved one who's passed over. It would be way, way cool if you talked to her."*

"Anything in particular you want me to say?" she said, almost mockingly.

"Seriously, go check in with her. It would be such a cool trip." I was now begging.

"Fine," she said shortly, and she disappeared.

Once she was gone my throat tightened up and my gut flipped. I instantly realized why I really wanted her to communicate with Joanne. It wasn't for fun. It was because I wanted someone else to tell me I wasn't crazy, that everything I'm hearing from Grandma is real. I tried to relax but found myself having difficulty breathing. All of a sudden the stakes felt very high. I knew that what I thought I saw was my grandmother telling me she would communicate with Joanne. If that didn't happen—if she didn't talk to Joanne—it would prove that it's all in my head and that everything up to this point was just make-believe. Time moved horrifically slowly at this point as I watched Joanne wrap up the reading she had been doing for the mother and daughter that sat in front of me. "Okay, I have another woman coming through."

Joanne started to describe her as the audience sat in silence, those who hadn't been read yet eager that it might be for them. "She is short and rounded around the middle. She strikes me as the type of woman who had a massive capacity to love. I'm getting a name that starts with J and contains an N."

My heart leapt. Grandma's name was Josephine. Those things fit, could it be her? I raised my hand to let the medium know it was resonating with me. Just then, the woman next to me raised her hand as well.

"So, both of you can relate to this information?" Joanne asked.

We both nodded.

"Who do you think is coming through for you?" Joanne pointed straight at me.

"I think it's my Grandmother."

"And you?" Joanne asked, pointing to the woman sitting next to me.

"It's a friend of my dad," the woman said.

It might not have showed on my face, but I was laughing inside. Here sat two women, one of which thinks a friend of her dad's is communicating with her, the other, a grandmother. I knew she was stretching, hoping to get a reading.

"Well, let me work this out," Joanne said. "It sometimes happens like this. We'll just get some more information and try to sort it all out."

She paused for a moment to connect again with the spirit that I was certain was Grandma. A strong feeling of surreal came over me. I was amazed that Grandma was really doing it. Maybe it's not in my head after all.

"The woman that is coming through shows that when she died there was something with her midsection," Joanne continued.

The woman next to me raised her hand immediately.

"Hold on," Joanne said.

I could tell Joanne knew it wasn't for her. I sat patiently.

Joanne continued. "She is showing me liver issues."

"That's my Grandma," I piped up, now tired of the woman next to me who was acting like a shopping addict at a department store sale.

"Okay, I agree," Joanne said, and then paused to gather more info.

After two minutes she started to speak again. "I am seeing art-work. Does that make sense?"

I nodded my head in agreement. As I did, I started to see my grandmother's transparent frame standing face-to-face with Joanne.

"She is telling me you did a painting of some sort for her. It looks like it's framed," Joanne continued.

I nodded again.

"I see you. Little, but blonde. Not a redhead," Joanne stated.

I laughed, along with a couple others who were close enough to see it. Blonde was the original, the red was purchased.

"The piggy tails are really tight?" Joanne asked.

"Yes," I answered. "Too tight, as a matter of fact." The crowd laughed again.

"And there's some sort of card game you played with her all the time?" Joanne asked.

"Yeah. That would be cribbage."

"Okay." Joanne paused.

After a few moments of silence, a smile came over her as if she had just discovered a deep secret of mine. She broke her gaze with my grandmother and turned to look me dead in the eyes before she spoke again. "You're a medium."

I stared back at her, frozen. I felt busted, as if I had been outed. "Yeah," was all I could muster.

Joanne smiled again, more peaceful this time, and continued with her information. "Your grandmother is showing me a duplex that is full of furniture, like way too much furniture. It seems to make it hard to walk through. Does that make sense?"

"Yes," I responded, thinking about the extra furniture sitting in my living room, waiting to go to my office.

"She is also showing me a big sign that says FEAR," Joanne continued, holding her hands up as if to show me she was reading a billboard-like sign. "She wants you to know that there is nothing to be fearful of. You should just go for it. Wait, actually, she is saying, quote, 'Get over yourself!'"

That broke the uncomfortable awkwardness I was suffering from pretty quickly. "Get over yourself" is exactly the phrase Grandma would use to shake me out of my doubt. I watched as Grandma disappeared from the front of the room and returned to my side, now laughing at me like that entire event was hysterically funny to her.

"Well," Grandma whispered to me, "you asked for it."

I shook my head slightly. *"Yes, I did."*

I thanked Joanne as I left and wended my way through the mingling crowd to my car. In payback fashion, I drove home listening to "I told you so" in countless different ways for most of the drive. Regardless, I was glad I went, and I was excruciatingly grateful for my short little guide who loved me enough to reluctantly give me the proof that I personally needed.

18

House Clearing 101

I was now seeing regular clients in my new office. Deep secrets were being shared with me. I was skilled at confidentiality. What I wasn't skilled at was not letting it affect me.

I found a therapist. I scheduled full-hour sessions with Dr. Joel Glenn Wixson, a clinical psychologist. "Emotionally taxing" were words I used when we spoke the first time. I explained to him that I didn't read the "What to Expect in Opening Up" manual. He explained to me that the manual didn't exist. I knew we would get along. I met Joel through his wife Heather, a fellow homeschooling mother. We were attending the kids' co-op together and I kept hearing about her husband, this down-to-earth and open-minded therapist. I asked her if he was taking on new patients. She said he was.

My first conversation with Joel went relatively well. We talked about what I did for work and how it was affecting me. I could sense he was partially on board but reserving the right to be a healthy skeptic. The best quality about him was his complete lack of judgment. I could tell him anything and he wouldn't blink an eye. I felt comfortable with him.

After one of the first meetings, I offered to help Joel and Heather with their old house. They had bought their dream home in Kittery, Maine, but were still sitting on a house they owned in Portsmouth, New Hampshire, just a few miles away. They were having trouble selling it and for some reason it came up that there might be something wrong with the house. I offered to walk through it to see if I could pick up on any energetic problems.

I arrived at the hundred-year-old house, the one that seemed as if it didn't want to change owners, and looked around. It was a beautiful New Englander with amazingly manicured gardens, the kind that made even the most homebound person want to go outside to linger in them. We entered the front door and I noticed the home was still filled with furniture. They left several pieces behind to make it more attractive to potential buyers. We went to the living room and sat down.

Since this was another new experience for me, I brought my favorite distracters, my Angel cards. I laid three of them out on the table, but none of them really spoke to me. They said a few things about Heather and Joel personally, but nothing that would help me understand why the home wasn't selling. After a few moments, however, I saw the shape of a male come into form behind Heather. He was wearing blue overalls and smiling at me with patience in his eyes.

"There's a man coming in. He's wearing blue overalls and holding something. I can't seem to make out what it is."

"What does he look like?" Joel asked.

I stared a bit harder hoping more details would come through, but other than the overalls and dark hair, everything was fuzzy. "I just know that he has dark hair."

"Well, why is he here?" Heather asked.

I watched the man raise his right arm and point at Joel. *"Are you related to Joel?"*

"Yes," he responded. He began to choke up emotionally and I could feel it run through me as if I was sharing his feelings. "I am so proud of him."

The pride was so solid I could feel it. "He is here for you, Joel. I think it is a father or grandfather. Not sure. He says he is proud of you."

"Okay. That could be my dad, or maybe even my uncle," Joel said. "The overalls would fit either of them."

The man, hearing Joel's attempt to place him in the family line, now came in more clearly for me—clear enough to show me what he was holding. "He is holding up a box-type object." I showed Joel with my hands that it was about the size of a book. "It says something on it. Fire? Fox? Fox Fire?"

"The Foxfire Book!" Joel burst out, as he leaned back in his seat. It was as if he had been hit with something unseen. "Wow, that's the book that I've been living my life by. It's the book that I've been learning from these last few years. He's proud of me for that?"

I was excited that Joel, the therapist who was now keeping me sane, was on the receiving end of such a powerful moment as this. We spoke about it for a few minutes, and the spirit moved on.

As beautiful as this was, however, it didn't help us with the house problem. I asked if I could walk through it.

Heather and Joel were more than happy to let me get started with whatever I needed.

I walked to the front of the residence and climbed the intricately carved staircase. I was stopped at the top by an overbearing female spirit in a long dress. While the man in overalls felt like he belonged here, she didn't. She felt somehow intrusive.

She peered down at me and began to speak. She told me she had lived in the house with another female and a male. Unlike the other female, the male, she explained to me, didn't live there long. "He was lost at war." She then pointed down the stairs at Heather, saying how much she loved her because she was so easy to manipulate. The woman showed me a vision of Heather settling into the house years earlier and finding herself becoming more and more obsessed with the house and the care of it.

The vision continued and I saw the female spirit's energy radiating out like a cloud of moving particles, the cloud wrapping around Heather. The spirit attached herself to Heather, like it wanted to change her behavior and take over her will.

"I had her from the day she moved in," the spirit growled.

"*You're dead! What are you still doing here?*" I asked.

"I'm supposed to be here," she said, and then she hesitated.

For a minute she seemed confused. I watched her demeanor change like she was melting off a belief that empowered her. She walked into a bedroom and I followed.

"You've got someplace else that you're supposed to be and it would be great if you could head that way soon," I said. *"They took good care of your home, didn't they?"*

"Well, yes," she responded, with a hint of defeat in her voice. "But I live here," she said. "It's *my* house."

I didn't know what to do at this point. I had heard about "stuck spirits" before in conversations with Ed, and Grandma mentioned them as well, but I never bothered to ask what I should do if I met one.

I decided to start with the obvious and asked the woman if she could cross over now and leave the house behind. The "no" I got in response was forceful and stubborn. Stumped like a contestant on a game show, I continued trying to think of something to do.

"Heather?" I called her over to the room I was in. "Can you come in here?"

Heather sat down on the bed and I filled her in on the situation. "I have this female spirit here and she is attached to you. When you moved in here did you feel more neurotic about house maintenance? More here than in any of the other places you lived?"

"Come to think about it, yeah. There's something about this house that I just can't seem to settle into, since the day we moved in. And now I'm having a hard time letting go of it," she said.

I wasn't sure how to explain to Heather what I thought was going on, so I just said it the best I could. "There is a woman here who wants you to stay. She feels like she's in charge of the house, and, for that matter, in charge of you."

Heather wasn't pleased. We talked for a bit about her experiences with the home, and any unusual feelings she might have had when she lived there. Eventually we drifted to what she knew of the house's history. She told me the original owners of the house were a pair of sisters. The spirit had mentioned living there with another woman, so it clicked in me that it was probably her sister.

With no other ideas to try, I decided to ask the female spirit if she wanted to see her sister again—and something very strange took place. Before I could ask anything, the spirit responded as if she had read my mind. She began to dissolve right in front of me. I couldn't understand what just happened—it was like she dropped her guard and left. I scanned the room and there was no sign of her. She was just gone. It felt like a shroud had lifted and the atmosphere lightened.

Then the doorbell rang. Heather went downstairs to find Joel talking to a young couple on the doorstep. I listened with curiosity as the man expressed his apologies for intruding, but that he had been at the open house earlier that day and wanted his fiancée to see it for herself. I quietly continued going through the house to clear out anything else, making sure to avoid the potential buyers as I went.

The only other energy I found was that of a man in his thirties rocking back and forth in the upstairs music room. He stood in front of the window and he seemed to have an intellectual disability.

"What are you looking at?" I asked him.

He turned and smiled, easing my tension. "They put those houses there," he said.

"*Those houses?*" I asked, as I pointed to the handful of houses across the street.

"Yep. Them. They built them," he said, not removing his stare from the neighboring homes.

"Were you here before they were built?" I asked.

He nodded yes.

"What was there before?"

"Fireflies and grass," he said.

I felt a sadness roll over me and I knew it was his. *"Do you see a light around you? There should be a light nearby."*

He nodded again as if to say he knew of the light I spoke of.

"If you see the light, you can go into it. When you do, you can see the fireflies and the grass again," I explained to him, feeling awkward about making a promise that I wasn't completely sure was true.

He turned to me and beamed a smile so big it moved his entire head. He put both his hands together in excited anticipation and started to fade.

From my right I could feel my grandmother pushing for my attention. I turned to her and asked, *"Is he gone? Did he cross over?"*

"Yes, honey. He did."

"Okay, that was easy. Both of them were relatively easy. Is it that simple?"

"Yes and no. Some are. Some aren't."

"Why was that one easy?"

"Because he trusted you. He knew you cared."

I let her words sink in for a moment, looking back on the two spirits I had just crossed over. I did care. Regardless of the woman's behavior and her getting under my skin, I did feel sorry for her apparent plight. I wanted to help them both, like it was something I was born to do. It was so natural and instinctual, I wondered about the source of my compassion.

I went back downstairs and filled in Joel and Heather on the male in the music room. The young couple had already left to get a feel for the neighborhood. Mission apparently accomplished, the three of us left too.

The following Tuesday another male spirit came through while I was in session with Joel.

"I want to talk to Joel," he said.

"*Dude, you're on my dime,*" I replied, half joking, half serious.

"Sorry. Just tell him 'seven days.'" He smiled and faded away.

I relayed the message to Joel as the session ended.

One week later—the following Tuesday—my phone rang. It was a very excited Heather. They had just received an offer on the house. Even better, the offer came from the young couple that happened to stop by when I was clearing the lingering spirits.

"Funny how the universe works, isn't it?" I heard the familiar voice come from my right.

"Yeah, Grandma. It is," I responded. *"So, was that all there was to it? I asked a couple spirits to cross, they did, and now everything is normal?"*

"Sometimes," Grandma said.

"I think I'm beginning to really like this work."

"I knew you would." She winked.

19

Lloyd Overstays His Welcome

Joel continued to be a rock, someone I could process my thoughts with regardless of how bizarre those thoughts were.

"So, where do I start?" I would say to Joel.

"Anywhere. Pick a place and go," was his typical reply.

I rested my elbows on my knees and looked down at my feet. A sense of desperation had been hovering over me.

"How about 'I wish I could turn all this off'?"

"Turn what off? Seeing spirits?"

I nodded. "More specifically, seeing them all the time. They're everywhere now." I sighed and hoped Joel would say something. He didn't.

"It came in waves at first which seemed manageable. I would see them around me for a few days, then I wouldn't. It kept going back and forth like that, and now I'm seeing them pretty much all the time."

I waited for Joel again, but he remained quiet. He does that a lot.

"The worst is at night," I went on. "I feel like I'm in a stupid horror flick. I'd hide under my pillow all night if I could. Do you know how hard it is to sleep when a stranger is standing there watching you?"

"So what do you do?" he asked.

"I drink wine. It's the only thing that shuts it off. I've tried meditation, wearing symbolic necklaces, I've tried everything I can think of. Wine is it so far," I sighed again. "But it doesn't last all night."

"And?" Joel prompted.

"Wine has other effects too I end up having to go to the bathroom," I said. "I have to cover my eyes as I walk." I showed him by holding my hands over my eyes leaving just enough room at the bottom to see where I would step.

Joel chuckled. "Does that work?"

"Nope. Not always. Last night I saw bloody work boots. Just off to the left, next to the bathroom. I'm pretty sure they were attached to someone," I said, as I fell back into the couch and pulled my knees up into my chest.

"Did you look to see who?"

"Ah, no! I peed as fast as I could, raced back to bed, and tried to fall back asleep, yes, with the pillow over my head."

Joel laughed again and then sat for a moment. "Humans can handle anything new once they have a context for what they're experiencing," he said.

"So, I'll just keep telling myself that I'm building a context for dead people around me?"

But talking about it didn't stop it from happening. A few nights later I was in my kitchen pouring my typical glass of "make the dead people go away" when a short, elderly man showed up out of nowhere. "*Who are you?*" I asked.

"Please call my daughter," he said, with a hopeful look in his eyes. He wore a mechanic's outfit and I could faintly make out the shape of an old sports car behind him.

"You want me to call your daughter?"

He nodded and I looked away, back at the empty wine glass. "*I'm not doing this right now. Please leave me alone. Please.*"

"My daughter...," he repeated.

"I'm sorry, but I'm tired. I don't want to do this right now; I just want to go to bed."

"Please!" He swept in just inches from my face as a chill ran up my spine.

"What if," I stumbled, *"I write down whatever it is you want to*

say on a piece of paper." I picked up a pen and an old envelope from the counter. *"I'll write it down and deal with it in the morning?"*

He backed up and began to flash images in front of me. I jotted it down as fast as I could, but nothing spoke of his daughter. I didn't ask. I didn't want to. I just wanted to go back to bed. As I finished writing "mechanic" on the paper, I looked up to see a blissful smile and both of his hands extended in front of him holding a partially molded clay pot. Drips of wet clay rolled down his arms and through his fingers. This was too weird, even for me. Could it all just be my imagination? I put the paper in the pocket of my robe and headed upstairs. As I was about to step into my bedroom, up popped the mechanic again.

"Put the information in the computer," he said.

"What?" I said out loud. "No. Nuh-uh. You agreed we could deal with this in the morning!"

"I lied."

"You lied?! You can't lie. You're dead."

"I lied."

I scowled at him.

Troy heard me talking to myself, so I filled him in. He agreed with the mechanic—to put the information into the computer, if just to get back to sleep. Two against one, I gave in. I entered "mechanic that loved pottery obituary" in Google. Fourth result on the page was a nearby funeral home. I found there was indeed a mechanic, named Lloyd, who had died three months earlier, a mechanic that loved pottery.

I was dumbfounded. This guy was for real. I turned the chair around to find he was gone. The hallway was empty. The next morning arrived. Lunch, errands, and dinner all passed by before I saw Lloyd again. He was sitting patiently on my living room couch. "Call my daughter, please," he said.

"No, Lloyd. What am I supposed to say? 'Hey there, I'm a medium with a message from your dead dad?' I can't do that Lloyd—it would be horrible!"

"Please?"

He seemed like such a sweet man. *"No,"* I said, feeling guilty.

For the next two weeks Lloyd was everywhere. He was in the garden with me. He was on the couch while I exercised. He was waiting on the stairs when I got up each morning. He sat at the table when we ate. He was like that pesky uncle that overstays his visit. Lloyd finally stepped way over the line by appearing in my bathroom just as I was stepping out of the shower. This *had* to stop!

"So, what do you think you should do?" Joel said, in our next session.

"I think I need to call the daughter."

I called her that night. I rehearsed what I would say at least ten times, and finally made the call. To my surprise it went okay. I expressed how I wanted nothing from her, that I just wanted to tell her what her father wanted to say so he could move on. Lloyd was worried about her. He explained that he knew her boyfriend was starting a business with her but had plans to dump her and run with the money. She said it made sense but that she needed to think about it, that she wasn't sure what to believe. I completely understood, and again apologized profusely for calling her the way I did.

As I hung up the phone, Lloyd smiled so broadly it made all the stress worth it. I could feel his emotions and see he was happy to have had the chance to warn his daughter. I looked at Lloyd with an odd newness now. I felt bad it had taken me so long to get the courage to call her. Here was this dear man wanting one last thing said to his daughter, and I was so worried about what she would think of me that I let it stop me from doing what I was supposed to do. Lloyd thanked me, and I thanked him. He faded away and I fell back into the pillows of my king-size bed. I stared at the ceiling and took one of the deepest breaths in my life.

"What am I doing?"

"You're doing what you're supposed to be doing, silly," I heard Grandma next to me.

I was excited she was there. I felt less alone. *"That whole situation was tough for me, lady."*

"Which part was the toughest? That you had to push yourself onto a stranger or that Lloyd lied to you?"

I turned my head to see her face. *"Both, as a matter of fact. You're like Joel. You both seem to be able to get down to details fast."*

"I'm not worried about anything other than what is affecting you. It's easy to get to the details that way," she smiled.

I felt normal again for the first time since Lloyd showed up.

"When it comes to calling a stranger, you have to ask yourself who is more important in the moment."

"Me, or the stranger? I feel like I'm being set up somehow to be the good guy or the bad guy."

"When I asked who was more important, I was talking about the daughter or Lloyd, not you or Lloyd. You have nothing to do with it."

"That doesn't make me feel any better."

"One day it will," she said. "Here's the deal. Lloyd is stuck. He's the important one here. So you upset the daughter a little bit. Who cares? She'll get over it. She received the information, which is all Lloyd wanted. She can use it or not use it. Besides, she's got a great dinner conversation now," Grandma laughed.

"So, he was stuck?" I asked. *"How does that make him more important?"*

"You already know that stuck means a person hasn't crossed over into the light. It was important for Lloyd to cross over. More important than keeping Lloyd's daughter in a life of sunshine and butterflies."

"Okay, so stuck people need to cross over. Got it."

"There are three places you can be," she explained, as an image followed along with her like a sixth-grade educational movie. "When you are living, you are on earth. After you die, you cross over into the light and go to the otherside. But in the middle—between earth and the otherside—is a place where people can become stuck or lost."

"So there actually is an 'in-between?'" I asked, recalling conversations with others about this mysterious place.

"You can call it that if you like," she said. "When you die, you first go to the in-between. You are still the exact same person, without the body. You can lie, cheat, manipulate, hate, cry, hurt, and so on and so on. It isn't until you cross over into the light that you let go of the emotional crap and find peace."

I watched the movie as the image of a person went through the death process, shedding a layer at each step. First the body, and then, when crossing over, the emotional garbage he carried in life. The next person went through the same process, but seemed to be stuck in glue or something when he tried to shed the emotional stuff. I imagined giving him a little poke with my finger to help him out, and it worked.

"See?" said Grandma. "It's all so simple."

"It really is," I said, as I waited to see if the next person would need a poke too.

"Some of them just need a bit of help," she added, "someone like you to give them a boost. That's all Lloyd needed." Grandma gave me a peculiar smile, and then faded out as she always does.

I told Joel what happened the next time we met.

Joel smiled a huge smile. "I always said, 'Show me a medium that channels your average Joe, the mechanic that works down the street, and I'll believe.' Now, here it is. Nice."

20

Heed the Whisper or Get the Shout

My newfound profession was not handpicked by me. It was not one I had been dreaming about since I started playing dress-up as a kid. It was thrust on me, so I decided to do it as long as it didn't interfere with the rest of my life. Fat chance that, eh?

Grandma kept telling me I needed to slow down. "You can't be intuitive if you're always distracted," she'd say. At the same time, I kept trying to cling to some kind of normalcy, even if it was just the comfort of my poor, dying car.

My purple Izusu Trooper had been in the shop a few times in the last month, each new repair bill larger than the last.

"It just doesn't make sense to keep dumping money into it," Troy said.

I looked over the steering wheel at the custom paint job and turned to Troy. "No way. I'm keeping it, and that's the end of the discussion."

Troy and I continued to weigh the options but, for a while, the Trooper and I won out.

One particular morning the Trooper and the four of us rounded the corner to the main parking lot where Troy worked and instantly discovered another car there. Or, more precisely, it found us when it hit us.

Just like people say when they speak of their accidents, time seemed to move slowly. I could see the metal on the front of the car fold in towards us like an old accordion. I wondered if it would stop before it got to us inside the car. It did stop, and the slow-motion ballet of chaos ended. I turned to check on the boys in the backseat—Michael was fine, Max was not. He was holding his head and complaining of pain. My anger for the man who hit us was growing, but I kept my focus on my son. I called 911.

Troy took care of Michael while I went to the hospital with Max. In between examinations it was just me, Max, and Grandma, sitting in the room while Sponge Bob played on the television.

"Why did this happen?" I pleaded with Grandma.

She sat silent, looking at me looking at Max.

"Hello? This is the time when you're supposed to talk, not just sit there," I said firmly, but with desperation in my inner voice.

She turned to look at me as she spoke. I could see she was uncomfortable. There was a quivering in her voice as if her heart was breaking but there was nothing she could have done. "I told you to slow down. I asked you to not take on so much."

"Yeah, but a car accident?! What the hell?! Punish me but don't punish Max!" I had an image of a spiritual path as one in which those on the otherside were supposed to protect you and help you, yet here I sat watching my son in pain.

"I didn't punish Max," she said firmly. "They punished *you*."

I took a deep breath. Arguing was going to get me nowhere. *"Is Max going to be alright?"*

She nodded yes.

"Alright then." I continued to breathe deeply. *"Why a car accident?"*

"They gave you signs. Plenty of them," she started to explain, as if she was trying to explain the color red to a blind man. "They told you to slow down. They've been putting your car in the shop for huge repairs, messing with your electronics, making appointments cancel on you."

Something in me let go, like a rope releasing its knot. Tears started to fall. Everything she said rang true, and worse, each time those things happened and I asked why, she always had the same response. "You need to slow down." Did I listen? No.

"Was there any other way? Did it have to hurt Max?" I asked her, trying to sniffle quietly so my son couldn't hear.

"They wanted you to lose your car and, well, this is hard for me to tell you, but the cold hard fact is that you wouldn't have stopped if the result was anything less than this." I could hear in her voice that she wished she could take away my pain just as much as I wished I could take away Max's.

"No, I get it. You're right." My head was now hanging down. *"If no one was hurt, I would've gotten another car in a day or two and filled my schedule back up again. I get it. Loud and clear."*

"It could have been worse, honey," she tried to comfort me.

"I know," I said, tears falling.

I watched Sponge Bob with Max, resting my head on the pillow next to his. The clock ticked more slowly now, and I held each moment close to me.

"He's going to be alright," said the doctor as he entered the room.

I dried my face. "Thank you."

Max asked me how soon we could go home.

"Soon, baby boy. Real soon," I winked. Max returned my wink by blinking both of his eyes.

I told Joseph what happened the next time we met. "An accident?" he said with surprise.

"Yeah. Now I'm spending my days researching bus routes and attending chiropractic appointments."

"So, you don't have another car?"

The conversation in the hospital with Grandma rolled through my head. "No, I think I'll chill out for a bit. The bus really isn't that bad."

Joseph shook his head. "I don't know if I could function without a car. Too much to do."

"Well, you could say my life slowed down. The big bummer is that the guy wasn't insured so I'm pretty much S.O.L."

"That sucks. Do you have a lawyer?"

"No, I don't think I'm going that route. I never really liked that kind of thing," I said.

"I don't care if you like it or not. You need to at least get out of it what you lost," he said. "I'll call my lawyer, get you set up. You'll meet him and he'll take care of you."

I shrugged my shoulders. "Alright, I guess." I looked to my right to check in with Grandma. She nodded her head yes, confirming for me that it was a good idea.

A few days later I was sitting on a grossly oversized leather couch in an office surrounded by mallard ducks, parchment certificates, and shiny trophies, waiting for my turn to speak with the attorney. Behind the counter sat a distracted secretary admiring her flawless nails.

"Follow me," she said, as she stiffly got up from her chair to head down a long hallway.

I gathered my paperwork and followed behind the four-inch heels to the last office on the left. When he finally walked in, I could see he was quite the stereotypical injury lawyer. Late sixties, salt and pepper slicked-back hair, and a light blue suit—crisp and attractive, but still light blue. He sat across a huge mahogany desk and dove right into the conversation. He asked me to lay out the details but was only interested in the main points. I tried to keep it simple.

"Yeah, yeah. Okay," he said, as he cut me off for the eighth time. "Listen. What happens is this. We find out what he is worth. If he's worth nothing, we go for your insurance company. One or the other will pay, I promise you," he said. "The important part is this: whatever you think you want, ask for more. Getting you a good size check is what I do. That's what I'm good at."

I stared at him. His speech was a perfect example of why I didn't want to see a lawyer in the first place. I wasn't there to get rich, I just wanted to get back on my feet. I told him I would think about it, collected my belongings, and headed out to the lobby. Just a few feet from the ten-foot-high revolving doors that would set me free, Grandma showed up.

"What's up?" I asked.

"You need a lawyer," she said, matter-of-factly.

"Ah, no." I attempted to walk around her, not caring who might be watching.

"Ah, yeah... you do," she said, as she popped in front of me again.

"Did you hear that guy? I'm not going to go forward with this."

She stared at me and I stared back.

"I refuse to use this lawyer."

As soon as I spoke, a screen appeared right between the two of us, as if it was resting on air. It was a map of Portsmouth. I asked her what I was looking for.

"There is a group of houses in downtown Portsmouth, right about there." She pointed to the map. "When you get there look for the blue-green one. That's where you need to go."

The image faded away and we were back to the revolving doors of the office building. I said I would try to find the blue-green house and Grandma stepped to the side.

"Hey," I said to Troy, as I climbed into the van.

"How'd it go?" he asked.

"It went alright, but I can't see using this guy. It's not a good fit for me."

Troy shrugged. "Alright. So home then?"

"Would you be open to trying something else?" I asked.

"Depends on what it is."

"Well," I thought carefully how I was going to lay this out for Troy. "Grandma showed me a map."

"A magical map?" Troy teased.

"No. A map that showed me where I would find the lawyer I need to see. She said it was over in a bunch of brightly colored houses just behind downtown." I waited for a moment before I continued. "It's on our way home. Will you drive me by them?"

"Alright, Scooby Doo, how will we know which house it is when we get there?"

I smiled. "She said it's the blue-green one."

"Great." Troy wasn't sure how else to respond, and it was written all over his face.

We drove to the area I saw on the map and scanned the houses. There were nine or ten clustered together with brick walkways separating them from each other. Only one was blue-green and my heart skipped a beat when I saw the shingle hanging off the front of it, "Law Offices."

Troy pulled over and looked at me with a huge smile on his face.

"I still have to find out if it's the right type of lawyer," I said.

"Whatever," Troy responded, as he rolled his eyes and smiled wider. He may have been a skeptic, but when things started to line up, he was quicker to get on board than I was.

I entered the front door of the blue-green house that had once clearly been a residence and was now used as a place of business. The receptionist was around thirty, her soft and warm brown hair pulled back purposefully. She was distinctly different from the last receptionist I met.

"Excuse me," I said. "What kind of lawyer is this attorney?"

"He's a personal injury lawyer."

"Thank you. Um, I think I need to make an appointment."

"Okay," she said, in a cozy voice. I was already imagining Troy giving me his "I told you so" face.

Two days later, the attorney agreed to take my case. To his surprise and mine, it settled far more quickly and easily than we thought it should have.

When he asked why I chose him as a lawyer, I bit my lip and steadied myself as I told him about my message from Grandma. To my sheer joy, he responded "Cool!" and began to ask me questions about intuition.

It seems kind of funny to me now, in a way. When I wouldn't slow down, slowing down was forced on me. Once I did slow down, things sped back up for me. Or at least went smoother, for a while.

21

"Look Mom, I Got a Psychic Reading at the Fair!"

"Hi, I'm calling to find out if you have any spaces left for rent at the fair," I said to the organizer of one of the largest county fairs in the area.

"Yes, we have a few spots left. What are you selling?" the female voice asked.

I paused for a second, not expecting the question. "Um, I'm a medium?"

"A what, dear?" she asked, as if I had mumbled. "A medium. A psychic. You know, I do readings."

"Oh, this is great! Our regular psychic hasn't contacted us this year. It would be great to have you," she said with excitement. I took her response as a sign I was doing the right thing—the fair was a friend's idea, so I wasn't sure.

Opening day arrived and I was set up among hundreds of booths selling everything from blow-up animals to personalized wooden signs that hang on your front door. I brought a pop-up canopy and settled into my eight-by-eight spot on the grass. I spent the hour before the fair laying out business cards and price information on the five-foot table at the front of my booth. Behind that table, hiding behind a strategically hung curtain, sat a smaller table with three chairs, one for me and two for anyone else that wanted a reading.

A few hours into the first day, with no requests for readings, I sat patiently thumbing through a book of metaphysics. I used the extra time to study up on how to work my weird new reality. Finally, as the sun hit its highest point and the heat poured in, I got my first customer. She was a woman in her mid-forties with long brown hair and a timid smile. The spirit who wanted to speak to her had come through so strongly I didn't have time to ask the woman if she had any questions. All I could do is watch the visions roll in front of me and repeat what I was hearing and seeing as quickly as I could.

"A woman is coming through," I said. "She is wearing a blue dress with small white flowers. She keeps showing me a picture of a fire station. I'm not sure why, but she is showing me that and then telling me she has two kids, one boy and one girl. She points to the image of the boy and then I see the fire station again. I think she may have a son that is a firefighter?" She interrupted me as she sat forward in her chair. "That's my mother-in-law. I'm married to her son. He's a firefighter."

"Okay, that makes sense." I paused for a second, asking the mother-in-law if there were any messages she wanted me to pass on. "She is showing two kids around you. One girl. One boy. I can see the girl clearly, the boy not so much."

"I don't have a boy," she said.

"I take it you have a girl?" I asked. "Yes, she's my only child."

"*Why am I seeing a boy?*" I asked the mother-in-law.

"Because he is coming. Just a few more months," the mother-in-law answered me.

I turned my gaze from the woman in the blue dress to look at the woman sitting in front of me. "She says the boy is coming in a few months."

The woman's eyes grew wide as she threw her hand over her grinning mouth. I sat quietly in front of her letting my brain put two and two together. "You're pregnant?"

She nodded. "Yes. Well, at least I think I am, am I? We've been trying for a couple years."

I kept reading for her, talking about her job, her friends, and so on and so on until the timer buzzed at the twenty-minute mark. She gave me a big hug, joked about stopping by 7-Eleven for a pregnancy test, and then headed out to enjoy the rest of the fair.

I didn't understand the magnitude of the reading until the next day when a man and his daughter came to see me.

"I'd like a twenty-minute reading for my daughter," the man said, as he held out a handful of cash.

"I don't read for kids. No one under eighteen. I just don't like, well, you know, to freak them out," I explained. I looked at the girl and she seemed strangely familiar to me.

"No, really. She's okay. She's fine with what happens," he said.

Behind them a small crowd was gathering, trying not to be obvious about looking into my booth. I turned back to the man and agreed to read for him and his daughter as long as he sat in on the reading with her. He was thrilled and motioned his daughter toward the chairs that were in the back of my booth.

I looked over the small table to the little girl. She had long dark hair parted slightly off center. Her eyes were simple, but eager to hear what I had to say.

I gave my standard pre-reading speech to the both of them. "Each reader is a little different from the next. I like to tell people everything I see, feel, and hear, and then I interpret it the best I can. If I just give you my interpretation, then we might miss something important to you. Does that make sense?"

They both nodded.

"Also, no one is one hundred percent accurate and if something doesn't make sense, let me know. I can try to clarify for you."

I sat back and took a deep breath as I looked at the ten-year-old. She was taking the reading very seriously. I shifted my attention from the girl to the space behind her, the space where family members typically appear. I watched as a spirit slowly took shape, an older woman with long dark hair that resembled the little girl sitting in front of me. I saw wrinkles appear as the rest of her came more into focus. Her aged presentation let me know she had passed when she was very old. Then, just as the necklace around her throat finished taking form, I saw the neckline of the clothes she was wearing.

It was blue with white flowers.

An odd sensation of "been there, done that" came over me and I looked intently at the spirit. "*Have I met you before?*" I asked in my head.

"Yes," said the spirit woman. "Yesterday."

I smiled slightly.

"What is it?" asked the young girl.

"Nothing. Just something looked familiar to me, that's all," I said. "I think I have your grandma coming through to talk to you."

The little girl nodded and squeezed her hands tightly together.

"Should I continue?" I asked the dad, still hesitant to talk to a child about communicating with the dead.

He nodded yes.

"Okay, so I think this is your dad's mom. She's smiling a huge smile at you. You really meant a lot to her."

The girl beamed and looked back at her dad for a moment to show her excitement.

I continued to stare past the right shoulder of the little girl and spent the next eighteen minutes relaying information from her grandmother to her. She showed me a variety of images, including fuzzy slippers, her granddaughter's love of building and engineering, and, most importantly, how much she missed spending time with her.

The man and his daughter were obviously happy with the reading. As they left the booth, I watched the crowd lingering outside—the crowd I thought was random—all turn to look at the three of us. The little girl walked up to one of the women and started to tell her about what happened.

"Do you mind if we take a picture?" the man asked.

The rest all looked on with excitement as the little girl came back over and stood to my left as the man stood to my right. Sandwiched between them I heard the word "cheese" and, like Pavlov's dogs, I smiled.

It all happened very quickly. I would have run and hid, but I didn't have time to think. I stood there. I smiled. And now I was looking uncertainly to the man on my right.

"You read for my wife yesterday," he clarified. "She was so excited about what you said that she told all of us and I couldn't wait to bring my daughter. She misses her grandma so much."

I held out my hand to shake his and forced a sweet smile on my face to cover up the uncomfortable feelings that were racing through me. He grabbed my hand tightly, shook it with confidence, and then walked away with the rest of the crowd. I was left standing alone, five feet out in front of my booth, dumbfounded over it all. They treated me like a "hero" instead of just someone doing her job.

I was shaken out of my thoughts by a six-foot biker with a three-foot beard. "Hey lady," he shouted, at the top of his lungs, "do you see my dead ma? What a joke!" As he walked away, I stared at two inches of butt crack hanging out of the back of his pants and shook my head. I snuck back into the rear of my tent to hide.

Grandma was there.

"What was that all about?" I asked.

"The good, the bad, and the ugly," she replied.

"Who's the good?"

"You are. You were good enough for a family to want a photo with you afterwards. They dragged you out on the lawn like a pink flamingo."

"No, no, no. See, that's just creepy. Why in the world would anyone want a picture of me?"

Grandma smiled, gently calming my nerves. "Get used to it."

"I'm going to pretend you didn't say that." I stared at the grass below my feet, my trusty feet. *"Okay, if I'm the good, then who's the bad?"*

"The big guy who needs a bath," she said, as she flashed the image of the biker's rear end in my face and then laughed when I shuddered.

"He made me feel stupid," I confessed. *"Tell me again why I'm doing a job that people make fun of?"*

"Well, little girl; there are plenty of jobs out there that people make fun of. Are you really going to let a man who can't pull up his own pants make you feel stupid?"

I chuckled. I knew she was right. I just needed all of me to know she was right. *"Okay, so who's the ugly?"*

She looked right at me, grinned just slightly, and spoke, "This fair."

A woman was now standing at the front of the tent.

"Looks like you should go and talk to her," Grandma said.

I got up to find out what the woman wanted.

"Hi there," I said, in the most chipper voice I could manage.

"Hi. Um, well," she said, as she sized me up, "I'm wondering how much it costs to get a, you know, reading."

I looked down at the large sign two feet from where she stood. It read "Twenty-minute readings for twenty dollars." I looked back at her, "Twenty-minute readings for twenty dollars."

She looked at me carefully, one eyebrow raised. "What if you don't get any information? What if you're wrong?"

"If I don't get anything then you don't have to pay."

There was a long pause. Her two small children were arguing as if it was one of their favorite pastimes. The woman herself was tired looking, with a slight slump in her shoulders.

"So, if you don't get anything then I don't have to pay you, right?" she repeated.

I tried to keep my sigh quiet enough that she couldn't hear. "Yeah. Sure."

"Okay then."

She nodded her head at me as if we had struck a deal in some dark basement.

I dragged myself to the back of the tent and dropped into my chair. I set the timer for twenty minutes and looked up at the woman. She was now sitting across from me, silent and waiting.

I recited my standard pre-reading speech. "Okay, give me a minute to relax and I will let you know what comes through," I said.

After an uncomfortable silence I started to speak. "I see a man coming through. He's in his late seventies, early eighties. He is about five-foot-nine, he has gray hair but it's a full head of hair. He says he is related to you," I said. He was coming through clearly.

"He is showing me a neighborhood. All the houses are close together. He says the house I'm looking at is your house. Now he's walking down the street to a house that is three or four houses down the road, on the same side of the street. He says he lived there."

The male spirit looked over to the woman. I could tell he knew her well. They had years together, and many memories.

"Do you know who this is?" I asked the woman.

Her eyes darted away from me for a second, "No, I don't."

I looked back at the man again and asked him for more information. "He's telling me something about your marriage. He's saying it's really rocky. He's showing me your husband walking out the front door not wanting to return." I paused for a second, then the spirit nudged me on. "And he says you do know him. I think he's your grandfather."

I pulled my attention off the grandfather and back on to her, looking at her with a question in my stare.

"I don't know who that is," she said, as she nervously rubbed her hands together and pressed them into her lap, her shoulders now creeping up her neck.

"Um, I'm not sure what to tell you," I said, as I looked again at the man, transparently standing behind her. "Let me see if there's anything else he can tell me."

I took a deep breath and spoke to him in my head. *"She says she doesn't know who you are. Can you tell me more?"*

"She knows exactly who I am!" he growled at me, as he turned to her and shook his head in disgust.

I sat frozen for a moment, not sure how to handle the developing situation. "*What else can I tell her?*" I asked him.

"Nothing. She knows who I am," he said, as he crossed his arms in front of himself.

I looked at the woman and saw a red glow wrap around her head. I had no idea what that meant so I ignored it and went on. "I'm sorry, but he's telling me that you know who he is."

"I don't," she said, with a quickness in her voice.

"Um, okay." I looked up at the man. He looked sad, as if she was denying his very existence. Anger built up inside me, and I chose to take matters in my own hands. "Well, looks like we're done here."

Her eyes popped open. "Wait. Ah, you can go on," she said.

"Go on?" I asked, somewhere between calm and sarcastic. "Why would I go on if none of this makes any sense to you?"

She leaned toward me just a bit as she calculated what to say. Her grandfather and I shared glances. Both of us knew his granddaughter was lying.

"But the twenty minutes isn't over," she said. "Maybe if you keep going, maybe if you tell me the messages that he wants to tell me, maybe something will make sense."

I shook my head. I had nothing left in me that day to humor anyone, let alone a woman who would deny her grandfather for the sake of a twenty-dollar bill. This woman wanted a reading for free and didn't care who she disrespected in the process.

With her grandfather and I on the same team, I ended the reading. "I think it's time for you to go."

"No, wait! Um, just keep going. What else is he saying?"

"It doesn't matter what he says," I replied. "You don't know who he is and you don't know what I'm saying. Thus, I must be completely off and there's no point in continuing."

"What if..."

"No." I stood up and walked to the front of the tent. She grabbed her purse and stormed out.

So ended my first fair. I learned a lot. I learned I don't like fairs. They don't pay well, they are exhausting and smelly, and they are full of sightseers, loud-mouths, and charlatans.

22

Fury Vs. My Self-Esteem

"I talked to my mom today," Troy said, when he walked through the door. "I told her what you do now."

I looked at him blankly as it slowly dawned on me what he meant. "Please tell me you don't mean 'do now' equates with talking to dead people?"

"I do."

"Nice. Very nice. You really told her?" I wasn't sure if I should be relieved or worried.

"Yeah. Why not? She should know." Troy, the son of a fundamentalist Christian, knew this was a touchy subject for me.

I pictured how she would look at me, what she would say the next time I talked to her. For some reason I imagined it all happening on the front steps of her church. Massive steps that led to a door overflowing with judgmental people. I watched as each one of them came down the steps, passing me by slowly, carefully making sure not to touch me as they passed. I felt like sinking into a hole.

"Honey, why would you tell your mother? She is totally going to freak out."

Troy smiled. "My dear Beau, maybe she'll quit asking *me* to go to church and instead start working on saving *you!*"

"Hilarious, Troy. Absolutely hilarious." I stared straight ahead, trying to stop the church thing from playing yet again in my imagination.

I started to panic, calculating when I would see her next. What would I say and how would she react to me? Would it be over Christmas dinner? That would make it all the worse. My once-hungry-for-dinner gut was now rock hard and felt like cement—the same kind of cement used by the Mafia to sink snitches and traitors.

"It'll be fine," Troy said, as he plopped down on the couch next to me. "Seriously. You shouldn't worry about what people think of you."

Troy got up to make dinner as I reached for my phone to contact my life support system, Molly.

"Hey, Chica!" she answered.

I could hear her boys in the background. "Hey you. Get this. Troy told his mom about me, about the psychic stuff."

She busted out laughing. "That's a good one. How's that working for you?"

"Not well," I said. "This is where I call you and you say, 'It'll be fine,' and then I feel better, forget about it, and go about my day."

"I'd be happy to say it'll be fine, but until you get used to flying that freak flag of yours you might not feel like it's fine."

"Freak flag?"

"Yep," she said. "Freak flag."

I laughed. The church image faded away and was replaced with a parade, me at the front, my freak flag flying high. "Okay, so fly the flag and don't care what others think of me?"

"Yep."

I hated it when Grandma, Troy, and Molly all told me to do things I didn't want to do.

"Love you," I said.

"Love you too, freak."

I hung up the phone. They were right. We all have to tell others what we do for a living. Sooner or later I'd have to get over it, I just wasn't sure how. Little did I know, on my birthday I would find an answer.

"Happy Birthday," said Sarah, a close friend and fellow mom.

"Thanks, man," I said with a big smile.

She smiled back, a warm smile that relaxed me. "So, what's up for you on this special day?"

"Just sitting here, trying to be in the moment and falling on my 'out-of-the-moment' ass," I responded, as I leaned back in an almost-antique easy chair.

Homeschoolers need a place for their kids to socialize and playgroups were the solution. Sarah and I had second shift off together and usually spent it parked in the corner of the adults' sitting room. We would chat about our lives, kids, goals, husbands, etc. She was one of a handful of people in my personal life I trusted with the knowledge that I was a medium. Talking to the dead isn't usually a topic of choice in the homeschool community and I was still dreadfully afraid of what people would think if they found out.

On the other side of the room from us sat Nikki, another mom I knew and trusted. A proud card reader, Nikki spoke openly with me about intuition. Thus, I shared with her what I had been going through. She had been my personal trainer, and each time she worked with me I would update her on what had been happening. She was one person I could turn to with unusual questions about this and that, moon cycles, energetics, etc. She was particularly excited to share her knowledge. It was as if helping me filled her with a sense of importance, a sense of being wise.

She was doing her own thing, however, while Sarah and I talked.

"How are things?" Sarah continued the conversation, as she curled up into her sunken chair, tossing off her shoes.

"I had a reading yesterday," I said. "It was really cool and I am really blown away by it. I was sitting there with a young woman who had her grandmother coming through, you know, in spirit form."

"You mean 'ghostly'," Sarah joked.

"You could say that," I followed, "Get this. She, I mean the grandma, showed me a poodle, a small one. Then, here's the cool part, she showed me how she would feed it green beans!"

"Seriously?" she said. "Did the client say it was right? Is the poodle on the otherside too?"

"Yep, and yep. I leaned back in my seat while we talked about the reading. I was excited because it was validations like this that kept my self-confidence alive and Sarah was someone I could share my excitement with.

"That just was plain cool. What an experience," she said.

The two of us filled the next thirty minutes with chit-chat until it was my turn to take over supervising duties with the kids. As I got up to leave, I smiled and waved at Nikki across the room. Her response was strange—like maybe I offended her. I shrugged it off and figured I'd ask her later if she was alright.

The rest of the day flew by, consumed with crafts, musical games, and kid play. The minute hand was creeping up on the hour just as I finished packing the new pieces of artwork created by Michael and Max into the back of the rental car I was driving. Running up and down the hills next to the building, the boys waved to me as if to say, "Five more minutes." I nodded yes and decided to kill the time chatting with the moms who were mingling on the front walkway.

"So, that's what I was thinking about how it should work," one of the moms finished her sentence just as I stepped into the group. She smiled at me as if to welcome me into the conversation.

Nearby stood Nikki, her five-foot-eight (and buff) frame began to rock from side to side, slowly and methodically. "Hold on! I'm not going to stand here. I'm not going to stand here with *her*." Nikki spoke forcefully as her head nodded in my direction. Her arms were crossed over her chest.

I felt the other moms back away slightly, unconsciously retreating from the no-contact zone that was now encompassing me.

"What?" I asked, trying to quickly wrap my head around the situation.

Nikki's hands flew into the air in frustration. Looking away and then back at me, her rocking now turned into an anxious pacing that ended two inches in front of my face. "You are a fraud! A fake! You lie! I don't want to talk to you like nothing's wrong!"

I stood frozen in time, my heartbeat becoming significantly louder. Shell shocked and hoping time would start moving again, I looked up at her. "Nikki? What is going on?"

"You! You! You're a fraud!" Nikki backed off from me and turned to the other moms, her finger remaining sharply aimed at my face. "Don't trust her! Don't trust her at all!"

"Wait. Hold up." I took a step back from her. My hands automatically rose up as if they were trying to stop buzzing hornets. "I don't know what you're talking about."

"Do you know she says she's a psychic?! A medium?" Nikki shouted at the other moms around us. "Well that's what she says, but she's a fraud! Don't believe her."

The rest of the world fell away in that moment. All that was left was the wild woman lashing out at me, and worse, outing me to the rest of the playgroup parents. I felt my heart press into the center of my chest and push forward into my ribs like it was trying to leave me permanently. Glancing quickly from one mom to the next, I searched desperately for reactions in their faces. I hoped I'd find support, but instead I found only shock. The panic and embarrassment were too much for me to handle and I started to cry.

"Wait, Nikki, what do you mean? I don't understand. Why would you say that?" I choked the last words out between sobs as the tears now poured down my face.

"Say that? You mean that you're a fraud? Because these people should know. They should know not to trust you! I trusted you!" She paused for a moment and backed up, giving me a little more space to breathe. "I heard what you said in there to Sarah, that bullshit about a poodle. No one gets that kind of information."

"Hold on. I don't get it," I said, now trying to catch up with the situation and stop it at the same time. "I just don't understand. What did I say to you that's upsetting you like this?"

"You don't have to say anything to me! I know you are a liar!" she howled.

"Okay, I think this should stop," one of the other moms said, stepping in just slightly. "This really shouldn't be something discussed here."

I prayed her brave attempt would work. Nikki would have none of it.

"I just have to get this out," Nikki said, with slightly less anger in her voice.

"Okay," said the other mom, "but can't this be done without the insults?"

Nikki didn't even consider the idea before turning to me and starting back in. "I also heard what you said to Ashley."

"Ashley? Who's Ashley? What did I say?" I asked desperately. I found myself wanting to calm her, convince her that I had done nothing wrong. I wanted to talk through the situation so I didn't have to walk away in total shame.

"Ashley, Diane's daughter. You told her that her mom had a demon!" she growled.

I thought of what I was being accused of, rolling everyone I had recently met through my head as the panic surged through my body like a fever until I landed on Ashley and her mother, Diane. "Oh. Yes, I did say she had a demon, but I said a personal demon, not a satanic, red-cape-and-pitchfork demon. I didn't say that to Ashley! I said that to Diane, and Ashley was standing there. We were just talking about how people have life issues that repeat over and over, that's all. We all have personal demons."

She paused and looked at me as if she was examining my response and looking for another reason to maintain her rage and hatred. "Well, fine. But I heard you in the lounge telling your 'out of this world story' about a reading you did. You are full of shit! There's no way you can get information like that!" she said, as she angled herself closer to me, squaring her shoulders to mine. I braced myself for what I was convinced would be a fist coming at my head. Her eyes were roaring as if I had done a deed qualified to send me to hell. "And I don't want anything to do with you!"

"But Nikki, I don't get it. Why are you doing this?"

"They should be warned about you. Everyone should. If I was going to do the right thing I would out you to everyone in the alternative community as a fraud. People should know so you don't take their money and scam them."

The initial strike to my gut was abating, pieces now falling into place in my anxiety-riddled brain. I stood there speechless. I had gone from frozen to desperate to broken in less than ten minutes. "There's nothing I can do. I'm just going to leave."

"Good riddance to you!" she said firmly, as she tossed back her long hair, pretending to stand a little taller.

The other moms stood there motionless, wide eyes on pale faces. One mother was choking back her own tears.

Stunned by what had just happened and not knowing how to react, they stared at me as I called the boys to go home. I walked to the car with my tail between my legs. It was my birthday, and now all I wanted to do was curl up in bed and die.

"I'm not going. Cancel the dinner," I mumbled to Troy, through my pink cotton pillow at the head of my bed. I had returned home a few hours earlier, spread out on the huge bed and not moved, hoping it would swallow me up. One of the mothers present for the verbal beat-down called me later and expressed her sympathy for what I went through. Nikki had spoken with her after the event. Nikki, it seemed, was frustrated over my "poodle eating green beans" reading. She had been doing intuitive work for twenty years and never had information come through like that. Thus, I must be lying. As I listened to this feedback a small part of me felt better. Nikki's frustration, albeit aimed at me, was really with herself.

"Beau?" Troy said gently, one hand resting on my back. "I think it might be better to go, to be with everyone at dinner. They're waiting for me to call back."

"Hmmmph. It's my birthday and this is how I want to spend it," I said. "Tell them that."

Troy stood up and walked out of the bedroom. I heard his work boots hit each of the wooden stairs as he headed down to the main floor. I heard the front door open and familiar voices start to rumble as they entered the house. Seconds later I heard footsteps climbing the stairs. There were too many to count.

The half-cracked door now opened wide with Heather and Joel pouring through it and making themselves comfortable at the end of my bed. I expected questions, discussion. How? What? Why? Instead, it was one sentence, spoken sharply from Heather. "If you sit here and let her affect your life, she wins." That was all I needed to hear.

It was a Happy Birthday after all.

Part III

Running With the Big Dogs

23

The Next Level

My birthday dinner was just one of many get-togethers I would share with Joel and Heather at their cabin in the woods. Despite being a city girl and not a huge fan of wilderness, I found more and more peace with each hour my family spent at their home. It was after one such visit that my path took a new direction.

I was still without a car, so Joel offered to drive us home. As we were leaving, I felt the hair on the back of my neck stand sharply at attention. It stopped me dead in my tracks. This feeling was new, and it was distinctly different from the Connection with Grandma. It seemed to flow around me with a strange force and will of its own. The Connection felt more internal, more rooted in my core. This new sensation was outside of me. I was forced to stand still for a moment, looking around to see who or what may be calling. I saw nothing. It was clearly localized to only the back of my neck, so I assumed the pull was coming from behind me. I turned back toward the house and was surprised to see the woods near the cabin filled with Native Americans. There were about forty, all appearing in full form. All standing at attention. All watching me. All dead.

Joel's woods were not too overgrown, but far from landscaped. Scattered throughout were men dressed in buckskin and carrying crude weapons. All of them were calm and focused, but one stood out from the rest. He was fifty feet inside the tree line. Around him was a perfect circle of space, as if all the other spirits knew to keep a respectful distance. His mere presence pulled me in. I was compelled to look at him just by his appearance.

Gradually, I relaxed. I was tempted to walk out there, to speak to him, to find out why they were all so focused on me, but the manners instilled in me from childhood won out and I decided it would be rude to hold Joel up from driving me home. I put my curiosity behind me and climbed into the passenger side of his truck.

"Joel, did you know that your woods are filled with Native Americans?" I said lightly, making small talk.

"No, I didn't," he said, as he climbed in. "Is that what you saw?"

The scene replayed in my head as I stared out the front window of the vehicle. "Yeah. I felt something odd, and bang! Native Americans, all over the place. They were just standing there, staring at me."

"Good thing? Bad thing?" Joel asked.

"Good thing, I think." The gears in my head started turning. "Maybe it's just history? Maybe your real estate agent forgot to put that on the description. 'Beautiful cabin nestled in prestigious woods filled with dead Native Americans.'"

Joel smiled, and I looked out the window at the scenery passing by, wondering if there was any truth to what I was saying. Was I really seeing history in his woods? If I was, could I see it everywhere?

Two days passed since my vision at Joel's and my curiosity was distracting me constantly. I forgot to feed the kids lunch. I didn't shut off the faucet and flooded the bathroom. Big things. Little things. Everything. I figured it was time to get this curiosity out of my head and find out what was going on. I went to Joel's cabin.

It was late in the afternoon when I arrived. The woods were empty of spirits, but I went out anyway. I was glad it was still daylight and made note of how long I thought I had before the sun would go down. I walked carefully through the brush, regretting my choice of shoes as I looked down at my new Birkenstocks. My feet sang for joy every time I wore them but, trendy or not, they weren't a good choice for traipsing through woods filled with sharp objects and bugs.

I found my way to the exact spot where I had previously seen the leader of the assembly and I laid down a blanket to make myself comfortable. I placed a notebook beside me in which I could record anything that might happen. As I sat there, I felt an openness around me, like I was in the middle of an empty football field. I looked about and noticed I had set my blanket inside a perfect circle of ten trees. The circle was twenty feet across and seemed to have some kind of purpose. I checked for tree stumps or any signs of landscaping but found nothing. This was a natural circle, not man-made.

The circle felt strange to me so I started to examine the trees that made it, one by one. As I got to the last tree, I felt the air in front of me begin to move. It seemed energetic—somehow human—but I couldn't quite make it out. All I could see was a vague shape of a man, large and transparent. It was clear and fluid, like heat rising off an Arizona highway. Something in my gut told me this was indeed the same Native American I had seen here two days before, and if this circle really was like a football field to me then the man in front of me, I felt, definitely had to be the Big Dog of the home team.

"Who are you?" I was squinting like an idiot to get a better visual connection.

There was nothing but silence. I turned to my right to look at Grandma, but she was gone. I felt anxiety push into my chest as I searched around frantically. I found her standing fifteen feet away, outside the circle, smiling and giving me a thumbs-up as if to say, "You're okay."

"What are you doing? Why are you back there?" I asked her. She didn't respond. Instead, with her palm facing the ground, she waved her hand toward me as if to say, "Turn around, don't worry about me." I did as she asked, slightly uncomfortable that she was so far away. Regardless, I turned back around to see that the spirit energy was still floating in front of me, unchanged since the time I first felt it.

"*Who are you?*" I asked again. Nothing.

"Are you some sort of Native American leader dude?" Still nothing.

I sat there for a while, staring on at the energy in front of me, hoping it would do something. It didn't. I looked around for any of the other Native Americans I had seen two days ago, but saw none. After a good thirty minutes of staring at the same spirit with no change or communication, I got up to leave. I shook the debris from my blanket and the hope from my mind, and started to walk toward the cabin. As my left foot stepped just outside the circle of trees, I heard a deep voice come from behind.

"I'll see you on Thursday," I heard, clear as birds chirping. Startled, I spun around to the direction of the voice. The transparent energy in the middle of the circle was gone. I turned back to Grandma with a questioning look on my face. She nodded her head, excited at the events that had unfolded in front of us.

I turned back to the circle again. "Okay," I said out loud. I hesitated for a moment, searching the circle with my eyes. I hoped saying okay would result in a better visual for me. It didn't. Instead, it was just me, surrounded by empty space, wondering what the heck I was doing. I started to walk away again. Two steps out of the circle I noticed that Grandma had now returned to my right side.

"What was that all about?" I asked her.

She smiled at me but said nothing. We walked together for a bit, her keeping pace with me.

"Playing games again, are we?"

"No," she responded firmly. "I'm just excited for you."

"You know what would be really cool?" I asked facetiously. *"What would be really cool is if someone told me what was going on."*

She rolled her eyes and faded back a step.

I continued to question her. *"I mean, what is this? Why do I feel this urge to sit out in the woods to talk to someone who clearly doesn't want to talk? If he did, he'd show himself and tell me who he was. It's like I'm stretching for something that is pointless."*

"Why would something pointless ask you to come back on Thursday?" she asked me with a smartness in her voice.

"Good question. Sorry," I apologized for my lack of patience. *"I just don't get it. Why can't I see him?"*

"Because he's not just a relative of someone you are reading for. You have to meet him halfway." She looked directly at me, a look that said, "Listen up." I stopped myself just as I reached for the handle of the van.

"I'm listening."

She stared at me for a few moments, waiting patiently for the information to come together in my head. "You know why he's important. Just think."

"I know why he's important?" I repeated.

"You have such a thick head for a cute little girl."

I looked her straight in the eyes. *"And you, darlin', are not telling me straight up what you want me to know."*

She sat for a moment. I could see impatience mixed with frustration. "I know. They won't let me say anything to you. I hate that."

I pulled back slightly in surprise. *"What do you mean, 'they' won't let you say anything?"*

"Well, thick head, you need to figure this one out on your own," she said, now more relaxed. "I'm excited for you though, just know that."

I opened the door to Troy's van and climbed in, placing the blanket and notebook on the seat next to me. That didn't seem to stop Grandma from riding shotgun like she always does. I looked at her, remembering when she was alive and how she would put up a stink about having to wear a seatbelt. She would typically win the battle and ride in the passenger seat with no restraints.

"Why were you standing outside the circle?" I asked her, as the van headed down the long dirt road.

"Now you're starting to think. Good. I think we might get somewhere now, or at least before Thursday." She smiled that sneaky smile of hers that let me know I was on to something.

"Ugh. I wish you could just lay it out for me," I complained in a soft voice. *"Okay, I understand you're not going to. Okay, okay, okay. Something to do with you not coming into the circle. The only thing I can put together on the surface is that this isn't just me seeing history."* I continued to work on any pieces I could with regard to the situation. *"And you didn't go into the circle. You couldn't go into the circle. Is it sacred or something? Is he sacred? Is that even a question?"*

"Everything is a good question," she said.

We sat in silence for the rest of the trip home. I was tired of trying to figure it out. It just didn't seem to make sense to me. Instead, I ran through the list of errands I had to do and how my time might have been better spent doing one of them instead of sitting in the woods for a half hour staring at nothing.

I returned the following week, as promised. The whole situation in the woods had been sitting on my mind like a squatter that wouldn't leave, and I was ready to see what might unfold. I made it to the circle before the sun went down and planted myself on my blanket. I looked over my shoulder at my grandmother as she gave me a thumbs up sign. I sat, and I sat, and I sat. Twenty minutes, and nothing changed. I could see his energy, waves of transparent movement that altered the objects behind him. I knew he was there, but past that, zip. Discouraged, I got up and walked to the edge of the circle toward the van.

"I'll see you on Sunday," said the deep voice, just as I stepped out of the circle.

I turned around, not as startled as the last time. *"Really? You will? Are you sure about that?"* I was annoyed. *"Listen, whoever you are, I know you can see me. I know you're standing right there, so what's the deal with the whole 'Let's not let Beau see us' thing?"*

I stood for a moment, silently waiting. There was nothing. No energy, no visual. Nothing. I shook my head in frustration and turned to walk toward the van again.

"I'll see you on Sunday," the deep voice repeated.

I whipped back around. Still nothing. *"Come on! You're like the worm that the fish can't catch. What is your deal?"*

The air was dead silent.

"I'll see you on Sunday," it said again, exactly as before. Purposely not responding, I turned to walk away. Grandma followed slightly behind me as I marched to the van, my pace quickened with frustration. I drove home and plopped down on the living room couch.

"How did the tree-hugging go?" Troy asked when I got home.

I huffed at him as I pulled off my new rubber boots, the ones I had bought because my Birkenstocks didn't work out so well. "Not sure how it went. Don't know what the heck happened."

"Well," Troy paused, realizing sarcasm might not be a smart idea. "Tell me what happened," he said seriously.

"Nothing. That's just it, nothing happened," I said.

I looked up at Troy and saw Grandma standing next to him, shaking her head. I changed my story to make it more accurate. "Okay, maybe not nothing."

"Care to elaborate?" Troy asked.

So, I did.

"Okay then, Sunday it is," Troy said.

"I've got stuff to do," I told Troy.

He chuckled and patted me on the shoulder. "Whatever, Beau."

The following Sunday I found myself knee deep in wilderness again.

"I'm here," I said sarcastically, getting ready for another twenty minutes of silence.

I laid out my blanket in the same spot and I nearly fell over when I heard the word "Good".

I stood up perfectly straight. *"We're talking now?"* I asked, as I stared at the translucent energy floating again in front of me. Suddenly, I was all ears.

I heard a low chuckle and I could see the energy in the air shift with his laughter. I hoped he would speak again. I pondered why I could hear him but not see him, and how he got his energy to dance like that when he laughed.

I looked up to where his head would be in this pool of energy and asked a question. *"What should I call you?"*

Long silent nothing in response. *"I've got to call you something."*

More quiet.

"Is it okay if I call you Big Dog?"

A pause, and he spoke. "Yes, and I'll see you on Monday."

"I'll see you on Monday," I growled. I turned and disappointedly packed up my gear once again.

I huffed back over the now familiar path to the van, Grandma again by my side. As I walked, I became more and more frustrated. So, I did what I always do—I channeled the frustration into a challenge. *"He's darn right he'll see me tomorrow. I'm not throwing in this towel. Now it's on, sir. It's on like Donkey Kong!"*

Grandma smiled as she climbed into the passenger seat.

24

Books and Signs

Stumbling on Big Dog was like finding a diamond in the sand. I just didn't know it at first. Time crept by with each session too short and each space between them too long. Sometimes I would only have to wait two days, other times it was a week. Each visit, however, seemed to fall perfectly into place with something that was happening in my life at the time. It often felt random, even though it never was. Why will Thursday be so important, or what should I expect now that he doesn't want to see me until Sunday?

Some days nothing new would happen and sometimes he would come through stronger and I might catch a glimpse of his feet, or the deerskin that draped his body. His long salt-and-pepper hair, or the numerous feathers draped down his back. He spoke to me in bits at first, one or two words that would eventually turn into sentences, which would eventually turn into hour-long sessions. I sat there in front of him, writing, trying to keep up.

The weeks rolled on and I arrived at Joel and Heather's late one evening. Late for me, anyhow, given my fear of the woods at night. Joel, who knew about my conversations with the mystery man and my fear of anything forest-related, lent me a massive flashlight. I turned it on, held it close, and made my way out to the circle. Big Dog had this way of constantly feeding me just a little bit, so I was always drawn in by my curiosity.

I entered the circle, leaving Grandma at her usual post just outside it. I held onto the blanket instead of laying it down this time, just in case. With my flashlight shaking slightly, I stood waiting for his voice.

"Are you there?"

No response. Just silence. I looked through the darkness and saw nothing.

I waited a few minutes and asked again. *"Hey there... it's me... are you there?"*

The ground rustled behind me. I could hear something moving but couldn't seem to catch it in my now quivering flashlight.

I decided on flight instead of fight and bolted back to the van, blanket dragging behind me all the way.

"Crap, whew," I said to Grandma, one hand resting on the van. I was completely out of breath. *"Was he, was he there? In the circle?"*

"Yes, but you left before he could talk to you," she said.

"Yeah, but did you hear that thing in the woods? I think it was a bear!"

"Sweetie, I don't think it was a bear."

"Well, it could have been one, you know."

Grandma smiled. "It wasn't one, I'm pretty sure. Are you going back in?"

"Ah, no." I looked at her as if she was crazy, or maybe like I was. *"I'll go tomorrow. Shoot! Will he be there?"*

She looked toward the woods, hesitated for a moment, and then turned back to me shaking her head. "No, he won't be there tomorrow."

"Crap! Crap! Did I fail? Did I royally screw this up?"

"No, honey. He said he understands you were scared," she reassured me. "Oh, and he wants you to come back on Friday."

I looked at her, puzzled for a moment. *"You can talk to him?"*

Grandma smiled at me.

"You know that's not fair, right?"

She chuckled. "Go home, sweetie," was all she said. Friday came and I sat in my usual spot, looking up at Big Dog periodically as I sketched him in my notebook. Over the days, my ability to perceive him in more detail had grown.

"I'm sorry I ran the other day. Dark woods and I don't work well together," I said.

Big Dog nodded. "Looks like you'll have to get over that soon."

"Why?"

He didn't respond so I changed the subject.

"I am so glad I can see you now. That was a long haul for me, you know. It was getting annoying not being able to see you, that is."

"You need to let go of getting annoyed," he responded, as he tilted his head up just slightly. I wondered for a second if he was posing for his portrait and he smiled as if to say he was.

"Let go of my fear of the woods. Let go of getting annoyed. Easy for you to say."

"Everything is easy for me to say. That's not the point," he added. "If you don't let go of the frequency in which you get annoyed, you won't move forward as quickly as I would like you to."

"As you would like me to?"

"Yes," he stated flatly. "You need to find your balance, and soon."

I raised my hand, like I was a third grader sitting in the back of the room. *"Ooh, ooh, pick me."*

Big Dog chuckled. "Ah, you!" he played along and pointed to me as if he was the teacher.

"Because you have plans for me that you aren't telling me yet just to be, um, annoying."

"Very good," he continued.

The relationship between us became lighter as the weeks rolled by. What was intimidating and somewhat overwhelming to me at first turned out to be much more comfortable than I would have expected. We had much the same sense of humor, and it made the interludes between serious stuff more fun. It became very relaxed, yet if a point had to be made, he would not hesitate to pull back from the fun and focus my attention on what needed to be heard.

"You know my name is not Big Dog, right?" he asked, as he noticed how I wrote BD by a number of his comments in my journal.

"Well yeah, but when I asked you if I could call you Big Dog you didn't exactly put up a stink," I explained. *"When I first met you, you were like the Grand Poobah of the woods. The King of the Hill. The Godfather. You know, Big Dog."*

"My name is Walking Elk," he said, as he looked away for a moment. As he turned, I watched him closely and could almost make out memories floating through his head.

"So, what are you thinking?" I couldn't help but be curious how this guide who seemed so powerful and strong could get swept away by nostalgia.

He collected himself and returned to looking at me. "Your name for me is perfect. Big Dog is more fitting because there is love in it from your heart. Walking Elk was one moment in time. The truth is I don't have a name. None of us do. The feathers you see in my hair are only memories, they aren't really feathers. My name is just a feather, a memory."

"So your name is from a past life?" I asked.

"One that you were in as well. I've been waiting for you for quite some time. I was given permission to help you this time, to see to it that you followed your path. To guide you."

"Given permission?"

A big smile rolled over his face. "Yes, permission. I am really excited that it is I that gets to walk with you."

"Walk with Walking Elk, you're funny."

"That wasn't a joke, but I'll give you that one. Very clever." He turned to face away from me. "Stand up."

I dropped my notebook and scurried up to the spot right in front of him. *"What is it?"*

"Hold out your hands."

I stuck them out and watched as he wrapped his transparent hands around mine. I started to feel warm waves wash over me. They started in my fingers and climbed up my arms, wrapping around me. It was a feeling of being held, not by a mother or lover, but by something much bigger. I started to sway back and forth gently, and, each time I started to think I should be falling I was caught and moved back to center. Just as I settled into the comfort of the experience, the feelings morphed into the memories of my past life with Walking Elk. Memories of me that were never mine, until now.

It was an incredibly moving moment. Tears rolled down my face. *"What was that?"*

"That is pure energy. It is our connection," he said. "I'll see you Thursday."

I smiled at him and I wanted to be able to hug him like a big teddy bear. I packed up my things and went home. The weeks crawled by, and Big Dog continued to share amazing things with me. My intuition and understanding flowed better when I was with him.

"Big Dog? You there?" I had shown up a day early and wasn't sure he would respond, but I felt the warmth rise from my core that told me he was near.

"Yes, I'm here. You're early."

"I couldn't help myself. I have so many questions."

"And so little patience."

"Yeah, yeah, I know." I flicked my fingers in the air like I was brushing off the statement. *"But listen, I have questions. Is it alright if I ask them?"*

"Can I stop you?" he joked.

I looked up at him from my notebook, where questions had been piling up for days.

He smiled. "Go on, ask your questions."

"Okay, so I haven't been able to find a book that talks about what I'm going through. I mean, I can find books written by mediums and such, but they all talk about having the ability since they were two or three or something like that. And, what's worse, none of them talk about being scared or how it feels or what it really looks like to see."

I paused and stared at Big Dog. He stared back as if to remind me that I hadn't really asked a question yet.

"Um, okay. Yeah, the question is, where am I supposed to find information on my path? More specifically, is there a book I can read?"

His head shook slightly from side to side as he began to speak, "There isn't a book for you, that's why you haven't found one yet. Your path is unique to you and if you try to follow someone else's path then you won't develop into what you are supposed to be. You are your own person. Don't follow anyone. Simply follow your own path."

"That's just it. I don't know what my path is. I don't know what I'm supposed to be doing, what I'm going to be doing five years from now, and so on and so on."

"You don't need to know what your path is. You just have to walk it. Why would you focus on what is going to happen five years from now? That just takes you away from what is happening right now," he explained.

"I get that we're supposed to be 'in the moment' and all, but it would be nice to know where I'm headed so I can work towards it or plan things for it." I remembered the phrase "in the moment" from a book I had read in the past. I thought using it would make me feel like I knew what I was talking about. It didn't work.

"What do you want to know?" he asked.

I gave him an example of a question that would fit with what I was trying to say. *"Like, how much longer am I going to be living in the house that I'm currently in?"*

"That's a stupid question."

I stared at him for a moment, frustrated, *"That's not a stupid question. It's a good one."*

"No. It really is a stupid question," he chuckled. "I don't want you worrying about when to move out."

"Why?"

"You should be focused on other things, not on the future." He sat down next to me. "No more questions. No more books."

I looked down at the list of twenty or so questions and started to wonder if any of them were important at all. He patted my knee gently as if to say "Sorry, but you'll be okay."

"I really have to figure out what is important and what isn't important, don't I?"

"Yes," he grinned. "I'll see you on Monday."

Ironically, a few hours after I got home from the circle, a friend recommended a book titled The Keys of Enoch. I didn't bother looking for it because Big Dog said no more books and I was trying hard to follow his orders. I slept very little that night. I couldn't get the book off my mind. Even the wine didn't knock me out. My head felt like it was filled with a hundred gerbils all running on their own personal gerbil wheels. So instead, I lay there all night imagining what the book could be about. By morning, Big Dog or not, my curiosity got the better of me and I hopped on the computer to search for the book. I found it and saw the fat sticker price of $100 attached to it. I looked around for Grandma—or anyone—to see if they had input on if I should buy it.

Nothing. Dead air.

"If anyone is out there and you really think I should drop that much money on this book, then give me a sign. Otherwise, I'm passing on it," I said in my head as I stared at the computer screen. No response. Clearly, no one felt it important enough to tell me to buy it and Big Dog had told me to back off from books, so I called it quits.

I pushed my chair away from the desk and headed downstairs to crank out a very late breakfast. Standing by the large glass sliding door was my faithful, furry, best friend, Apple. With tennis ball in mouth and wagging her entire back end, she let me take the ball from her mouth. I opened the slider and stepped out to throw.

I expected to feel the brown scruffy doormat under my bare foot, but instead I felt fur. I stepped on a groundhog. My foot pushed down and the groundhog pushed back. Even after I screeched and pulled my leg back, I could barely see the animal against the dark mat until he waddled away.

He harrumphed off the porch and around the corner, giving me an angry look as he went out of sight.

Apple gave it an amazing chase, considering she was blind in one eye and totally deaf. Me, I just stood there, dumbfounded.

Back in the house and looking to my right, I noticed a book I had recently purchased. "*Animal Speak.*" I bought it specifically to learn about the animal world, how we are connected to it spiritually, and how animals send people messages by coming into their lives in peculiar ways. I picked it up and flipped quickly through the alphabetical listing. For "Groundhog" the book stated the animal appears at a time when a new area of study is about to open up, and its gift lies in its ability to get deep into an area of interest. I closed the book, got Apple back in the house, and headed upstairs again to order "The Keys of Enoch" after all.

There are signs, and then there are signs, I guessed.

25

Always Use Protection

"I bought a book," I said, the moment I felt Big Dog come into the circle. Guilt had been building up ever since I clicked "purchase" on Amazon.com, and I spat out my confession.

He floated in close and sat next to me on my blanket. "There's a difference between aimlessly browsing the aisles of a bookstore and buying a book that calls to you. You're supposed to step into what calls you, versus floating around hoping something will stick!"

"I didn't know you guys were up to date with your shopping experiences," I joked.

He rolled his eyes.

"So you're not mad at me for buying another book?" I asked with hope.

"No, I will never be mad at you. That is not my job. My job is to help you," he explained.

I sat for a moment, watching a bug crawl up on the edge of the blanket. *"So, I can do anything wrong and you won't get ticked off?"*

"Ticked off? No. But I will take the opportunity to say, 'I told you so,'" he chuckled. "The book was a good purchase. It was a purchase you thought about. That is all I ask."

"Easy to do," I said, as I felt relieved that I wasn't in some kind of trouble. The lessons he was teaching me weren't necessarily rules carved in stone. They were guidelines. *"So, are you an angel?"*

"I prefer the term 'guide'."

"Me too. It fits better. You know, with the lack of wings and all. So, what do you have in store for me today? What do I get to write in my journal?"

"You need to start protecting yourself," he said, still sitting by my side, staring out at the scattered trees.

"Any chance you care to tell me what I'm protecting myself from?" I turned to look at him, but he disappeared and instantly reappeared one foot in front of me.

I looked at him, confused. *"Um, okay. I still don't get it."*

"That is why you need protection."

I looked around as if I had missed a key piece of the lesson. I didn't notice anything different, so I turned back to Big Dog. *"Nope, I still don't get it. I don't see anything that I need to protect myself from."*

"That's just it. You are dealing with energies, many of which you still can't see."

"Sorry?"

"You thought I was next to you. Now I'm in front of you," he explained. "That was not done by you. That was done by me. It is my choice to affect you, your mind, and your space, as I see fit. It is up to you to put up an energetic barrier, to hold your space so you have control over it. You are going to be dealing with strong situations, strong spirits. I need you to work on protecting yourself and your energetic body."

I heard the seriousness in his voice and didn't know whether to be grateful for the heads-up or scared about what was coming. Instead, I felt frustrated and anxious.

"Protecting yourself is not like shoe shopping. You don't pick the type of protection, you just do it," he said.

"Okay, protect myself. What's the magic formula?"

A few moments passed silently before I looked up at Big Dog.

"I'll see you Friday," he finally spoke.

"Hey! Wait! Did I ask the wrong question?"

"I'll see you Friday."

I stood frustrated and smoldering as he looked at me with soft eyes.

"Annoyed, impatient, and curious," he said.

I looked at him, relaxed my stare, and smiled a very small smile.

"I'll see you Friday."

Friday didn't come soon enough.

Between seeing dead people and all the "reality" ghost hunting television shows, I was becoming more and more interested in the subject. The idea of capturing a ghost image on film was exciting and I decided the best place to do it was in the largest cemetery in the area, South Cemetery. As I walked up and down the rows of headstones, I saw some of the most breathtaking monuments I had ever seen. Tombs were scattered throughout the graveyard like Monopoly hotels. Deep in the center of the cemetery I stumbled upon a mausoleum that looked like I might be able to see into through its tiny carved window. I walked up to it and took pictures of the interesting markings on its walls.

Overall it was an uneventful ghost hunt, so I headed out to tackle the remaining errands for the day, including a meeting with Joseph to discuss my ever-developing website.

"Hey, all!" I said, as I walked through his office door.

"Hey, Beau. Come on in," Nicole called out from somewhere in the back.

When the big green door shut behind me, Kodiak traipsed out across the wood floor and I leaned down to give him a hug as I had done countless times before. Instead of his usual affectionate hello, he skidded to a stop, his hackles standing on end. Stunned, I then watched as the side of this mouth curled up to show his massive teeth. Joseph heard his growl and raced up to grab hold of his collar.

"Beau," Joseph said. "I have no idea what's gotten into him. Kodiak, sit!"

"Thanks. Maybe he smells my dog, Apple?" I asked.

Joseph shrugged and sat back down at the computer.

"Don't worry about it, Beau. Did you bring the paperwork I asked for?"

"No," I said, snapping my fingers. "I forgot. Do you want me to run home and get it?"

"Probably. It'll make it easier."

Less than a minute into the short drive home and I felt a foreign rage start to boil inside me. My fingers melted into the steering wheel as I gripped it with all the force I could muster. I was all set to chalk it up as frustration over being forgetful until I saw a tall and lanky male with a bounce in his step, walking on the sidewalk just ahead of my car. He was wearing a florescent pink sweatshirt and listening to music. The rage that had started a quarter mile back was now in full swing.

"What the fuck!!" I screamed from my car. "Are you insane?! Pink!! You are such an ASSHOLE!"

I gripped the wheel tighter, passed the unsuspecting pedestrian, and took the right turn onto my street. I pulled into my driveway and looked at my front door. It looked different, like I didn't live there. This is not my home, I thought for a second, and then I marched up the steps to my house. As I unlocked the door and crossed the threshold, I was overcome by a strange thrill. Excitement rushed through me like I was breaking the law. Trying desperately to ignore the sensations, I ran in, grabbed the paperwork that was sitting on the front table, and headed back to the car as quickly as I could.

Once inside my car I thumbed through the folder and discovered it wasn't my forgetfulness I was angry at. Something was wrong and I didn't know what. My personality was off the rails, and for the second time in my intuitive journey I thought I might be losing my mind.

"Joseph," I said, as I walked back through his office doors, Kodiak growling in the background, "I think there is something wrong with me."

Hearing the rare serious tone in my voice, Joseph stopped what he was doing. "Yeah, I didn't want to say anything, but Kodiak has never acted like that with *anyone*. I think you might have an attachment."

"Attachment? I started to panic. "What the heck is an attachment?"

"It's when you pick up a spirit, like a hitchhiker, but they don't have the best intentions," he explained.

I looked down at my body and saw nothing. "Wouldn't I see it?"

"Nope. The last thing a hitchhiker wants is for you to spot them. If you do, then the ride is over," he said.

"What do I do?"

"Call Ed."

I took the advice and headed to Ed's office. I called him from the car. He could hear the urgency in my voice so he agreed to squeeze me in at the end of his busy day. After an hour on his acupuncture table I was cleared of the attaching entity. Whatever Ed did, I don't remember it involving needles. I do, however, vividly remember feeling relieved that I didn't have to go through a night knowing there was a dude that I couldn't see hanging out in me.

The next day was Friday and, as assigned, I headed directly out to see Big Dog.

I called out his name, as I stepped into the East side of the circle.

"Hey, Beau," he said, with a casualness about him.

"I'm taking a small leap here, but I suspect we'll be talking more about protecting myself. I'm thinking you already know what happened?" I asked, with humility in my voice.

"What do you think?" Big Dog laughed a bit, as he settled in to sit down in front of me.

"I think I wasn't taking protection very seriously the first time you talked about it. Thus, I can speculate that you most likely called the meeting short because of my lack of interest?" Big Dog nodded, so I continued. "*So, um, I'm serious now.*"

"Then it's time to discuss protection." Big Dog took a spiritual deep breath before he continued. When he inhaled, it was like he breathed in the forest around him. "There are two ways to protect yourself. You can protect your energetic body, and you can protect the space you are working in."

"Wait. I can protect a room? Does that mean I can protect my kids?" I interrupted.

"The person who needs protection is best served by protecting themselves first. You can shield your children, but you cannot protect them. That is something they must do themselves," he explained.

"Make my boys protect themselves. Check." I pretended to write in my journal.

Big Dog smiled.

"Protecting yourself is something you've heard before, just in pieces," he continued. "You need to ground, clear, and protect."

Big Dog waited for me to search my feeble memory banks and put the concepts together.

"Grounding is that cord into the earth thing, the thing that stops me from blowing up cars. Clearing is that washing away type stuff with imaginary water or whatnot that makes me feel better if someone is pissing me off. And protecting is, um, the one I haven't learned yet," I said.

"Yes. That's why we're covering it here. It's good to ground, better to clear, but pointless if you do not contain the work you've done and protect."

"Contain?"

"What I want you to do is this. After grounding and clearing, create a bubble around you. One that is thick enough for you to believe it will not burst," he explained. Big Dog stood up and asked me to join him. "When you protect yourself, you need to believe it. Intention is the key to all energetic work. What you decide will happen, does. You just have to believe."

With that statement, Big Dog encapsulated me in a magnificent bubble three inches thick and flowing with a brilliant golden light. It was like a shiny wall between us, making Big Dog seem farther away then he really was. When I reached my hand out to touch it, it started to fade.

"Hey. Why is it going away?"

Big Dog crossed his arms over his chest. "Because this was the protection I created for you. It will fade quickly. You need to do this for yourself."

When the bubble faded into nothing, I focused with my mind to create one of my own. It was more of a dull lumpy blur than anything else.

"It's not working," I said.

"Patience, my dear," Big Dog said gently, "and commitment. Do this every day. Every time you rise and each time you feel that you need it. Eventually, it will be there for you, like a second layer of skin."

"Grow another layer of skin. Check," I joked.

"In a sense, yes," Big Dog said, as if he had completely missed my lighthearted moment. "And the statement 'for the highest good of all' is a good one to use as well."

I walked back over to my blanket and sat down. As I pulled my second foot into a cross-legged position, I noticed a Native American to my left wearing very little and holding something painfully sharp, eyeing me as if I was to be his next victim.

"Who's that?" I asked cautiously.

"He is a warrior," Big Dog replied.

I looked on as this warrior crept toward me, slightly hunched down, taking careful steps through the brush.

"What is he doing?" As I felt the hairs stand up on the back of my neck, I leaned back instinctively on my blanket.

Twenty feet from me he raised his spear, and I shouted. *"Big Dog! Get rid of him!"*

"Protect your space," Big Dog said calmly. "Use wings." Without thinking, I waived my hands in front of me beginning at face level and working out and down. As I stroked the air around of me, I imagined brilliant white angel wings pouring from beneath my hand, and they did. I envisioned a massive wall between the hunter and myself, and it appeared. I stared in disbelief for just a few moments, then I turned to my right and my left, painting with my hand a room of angel wings, finishing off the image with a ceiling and floor to match.

Once surrounded, I turned to Big Dog, standing inside the white room with me. "See?" he said. "You knew what to do."

I lifted one eyebrow, expressing my extreme disapproval of his methods and sank into the blanket.

"See you Wednesday?" Big Dog asked, this time without the hint of demand in the tone.

"Absolutely," I responded.

26

The Shoe Factory Lady

The next day, I arrived at the fair excited to be surrounded by like-minded individuals. This particular event was a one-day specialty fair with a strong focus on health and holistic lifestyles so I was hoping this one would go better than my last. Held inside a local convention center, it was created and organized by Joseph and Nicole. When they asked me to do readings there, I chuckled. If it wasn't for my friendship with them, I would have quickly shouted "No!"

I walked through the building looking at all the different types of vendors as I made my way back to the "Reader's Tables." There were naturopaths, massage therapists, and people selling beautiful stones and crystals, just to name a few. I walked past the last row of booths to find an open area in the corner of the building. In it were five large round tables laid out in an "x" like the pips on a die, one for each psychic reader scheduled to be there that day. It was instantly clear that my table was the one in the middle, it was the only one that wasn't set up yet.

The readers at the other four tables had already draped theirs in beautiful linens, covered them with brochures, business cards, crystals, and so on. I looked at my poor barren table, covered in a clean, stark-white sheet in the center of the space, and walked toward it. I removed my coat, hung it over the back of the brown metal chair, and sat down. I nervously clutched my purse on my lap and set my water bottle on the edge of the tablecloth. Something else should be sitting on this table, I thought. I watched each of the readers as they put their final beautifying touches on their space for the day, each reader wearing equally beautiful clothing that perfectly matched their table. Some wore long skirts and multiple necklaces. Some wore more businesslike attire complete with high heels. And then there was me. Blue jeans, Birkenstocks, and an unbuttoned shirt over a T-shirt, at a table that looked as naked as I felt.

Yep, I was uncomfortable and nervous. I got up and walked over to the check-in desk. This was where customers would sign up for their readings and pay for them. Nicole was manning the position, arranging the empty schedules for each of us.

"So, Beau, I know you haven't done anything like this before. Here's how it works," Nicole said, with the tone of an organizer. "People come up to this table, pick which reader they want, and buy a ticket from me. They pick a time slot on your sheet and sign up. I'll send the people back to you when it's their time to get a reading. You collect the tickets. Give the tickets to me at the end of the night and then I'll pay you your portion of the money."

I nodded yes and wrapped my arms around her for an impromptu hug and she chuckled a bit as she stepped in to receive it.

I headed back to my empty table and dug my hand into my purse looking for the business cards Joseph had created for me. I was grateful my water bottle was no longer alone on the table.

People began to arrive, strolling up and down the aisles looking at what each booth had to offer. Nicole spoke with the first woman that approached her, wrote something down on one of the five sheets, and took her cash. She handed the lady a ticket and then pointed back toward me. Only two minutes after the event started and I was up to bat. It was the first of twenty readings that day.

Three hours into the fair I took a desperately needed break. I enjoyed a bowl of soup and wandered through the rest of the convention center looking at the different booths. When I arrived back to where Nicole was sitting, I glanced at the paperwork on the table. I was the only reader with a sold-out schedule. My first reaction was relief that my lack of decoration didn't stop people from wanting to see me. My second reaction was panic as I started to feel the weight of the situation. I had already done a number of readings so far and was wondering how I was going to make it to 6 p.m.

I returned to my table and looked up to see my next client making her way toward me. She was a plain-looking woman with shoulder-length, straight black hair. She wore bargain store jeans and an unassuming shirt.

"Listen," she said sharply, as she sat down and slammed her ticket on the wide-open tablecloth. "I've seen three other mediums. None of them impressed me. Let's see if *you* can."

I stared at her like a deer stuck in headlights as panic and four-letter words floated through my head. I felt perspiration start to build under my arms and mentally reminded myself to take a deep breath. "Um, okay then." I looked down at my feet for a few seconds to get a grip. Stalling to give myself space to calm, I said, "Well, you clearly know what a medium does, so at least I don't have to explain that part of it."

"Yes, I do. Just go ahead." She flicked her wrist at me like she was dismissing an errand-boy.

"Um, okay." I paused and stared past her to see if there was anyone around her coming through from the otherside. To my surprise, there was, and he was visually very clear to me. I glanced back at her before I started to speak. She sat perfectly still and obviously skeptical. It was like looking at a frozen scientist. "I have a man coming through on your dad's side."

"How do you know it's my dad's side?" she blurted, arms now crossed in front of her chest as she leaned back from the table.

"He's standing behind your right side. That's your dad's side of the family, usually. For me, at least." I wasn't expecting her question.

"Fine. Go on." Another flick of her wrist.

"Okay. He is older with gray hair, but not a full head of gray. He's right around six feet, just a hair shorter than that. He is lean and um, well," I paused because that was all I could see. He was coming in clearly, but he wasn't giving me any information. He simply stood there, hands folded into each other and resting in front of his midsection, looking like he was ready to twiddle his thumbs at any moment. He looked at me with a challenge in his stare, as if he knew I was asking for information, but he wasn't going to give it.

"Umf," she mumbled, as if that was all I was worth. "That could be anyone. Can you be more specific?"

"I'm sorry. I'm not sure. He's just standing there, looking at me. He's not talking or anything. His shirt is blue." I kept staring past her shoulder at the male spirit, wanting desperately for him to tell me something more, anything more.

"Help me out here, guy," I said. *"Give me something to tell her. I'm sure there's a message that you'd like her to have, right?"*

He stared at me but said nothing.

"*Dude! I'm dying here,*" I said to him, trying to point out the pressure I was feeling from the woman's drilling stare.

He moved just enough to shake his head "no."

The woman, who clearly was bored with waiting, spoke up. "Alright, so it might be someone I know. You really can't tell me who?"

"No. I typically ask for a clarifying piece of information, but he's not giving me anything," I explained.

"Nothing?"

"Nothing," I said.

She sat back in her seat, releasing the air from her lungs with a huff, as her back hit the metal chair. "Well?"

"No, it's okay. I'll keep trying," I said, as I stared at the male, hoping he would hear the desperation in my voice. This stalling went on for what seemed like a psychic's eternity in hell. Then, just as I had run out of ways to rephrase the sentence "Sorry, I'm just not getting anything," the male took one step back with his right foot and opened up a vision behind him. Keeping a seriousness in his face, he held up his right hand as if to say "Here it is." Behind him I could see an enormous shoe factory. I flashed back and forth between glimpses of one man holding the body of a shoe as he hand-stitched the sole onto it to hundreds of shoes lined up like soldiers on an automatic belt. I knew what I was seeing, and I sighed with relief.

"He is showing me a shoe factory," I said.

The woman sat bolt upright in the chair, dropping the notebook she was holding in her left hand, her head now stood just a bit higher on her neck. "Oh my. That is either my grandfather or my uncle! That factory has been in my family for years!"

"Cool," was all I could say at this point. Just getting this far under this type of stress was enough for me.

"Well? Which one is it? My grandfather or my uncle? Oh, I hope it's my grandfather," she said as she sat there, a completely different person than she was moments ago. She leaned forward and sat on the edge of her seat hanging on my every word.

I looked at the man, feeling so much better now that it had finally started to flow. *"Thank you! Thank you for showing me that! So, who are you? Grandpa? Uncle?"*

"Time's up," was all he said.

"What?" I asked, as I watched him start to fade.

He pointed to the timer that sat next to my side, the one that was necessary to keep to my tightly packed reading schedule. The timer clicked over to the twenty-minute mark, he smiled at me, and waved goodbye.

Just before he disappeared completely, he flashed me a strange expression. It was a smirk, a smack-in-the-face type look. He was making a point to the woman and using me to deliver the message.

"Wow. Sorry. Gotta tell ya, he just left," I said to the woman. "And, looks like your time is up."

"But doesn't he have anything to say? Please," she begged. "Please."

"I guess that was all he wanted to say," I said, as I stood up to walk to the check-in table. I knew Nicole would move the woman along. "Sorry, I can't give you any more time."

She followed me over to the table and as I walked away, I could hear her arguing with Nicole, trying to get more space in my already booked schedule. This woman sat with me and countless other mediums trying to connect with her grandfather but refused to accept whatever information came through. Instead, she insisted on specific details to verify I was legit before she would accept it was indeed a loved one talking to her. I wondered how much she had missed out on, and how much money she had blown, if she was waiting for it to fit the way she wanted it to.

I looked back toward the front table to see her finally walk away disappointed. A handful more sitters, and I wrapped up my day, dragging my tired self out of the building and sinking into my car. I called Troy and complained about how drained I was. He suggested I chill for a bit to re-energize before I came home. I agreed, and headed straight to the circle, figuring it was the best place for me to find energy.

"Big Dog?" I asked out loud, as I settled into my usual spot.

"Yes?" he said, without showing himself.

I curled my knees up into my chest. *"Just seeing if you're here."*

I sat silently for almost an hour, wrapped in my blanket, watching the trees, the birds, and the smallest of bugs. The woods had slowly become a place to recharge, and the circle a massive battery.

Pushing my tired body up to a standing position, I gathered my blanket feeling recharged with gratitude and a peace that I had lost just hours before, I was ready to head home.

"Beau?" Big Dog's voice echoed through the trees.

"Yeah?"

"You won't always work at fairs."

Somehow it was the perfect thing for me to hear. *"Thanks, Big Dog. I think they are good training, actually. I believe if I can get through that, I can get through anything."*

"Well said," he responded.

"One question before I leave?"

"Shoot."

"Why couldn't I get more information for that woman? You know, shoe factory lady."

"Those on the otherside will only give you what they want to give you," Big Dog explained. "You are not in control of what comes through," he said. "What is most important here is for you to acknowledge that you are just the telephone line. Nothing more than a cord, put here to transfer information. The person's experience will be determined by their loved one or guide, not by you."

"Yeah, I can see that. I kind of thought she might have upset her grandfather."

"The grandfather was disappointed in the way she treated the people he selected to pass information through, the other readers and yourself. This is why he used you to teach her a lesson about respect, respect for the reader and respect for the spirit that is her loved one."

"So, recap. The man that came through from the otherside will only say what he wants to say. I can't pull information out of him?"

"Exactly."

"That makes it interesting, doesn't it?"

"Sure does. For you, at least."

27

Carol's Death

I sat across from Heather in the lounge of the homeschool co-op as we talked about the standard school topics. After a while the conversation shifted to the stress Heather was currently dealing with in her life. Her mother was dying.

Carol, Heather's mother, had been diagnosed with a lung disorder and wanted to spend her last months at home with Heather, Joel, the grandkids, and her husband, Roland. Since the diagnosis, the two families were living together in the familiar cabin that sat yards away from the sacred circle where Big Dog and I spent so many hours.

I asked Heather if there was anything I could do. Two days later she called to say that her mother was excited for me to visit. I quickly agreed to come over that night. I walked into the cabin to find the family waiting in the kitchen while Carol was resting in a back room. I could feel anticipation mixed with anxiety, which made the air heavy with importance. I had no idea what I was going to say. Carol and I had never met. I didn't even truly know what I was doing there.

I could smell the odor of hospice as I made my way closer to Carol's room, a room that was most likely a den before she arrived. There was no door to it—it was a simple twelve-by-twelve box at the end of the hall, with windows on two sides and a sliding glass door that led to the back yard. The area had been turned into a bedroom, modified to help Carol feel comfortable.

I stopped at the end of the hall when I saw her. Carol was in her hospital-style bed, lying on her right side looking away from me. Behind her sat a translucent man dressed in a white suit, clearly there for her and obviously content to stay by her side. I made the fast assumption he was an angel watching over her. When he "heard" that he laughed at me. "I'm not an angel. I'm her dad."

I apologized. He smiled, and pointed toward his daughter as if to say, "What are you waiting for?"

I walked around the foot of the bed and found an old wooden chair. I tenderly pulled it over so I could be close to her.

"Hi Beau," she said, as I sat down.

"Hi Carol. It's really nice to meet you." I tried to stay calm and sound relaxed.

She smiled at me and sat silent, examining my face with her eyes.

"I hear that you have been doing a lot of thinking lately," I said.

"Yes," she responded, with a subtle wind within her voice. "I'm in an interesting situation."

Her eighty-three-year old skin was white with shades of brown and yellow. Her hair, thin and white as the rest of her, was sunk deep into her pillow. Her left hand was draped close to the edge of the bed and I reached out to take it. When my hand touched hers, I saw a shift in her eyes, as if that touch was a gift.

"You look like you're thinking," I said, as she began to squeeze my fingers.

"I have a lot to think about and not much else to do, really."

"Are you thinking about your upcoming journey?"

She nodded her head slightly on the pillow. "I am not sure what it will be. It's kind of frightening."

I thought for a while before I spoke. I kept picturing a friend saying goodbye to their astronaut buddy just as the astronaut is going to head out to space, and the friend giving them advice on what to do when they hit outer space. The image kept me humble. I wasn't the one going on the journey of death. Carol was.

"Do you have any particular faith that you follow?" I asked.

She shook her head no.

"What do you say we talk about energy then?"

She seemed to welcome that idea, so I continued. "Do you see your eyeglasses lying here on the table?" I picked up the glasses to show them to her. "They can't see. You are the one who can see. These eyeglasses are just like your eyeballs. They are made up of carbon and miscellaneous different types of materials that each have fancy names that scientists like to label, but nothing that can actually see." I paused for a moment and took a second to look into her eyes as she looked into mine. "Your eyeballs cannot see any better than these glasses can. It is the observer behind the eyeballs that can see."

"Yes," she said, with a hint of "go on."

"Our spirit is made up of energy. If it wasn't, we wouldn't exist. Do you remember hearing the theory that energy never dies?"

She nodded once.

"Well, when we pass, our spirit's energy simply steps out of the body. It doesn't die. It separates from the body and takes a different form, like water evaporating."

We sat for a few moments, the corners of her lips turning slightly up, and her eyes focused sharply on mine. I asked Carol if she would like another example and she nodded.

"Okay. So, our physical body is like a vehicle and our spirit is the driver. When the car gets old..." She pointed her thumb toward herself and grinned. "Yep, when our car gets old, we simply step out of it. And this is where the fun begins. We can get another car if we want to or we can decide to be without a car for a while. Best of all, when we step out of the car, we realize that the car was very limiting, and without it we are free to do so much more."

"I wonder what that is," she said. "I wonder what there is to do."

"It will be beautiful," I said.

"Do you think I can do it?"

I nodded my head yes and smiled in the silence as I let the idea of her passing settle into the moment.

"Are you scared to leave your family?" I asked.

She nodded, clearly too touched by the topic to speak.

"That makes sense," I said. "You have an amazing family and an amazing life."

"Had," she said.

"I have to argue with you on that." I repositioned my hand just slightly in her grip so I was holding her tighter. "You will still have them. That will not change. You just won't drive here in your car." Her eyes started to shut; I felt her exhaustion. "I'll leave you for today," I said.

"Come back tomorrow?" she asked, with her eyes still closed.

"Absolutely," I said, as I kissed her hand goodbye.

I walked back through the house, filling in the family on the topic of the day and asking if I could come back tomorrow. They were more than happy to have me return, so that's what I did.

"Hey, Carol. I'm back," I said, with more comfort this time.

"Hi, Beau," she said, as light rolled onto her face. "I was hoping you would come back and talk to me. I like to talk to you."

"I like to talk to you too. You know you told me yesterday to come back?"

She closed her eyes and chuckled once. "I forget, you know."

"I know, Carol. So, what's on the menu today for discussion?"

"I just like to hear you talk," she said.

I leaned into the edge of the bed, feeling the ease of being near her. "Okay. Well, let's talk about your family. Do you have any worries about leaving them?"

"My mom left when I was young," she said, as she grabbed my hand again and squeezed it tight. I saw the sadness come over her face and I knew this was a big part of what was keeping her here.

"Are you worried about your kids feeling the same thing?"

She looked at me, the sadness still in her eyes. She said nothing. She didn't have to.

"Carol," I continued. "I can't imagine losing my mom so early. That had to be incredibly difficult." I paused to gauge whether or not

I should continue. "The pain of losing a mother is very, very hard. I can see how you don't want your kids to feel that way."

She looked away from me, drawing her eyes down to her bed. I could feel a sense of defeat flow through her hand to mine. I wanted to take her pain away—to tell her it would be fine, but I knew this was *her* process and I would be far more effective supporting her if I was just present.

"How about I just sit with you for a while today? We can talk later?" I asked, with more lightness in my voice.

She smiled, and we sat.

A few weeks went by with Carol. Each day I would wake up in my bed and think about when I could be with her next. Most days I spent at least a short bit of time with her, some days I couldn't. I was taken with how comfortable I had become around her, how much I wanted to simply sit and be with her. It wasn't like I was sitting near "death," it was as if I was sitting near someone preparing for an incredible journey and I couldn't help but be both sad to see her go and excited for her trip.

She spoke of her mother's death repeatedly. Many times, I would look to her father for guidance, asking him the best way to handle such a tough topic. He was kind and compassionate, making sure to advise me in ways that made Carol the most comfortable. Each time she shared with me, I could feel a lightening in her spirit.

"Mom's not doing well today," Heather said one afternoon, as I let myself through the front door. I had been welcomed by the family in a lovely way—I wasn't allowed to knock anymore.

"How so?" I asked.

"She isn't speaking," Heather said.

We sat uncomfortably silent for a few minutes.

"It's very exciting Beau," Heather continued. "She said she saw three women last night standing at the end of her bed. She talked about it like she really saw them. I think she did."

"Wow. That is cool," I said. "And now she's not speaking?"

"Yes. Well, we don't know if she will speak. She seems to not be able to right now."

I looked down the long hallway that ended in Carol's room. I couldn't see her bed, but I could see her dad, sitting, looking on at her. As I stared down the hall I began to see a variety of smoky colors flowing in and out of the hallway. Sometimes, one would shift in or out of a human shape.

"I think it's really crowded down there today," I said to Heather.

"What do you mean, crowded?" she asked, as she leaned over the island to peek down the hallway.

"Spiritually, it's really crowded. She has a lot of people, you know, spirits, down there," I said.

"Is it the three women?" Heather asked.

I took a moment to silently ask Carol's dad. He shook his head no. "No," I relayed to Heather. "I don't think it's the three women. It feels more like they are there to do work. Like they are there to prepare Carol."

Heather was now crying. I felt horrible and immediately apologized. I made a quick mental note to be more careful with what I said around family members.

I walked down to be with Carol, passing by colors and shapes that were weaving through the air. As I turned the corner I watched her dad stand up, tip his head to me slightly, and then fade away.

The colorful spirits that surrounded the room didn't feel like family members of Carol. They felt like workers, amazing and compassionate workers. I stood frozen in the entryway, knowing that stepping in further would somehow interrupt the process. I watched as they twisted and swirled around her, like watching a beautiful, weaving embrace. Ten minutes went by and the graceful dance of color around Carol slowly morphed into a deep rose hue that circled counterclockwise around her. She looked more peaceful than I had ever seen her before.

When the light faded and the room calmed, I tip-toed over to her side and quietly leaned over her. Her eyes were distant, as if she was paying more attention to somewhere other than the room we were in. A visual flashed through my head of her holding her father's hand with her left as if he was pulling her up a cliff and holding Heather's hand with her right as if she just couldn't let it go.

As I smiled at her peaceful face I heard her voice speak through motionless lips, "Hi, Beau."

I gasped, and tears started to roll down my cheeks. Excitement and bliss poured through me. She could see me. I could see her. She was so beautiful.

"Can you hear me, Carol?"

"Yes." Her lips remained still but her voice poured through my head. "Look, Beau! Look!"

"I know. I can see you. You are so beautiful," I said.

I stood motionless for a few moments, watching as images of her floating among waves played out, waves that looked like, I don't know. Freedom? After some time, the images faded and her human body came back into view as if my focus was pulled away without my permission and forced to plant itself back onto Carol's body—a body that started to cough and moan. She had returned. I stepped to the side as Heather came into the room and began taking care of Carol's basic needs, clearing out her mouth with a soft toothbrush, wiping back the hair on her forehead. I went back to the kitchen and made myself some tea.

As I sipped the last of my tea, I felt something pull through me like the house had been emptied of all of its air. I stood up slowly so not to alarm anyone, and casually walked down the hallway, all the while wondering if I was going to find Carol had died.

I stepped into the open room and felt as if I was standing in a desert. There was not even an inkling of life. I walked quickly over to Carol and watched as her chest rose and fell. She was still alive. I sat in the wooden chair and looked around the room, desperately searching for anything spiritual that could help me to understand the empty feelings I was experiencing. Nothing, just open empty air. I turned back to Carol, hoping I could see her spirit again. Nothing.

Puzzled, I walked outside to see if Big Dog would help me understand what was happening. As I approached the circle, I saw him cupping his hands in front of him casually as if he had been standing there all along.

"Hey. Thank you, thank you, thank you for being here," I said, as Big Dog welcomed me into the circle.

"Anytime," he said, with seriousness about him. He knew I was struggling.

"What is happening to her? Where is she?"

"You noticed she isn't there," he said. "You are right, she is not there."

"But she's alive," I said in disbelief.

"Her body is alive. She, however, is not there."

"Okay, back to the beginning. Where is she?"

Big Dog stepped closer, close enough that I could reach out and touch him. The pull to rest my head on his chest and let him comfort me was intense. "You care very much for her, don't you?" he asked me.

"I do," I said, as I started to sob. *"I just, I just, I'm trying to help."*

"Simply being there is all the help she needs," he explained. "You are her witness. It is in the witnessing, in the actual acknowledgement of her process, that you are allowing her to transition."

"Transition?" I sniffed.

"She is going through her book. There is a lot of work for her to do over the next two days," he said, as he held up the image of a book to me. Somehow I knew the book held Carol's life inside it.

"She is passing in two days?" I asked.

Big Dog nodded yes.

I walked back up to the house and peeked into Carol's room again. It was still bitterly empty. I said goodbye to the rest of the family, keeping the information of the time of Carol's death to myself, and came back the next day to find the room still feeling empty.

Carol was off doing her thing again and her body was lying in the bed, breathing and holding space. Figuring I'd pass the time until she came back, I walked out to the circle. Big Dog was not around. No one was. I sat for a while, staring up at the treetops and contemplating as birds swooped and darted by. Ahead of me was a small pond, big enough to float a canoe but not quite big enough to take it anywhere. I walked to the edge of the water, careful not to slip in through the marshy green. I stared at the surface. It was perfectly still except for one or two water bugs dancing across it. I felt a rustle in the middle of my back, my hairs started to rise, and a sensation climbed upwards to the top of my head. Above the pond the sky seemed to become lighter and lighter as if a blaze of brilliant white was settling in above it. I looked up to see a flattened sphere of white and gold light form and hover above me, stretching out over the pond. My eyes glued to the light, the obvious question ran through my head, *"What is it?"* As the question finished forming in my mind, her voice startled me.

"Beau!"

I felt a bolt of energy pound directly through my body, ripping the breath out of my lungs. Shaking, I kept my stare on the object, and worked to stay upright on both feet.

"Carol?" I shouted out loud.

It was definitely her. I stood there in awe until the light faded and the sharp colors of the forest came back into view. I dropped down to my knees and started to weep. I knew I had touched the otherside. The moment was brief, but is now etched in my soul for the rest of my life. *"Thank you, Carol. Thank you."*

The next day I returned again, this time to find the entire family gathered around Carol's bed. She was still with us here on earth, but it was becoming very clear that she was close to departing. The family welcomed me into the room and we sat together, talking and not talking. Occasionally, without moving her lips, Carol spoke softly, making subtle requests. *"One more kiss,"* I heard her say in my head, as her spirit looked on at her husband, Roland. I watched as Roland got up from his seat and bent over the body of his wife, kissing her on the forehead. I sat in silent amazement that words unspoken were clearly heard. Moments like this were treasures.

The night rolled over the day. Carol's room was never empty, her bed always surrounded by family members, living and dead. As the clock ticked closer to midnight, I told the family I was going to head out for the night and return in the morning. They all said goodbye, their hugs extra tight.

I made my way down the hallway, out the front door, and half-way to my car. I stopped for a moment, feeling pulled to turn around. Carol appeared behind me, in full form, with a huge smile fixed on her face.

"Goodbye, Beau," she said.

I started to cry, *"Did you die?"*

"Not yet."

"I'll see you tomorrow?" I asked hesitantly.

"Thank you, Beau," was all she said before she faded away. I went home that night and slept maybe an hour. I lay in bed, periodically opening my eyes thinking I might see her there, but I didn't. Eventually I fell asleep and woke up groggy. I skipped the shower and breakfast, changed into new clothes, said goodbye to my family, and burst out the door to head back to Carol's side.

I reached over to change the radio station as I drove over the massive green bridge that linked New Hampshire to Maine. I saw someone sitting in the passenger seat out of the corner of my eye.

"Hey, Grandma," I said, assuming it was my usual co-pilot.

"Nope. It's not your grandma," Carol's voice said. "It's me!"

I turned my head and saw Carol sitting beside me. She was dressed in a long blue dress, her cheeks filled in and rosy. *"Carol!"* I shouted.

"Yep. It's me, Beau," she said with excitement. "I did it! I did it! Can you believe it? I really did it!"

"You did it," I said, not sure how to respond—then it sank in. *"You did it? Oh, wow. Are you gone?"*

She nodded excitedly.

I looked at the road and chuckled a bit, unable to block out the carefree feelings radiating off Carol. I never expected her death to unfold for me like this. I had pictured tears by a bedside, not excitement on the freeway.

"I'm really proud of you," I said. *"You did it."*

"Me too." She sat back a bit in the seat now, looking around at the world outside the car for a moment before she turned her eyes to me again. "Tell them thank you for the song."

"The song?"

"Yeah. They sang to me," she said, as she held her hands over her mouth as if the song they sang for her was the most amazing gift anyone had given her.

"I'll tell them," I said, as I took the left onto their gravel driveway.

I walked into the kitchen to find it empty. I made my way back to Carol's room and found everyone gathered around, holding hands and weeping gently.

"She's gone," I said.

Heather nodded as she looked up and raised the sides of her mouth just slightly, welcoming me to this moment. I sat down next to Carol's still body lying on the hospital bed and experienced the surreal moment of also seeing Carol's spirit standing directly behind Heather. Carol nodded at me as if to say I should share.

"Carol was in my car this morning," I said to the family. Joel smiled and reached out to squeeze my arm in gratitude. "She said to tell you thank you for the song you sang to her."

Heather gasped, Joel smiled, and Roland began to weep again.

"Oh, Beau. She heard it!" exclaimed Heather.

"I take it you sang to her?"

"Yes. Yes, we did," she said. "It was our way to honor her."

"Your entire family is so beautiful. Carol is so lucky to have you," I said, as I was moved to tears.

We sat around Carol's body for another hour or so, singing songs to her and periodically reaching out to embrace each other and the moment.

Later, two men from the funeral home came to the cabin to bring Carol to the crematorium. They were wonderfully respectful of the family and walked through the front door with their heads slightly lowered and their moods somber. When they started toward the back of the house to collect Carol's body, Joel stopped them and informed them that the family would be walking her out. The two men stepped back and simply witnessed, as I did as well, the solemn moment when the family pushed Carol's hospital bed through the house and down the front steps to the driveway. Each family member holding onto the bed at all times, they walked slowly and methodically, embracing the experience, making sure even the smallest family member, their son Cayden, was able to participate for the entire walk.

At the end of the walkway the family handed Carol over to the two men, who delicately lifted her into the van. They gently closed the doors and ceremoniously turned to the family, looking down slightly as if they were willing to stay there as long as it took until they were dismissed. Roland stepped forward and placed his hand on one of the men's shoulders, squeezing it gently and thanking him for taking care of Carol. The men, clearly moved by the experience, walked slowly toward the front seats of the van, climbed in with care, and started to drive away. Ten feet down the driveway the brake lights lit up when the driver noticed in the rear-view mirror the family was walking hand in hand, slowly behind the vehicle. I saw the look on the driver's face and watched a slight sob and a sniff as he witnessed the amazing scene. The van rolled no more than one mile per hour down the driveway for over a hundred feet until it crested at the top of a hill and the family stopped their march. A pause and a moment of silence, and the van again began to creep up and over the hill, this time alone.

I stood on the walkway watching the events unfold, Carol by my side.

"Aren't they beautiful?" she asked me.

"Amazing. You are so lucky," I responded.

"I know."

28

Out of the Woods

It had been a while since Carol had passed and I was back to speaking with Big Dog on a regular basis. I paused for a second at the East side of the circle, feeling an odd sensation. Stepping into the sacred area just seemed like something I shouldn't do. I stood puzzled for a second. To my left I felt an anxious pull, with heaviness behind its grip. I looked over my shoulder to see a young man, about twenty years old, in spirit form, shaking and nervous.

"Who are you?" I asked.

"I'm waiting for the chimney man to come back," he said. I stepped away from the circle and turned toward him. *"Who's the chimney man?"*

The young man looked over his shoulder toward the cabin, looked back at me, and then disappeared. I shifted my puzzled gaze to Big Dog who was standing in the circle.

"I'll see you tomorrow," Big Dog said, as he also disappeared.

"Of course you will," I said sarcastically.

Now alone in the woods, I went up to the cabin and called out to Joel. "Do you know who the chimney man is?"

Joel looked up from what he was doing.

"I was down at the circle and saw this boy who said he was waiting for the chimney man," I explained.

"Living or dead?" Joel asked.

"Funny, I get that question a lot," I joked. "Dead," I continued more seriously.

"Wow. That's interesting. We just installed a chimney. Tom did the work, so I suppose that could be who he was talking about."

"Why would a dead teenager be waiting for him?" I asked, now getting more curious.

"Well, Tom and his wife lost a son a little while back. Bobby. I believe he was about that age. Do you think it was Tom's son?" he asked.

I thought for a moment. "Not sure. I know that he had long hair. He was thin. Who else would ask for a chimney man?" I filled Joel in with everything I could remember.

"I can call Tom and we can see," Joel suggested.

I stared at Joel for a moment, trying to decide what to do. My hesitation must have been obvious.

"Are you okay?" Joel asked.

"I'm just wondering if this is going to keep happening forever or something. You know, like Lloyd."

"The mechanic who did pottery?"

"Yeah," I sighed.

"They're not really the same thing, you know," Joel said.

My expression must have changed dramatically because Joel didn't wait for me to say anything.

"Lloyd insisted," Joel said. "This boy didn't."

"Are you saying I shouldn't get involved?"

"No. I'm saying they're not the same situation," Joel replied. "What do you think you should do?"

I remembered the little boy at Disney World. It wasn't a fair comparison either. "That's just it, I don't know," I said.

"Did you ever think about asking your guides? You know, Grandma? Big Dog? Seems like they would know if you're supposed to intervene or not."

"Good idea. How did I not think of that?" I paused for a moment and looked around. "Well, maybe I should go down and talk to the boy in the trees," I said cautiously. "He seemed stuck, really upset. If he is stuck, maybe I can help him cross over."

"Makes sense. Want me to go with you?" Joel asked. I nodded yes and walked back down to the circle, this time with Joel following me. When we arrived I took Joel's advice.

"Big Dog?" I said out loud. "You there?"

He came into form right in front of me.

"Big Dog," I continued, *"is there something I should be doing for this kid?"*

"Go and talk to him. He could use your help," he responded.

"I'm not interfering?"

"No, you are not. There will be times when you will see things that you shouldn't act on, that is simply the pool of knowledge. But there are times that you will need to do something," he explained.

I walked to the same spot I was in when I saw the young man before, hoping I could reconnect with him. With Big Dog's advice in my head I now focused on how I could help and waited silently. From my left I started to hear creepy sounds—screams, nails scraping, moans. As I looked toward the source of the sounds I found the chimney man's son.

"What are those noises?" I asked him.

"Can you hear them?" he said. "I can too. I, I can't leave. Tell him that I'm here."

"Tell who? Your dad?"

He nodded yes.

"Are you Bobby?"

"Yes. But," His hands shaking violently, he looked around with fear in his eyes. "I can't leave here. Please. Please, tell him."

"Bobby, talk to me. What is going on?" I asked. *"Why are you scared?"*

Bobby looked around frantically. "I can't leave, they'll get me."

"Who's they?" I asked, as my heart started to match the tempo of the young man's fear.

Bobby cried out in pain, buried his face in his hands, and images began to flash in front of my face. The woods faded away and I was left alone in a vision, standing on a dark road littered with drug paraphernalia. I could see Bobby walking through it, mad at himself for falling off the wagon yet again. I watched as he dropped to his knees on the pavement and buckled over to his left side. The vision faded, but I could still feel pain radiating through my entire left side as if I had been crushed.

"Joel," I said out loud.

"Yeah, Beau. I'm right here," he said. He was standing behind me.

"I think he was involved with drugs. And there is something really intense about my left side, like it's been crushed."

"Okay. Has Bobby crossed over?" he asked.

"No, not yet," I said. "He is trapped in something that I don't understand. It's like he's put himself in a black box and I can hear the sounds that he hears outside the box. They're horrible. I'm not sure what to do."

"There's got to be something," Joel said with encouragement.

I looked at Bobby again and waited for him to pull his hands away from his face, but he didn't. Instead, I heard his voice, shaky and muffled. "I can't leave here. If I do, the demons will get me. Just get the chimney man."

"Why do you call him the chimney man?" I asked.

Bobby started to sob. Without raising his head, he sunk down to the bottom of his black box. "I can't remember his name!" he screamed from a broken heart. "My mind. My head!"

"Bobby, stop. Relax." I knelt down to look straight at him. I looked around to see if there was anyone or anything nearby to help Bobby cross over or release him from his pain. I felt completely unprepared to deal with something of this magnitude. Off to the left I saw an older female, shimmering in white, waiting patiently. She was shorter and round, with neatly cut white hair, her hands resting by her side.

"Are you Bobby's grandmother?" I called out to her.

She shook her head no just as Big Dog came up from behind and stood to my right, a few feet from Joel.

"Big Dog," I called out. *"A little help here?"*

"She is a Collector. She is not related to Bobby, she is here to help," Big Dog explained, and then faded back toward the circle again.

"Bobby," I said with urgency, *"You have a Collector waiting for you. She can help!"*

"She's not here to help me," he said, as he slightly pulled his head up from his hands. "If I look at her, then she'll take me."

"Where exactly do you think she is going to take you?" I asked, losing my patience over his firm desire to stay in the box.

He whispered softly as if he didn't want the Collector to hear him. "Can't you hear it? Outside the box? It's hell. That's where I'm going."

"Bobby," I waited for him to look directly at me. *"Listen to me very carefully,"* I said with purpose. "*You are not going to hell. Hell doesn't exist. Do you hear me?"*

The nod from his head was so slight that I didn't completely believe he was on board with what I was saying.

"Bobby, the chimney man's name is Tom. You told me he is your dad, remember?" I said softly, changing the subject.

Bobby sobbed again and I felt a stronger connection to his emotions. "Yes, that's my dad."

"Yes, Bobby. Your dad. He would want you to be safe, not sitting here in fear. Please, Bobby, just look at the woman. She's here to help you," I said gently.

"So, what happens if I look at her? Do I get to see my dad?" he asked.

"Yes, you can. Whenever you want. Do you believe in heaven?" Bobby nodded yes. He was listening intently now. *"Well, when you have a guide like her, that means you are going to heaven, not to hell."*

"Are you sure?" I could feel him reaching out to me.

"Yep. That's her job. Just look at her. You'll see."

"But what if she is one of them? One of the people outside this box?"

"Bobby. Look at me. Can you see me?"

"Yes. Yes, I can see you," he said.

"Bobby. Can you see that I would never hurt you? Can you see

my heart?" I asked, not sure what in the world made me say what I had just said.

I waited patiently. Bobby's sobbing slowed to a weep, his fists released from their clench, and, most importantly, the horror sounds began to fade.

"I can see you," he said.

"Hold on to me, Bobby. It's just me and you." I decided to sit with him for as long as it took to make him feel safe.

In the silence I became aware of everything around me. Joel standing next to me. Big Dog ten feet away, in the circle, watching. The female Collector was ever so slightly coming closer.

"Bobby?"

"Yes?"

"I think it's time now that you look at your Collector," I said, softly demanding.

"Okay," he said, with the look of a child going to school for the first time. "I can do it. Just promise me I'm not going to hell."

"I can promise you you're not going to hell. You know I wouldn't lie to you."

I began to see clearly the box that enclosed him, the box that kept him safe from the demons he believed were waiting to take him away. Through the faded black wall that divided Bobby and myself, I saw one steady hand reach out toward me. I raised my hand up to meet his and imagined myself pulling him forward out of his prison. I watched an arm, a shoulder, his head, and finally the rest of him fall forward into the space in front of me. Still holding on to me, he turned to look at the woman in white. Time felt as if, for one beautiful second, it was suspended. His eyes called out to her, and she swooped in around him, swaddled him in light, and held him in her compassionate arms.

Bobby turned to me one last time and thanked me. As he did, I could see life pouring through him again, as if that last step he took peeled away all the fear and lifted him out of the gloom. Seconds passed, and he was gone. The woods, that moments before were alive with light, color, and activity, were now dark and quiet. It took a minute to sink in.

"Joel?" I said, turning around to find him. "Yeah?"

"I did it."

A big smile rolled onto Joel's face and he stepped forward to help me back up to my feet.

"I'll be up in a minute," I told Joel as I leaped toward the circle, eager to talk to Big Dog about what had just happened. Joel nodded and walked toward the house.

"Hey Big Dog!" I said.

Big Dog smiled at me like a coach proud of his runner coming in first place. "You did well."

"Not bad, considering I didn't know what the heck I was doing," I said.

"You did know what you were doing. You've crossed people over before," he said.

"Yeah, but not like that."

Big Dog laughed at me yet again. "Just go home knowing you did well."

I stood there with a smile plastered across my face.

I walked back to the cabin to talk to Joel about what had happened. Several days later we would learn the full story of Tom's son. His addiction, his recovery and his getting hit by a car walking home from church. As the father spoke of his son, I could feel the pride and the love in his voice, talking about the obstacles his son had overcome and the strength with which he walked through parts of his life.

The night ended and I climbed into the van to head home. As I drove down Joel's driveway, I saw a stocky male standing perfectly still in the center of the road. I rolled to a stop. He stood calmly between my two headlights, but untouched by them. A deep chuckle—a familiar deep chuckle—ran through my head. It was Big Dog.

"You can leave the circle?!" I shouted through the front window.

He waved at me with his right hand, slow and deliberate, like an old highway advertisement for a truck stop, and then disappeared. He reappeared in the passenger seat.

"Dude, you're not in the circle!" I said.

"Of course."

"Could you always leave the circle?"

"Of course."

"Then why all the appointments and schedules and stuff to make me come out here?"

"Which has more value, the gift that you stumble into, or the gift you have to go after yourself?"

It was feeling like a Yoda moment. "Go after?" I said out loud.

"Exactly," said Big Dog. "By having you come here to get it you're accepting not just a gift but a responsibility."

I couldn't think of anything to say.

"Tomorrow night?" Big Dog said.

"Tomorrow night," I replied, as Big Dog faded away.

29

Sadie's Haunting

Weeks passed, and I continued my sessions with Big Dog at the circle. I knew I didn't *have* to go there for them, but somehow it felt more official, more studious. Then, through a referral, I was contacted by a woman named Paula. She had lost her best friend, Sadie, to suicide.

After Sadie died her husband and three children decided to move out of their home. The intensity of being in the house was too much for the kids and people were speculating that there might be "something" in the house. Their biggest fear was that Sadie might now be stuck in the house with that something. I agreed to meet with Paula and the widowed husband at Paula's house the next night. She was thankful I made such a long drive to help her on such short notice.

When I arrived I made a last minute decision to bring Grandma's pink rock. Dealing with a suicide and a potential haunting, I hoped holding it would help calm my nerves.

I walked up the dirt driveway feeling unprepared (as I always do), yet glad I was given the opportunity to help. Paula was standing in the entryway next to Sadie's husband, John. She opened the door a bit wider as if to say "come on in."

The three of us gathered in the kitchen. Paula stood in the center while I sat at a high-top table, with John seated on a nearby staircase. I felt a wall around John, like maybe he was conflicted with my being there. "John, are you a skeptic?" I asked gently.

John shifted in his seat. "We're Catholic, and this is not really my thing."

"It's okay by me. I'm totally comfort..."

"I'm just worried about Sadie, that's all," he interrupted me delicately.

Hearing the love in his voice for his late wife, I nodded and moved on to speaking with Paula. "Thanks for calling me in. I'm sorry about Sadie's passing. If it's okay with you I'd like to just get an idea of what's happening intuitively and then ask you questions."

"So, do you want me to tell you what's going on?" Paula asked me for clarification.

"No," I responded. "I'd like to sit with the energy for a little bit first and then ask you questions. I want to make sure I'm connecting to the right stuff before I say anything."

I sat for a moment and saw a flash of children race through my head. I counted them the best I could. Two boys and one girl.

"I know that Sadie and you were parents," I said to John. "Do you have three kids?"

John nodded yes.

"Okay," I said. "One of the kids is very much like Sadie. I suspect they are saying that the girl is the spitting image of your wife."

John nodded again.

I looked on at the energy that was giving me the information. I knew it was female, but it didn't feel like it could be Sadie.

"Who are you?" I asked.

The spirit didn't respond. She seemed to fade as a second vision swept in behind her. It was an image of a young woman, thin, in her mid-thirties, sitting on a bedroom floor. She was reaching toward me, crying.

"Paula," I said, "I think we have to go to Sadie's home. I was hoping I could connect with her here, at your house, but it looks like I'm not going to be able to." I paused for a moment before going on. "Was Sadie very thin?"

Paula nodded. "Do you see her?"

"Yes, but she's not here. I think she's still in her home, and it looks like I'm going to have to go there to connect with her."

John nodded, pulled himself up from his sitting position, and grabbed his keys as if to say, "Let's go."

A few minutes later, two cars rolled into the driveway of John and Sadie's house. I was the first one to enter, walking directly into the kitchen and doing my best to swallow the lump in my throat. I felt a heaviness fall over me like a lead vest. I stopped in the middle of the linoleum and stared straight ahead, half hoping I would see nothing because whatever was attached to the dark feelings pouring through me could not be a nice thing to see. A few seconds went by and I was startled by Sadie's spirit flashing in front of me with a look of panic in her eye. She pointed upstairs and tried to speak but her voice sounded like it was muffled, underwater. With that she was gone.

John and Paula were standing directly behind me.

"John, can I go upstairs?" I asked.

I looked up the stairs knowing that whatever was going to happen was waiting up there. I gripped Grandma's rock so hard I thought my fingers might bleed.

I crept up the stairs, focusing on the safe-looking white wall at the top. With each step up, however, that white wall seemed less and less safe. Two steps from the top the wall turned black, a pool of dark oily liquid crawled across it, engulfing it. My heart jumped and my feet stopped.

I couldn't move forward, but I couldn't move back, either. With Paula and John right there behind me, I couldn't bear to tell them we had to turn around because I was chickening out.

So, I did the only thing I could think of. I scrunched my eyes closed as tight as I could and yelled "*Stop it!*" in my head to anyone or anything around. When I opened my eyes I was both surprised and relieved to see the wall was white again. The heaviness lifted and I made a mental note that I had to stay in control.

I continued up the stairs, reached the top, and was energetically pulled to the right—John and Sadie's former bedroom—and went in. Another flash of Sadie sparked in front of me calling out my name. Somehow, her voice and the distant sound of my name echoed in my heart. It reinforced my impression there was something else here—something between Sadie and me—and that boosted my motivation to get through it to help her.

I stepped out of the master bedroom and checked the other three rooms, all children's rooms, all empty except for a few personal belongings scattered about the floor. There was a huge difference between how I felt in the kids' rooms and how I felt in Sadie's room. It was as if nothing was wrong when I stood in the children's rooms, like they were all inside some kind of protective bubble. I heard a woman's voice behind me say "She kept them safe from him." I whipped around to see the same female spirit I had seen in Paula's kitchen.

"She was an amazing mom," she said. "She wouldn't let him touch them."

As she spoke, I saw a vision of a male spirit in front of me, trying to get into the kids' rooms and failing, and Sadie standing behind him with a warrior look in her eyes.

The vision faded and I walked back into the master bedroom looking for more information. I began to ask John questions.

"John, I'm wondering a few things. I feel like the biggest problems happened here, in this room."

John nodded.

I continued. "I know that she committed suicide and that you think there is 'something' in the house that is harming her."

John nodded again. I could feel his energy tighten up. He was getting uncomfortable, but the thought of helping his wife overrode that discomfort and kept him by my side through the process.

I looked around the room. The head of the bed was against the right wall, the foot pointing toward the door. Dressers still lined the left and back wall, a closet just off to my right.

Another vision began. The bed was no longer on the right wall, it was directly in front of me. Sadie was lying on the left side of it, holding herself as tightly together as she could, curled up into a ball. She was crying and rocking as a male spirit floated very close above her. She was alive, but he was dead and slowly stalking his prey. I could feel her fear as she struggled to move away from him. Her panic turned to terror and she fought back at whatever it was that was hunting her. All I could do was watch as he pulled her arms apart and pressed in closer. I witnessed her horror unfold and could only stand by as she then got up from her side of the bed, turned to look at the image of John fast asleep beside her, and headed downstairs.

"I think that the 'something' you think was harming her, was something real," I said to John and Paula. "I'm looking at the bed, but it doesn't look like it's on that wall, it looks like it's on the wall in front of me."

"Yes, we moved it," John said.

"Well, it looks to me as if, um," I paused, not sure how to relay what I saw to the husband without completely freaking him out. "Tell me something, John. Did she ever say to you that she was being attacked at night?"

John took a step back and caught his breath. "Yes. She did," he fought back his emotions. "But I didn't know. I just, didn't know."

"It's okay, John. I'm just getting information on what happened," I said, hoping to comfort him in an uncomfortable situation.

I waited for a bit, hoping to give John time to process. I looked over to the bed again, this time seeing a completely different scene. Sadie was there alone, the house felt incredibly empty. The vision flickered in and out, making it difficult to see the flow of events. In one flash she was sitting on her side of the bed, strategically wrapped up in blankets. In the next flash she was lying down, a gun by her side, and red pooling in the crevices of the sheets.

"I take it she killed herself here, in her bed," I said out loud.

"Yes," John said. "With a gun." I nodded solemnly.

John continued. "I went to the store. She told me to go, and to take the kids. I had no idea what she was going to do. I didn't know that she would do that. And then, I came home."

He ended with the word "home," and I walked a few steps toward the edge of the bed. I hoped to reach out and connect to Sadie's energy. I still wasn't able to grab onto her even though the scenes that had played out in front of me made me want to help her more urgently than ever. I looked from left to right, calling out her name in my head.

"Sadie?"

A dark, deep voice answered me. "You won't find her," it said. "She's mine."

I gasped slightly, and quickly pulled myself together to not frighten John and Paula.

"Who are you?" I asked.

"She's mine," he spoke again.

I stepped back. I began to feel more like I was in a dungeon than a second-floor bedroom.

"Where are you?" I called out to the male voice.

"Right here," it said from behind me.

I could feel the form of a body pressing up against my backside, a hand sliding around my waist. An image rolled through my head of me being pushed to the floor and attacked. My heart started to pound and my feet screamed at me to run. Flashes of dark, wet street corners and crying women burst through my head. In that moment, I was sure I was next on his list. His hunt had begun and the more he pressed into me, the more the bedroom faded from my mind. The pull to bring me into his twisted vision was strong. Almost too strong.

I felt a pebble of anger start to rise in my core. As it rose, I clung to it like a rope hanging over the edge of a cliff. The tighter I clung, the more it grew. Soon, I was no longer prey on some dark street corner. I was Beau, and I was pissed. When I embraced the rage, the bedroom came slamming back into view. Something in me snapped and I wasn't about to take it anymore. I turned and watched as he floated backwards, slowly and timidly fading away through the wall in front of me.

When he was out of view I turned to my right. Sadie was now standing next to me.

"There you are," I said to her.

"Will you come downstairs?" she asked. "It's easier for me to talk down there."

"Absolutely," I said. *"Lead the way."*

I turned to John and Paula, who had been silently standing a few feet behind me.

"Regardless of what caused her death, right now she needs our help," I said.

John asked if someone was hurting his wife. I hesitated, but I explained that his wife had been victimized by a spirit, and then quickly switched our focus back to Sadie's role as mother and the efforts she expended to protect their children.

"She was such a good mom," Paula said, with tears in her eyes.

"Sadie wants us to go downstairs. I haven't gotten rid of this man yet, but I will. In the meantime, Sadie wants to talk to us and says it's easier for her to do that downstairs."

The three of us went down to the living room. It was lined with three couches and three overstuffed chairs, creating a u-shape. Sadie's spirit showed up in one of the chairs and she tapped the armrest as if to tell me to sit where she was sitting.

"That's where she would always sit," Paula said, as I lowered myself onto the seat.

I leaned to my left, following Sadie's orders to curl my feet up into the chair and rest my head on the armrest. "Sadie is telling me she liked to sit like this," I said.

"Yes, that's exactly how she sat," John said, as he positioned himself across the room in another chair.

"She has some things to say, so I'll just say them as they come through."

John nodded.

"Okay. Well, she is here. I can finally see her clearly. I think I just needed to separate her energy from that man's," I continued on. "You are right. There is something in this house and the something is a male spirit. Sadie is telling me that he attached to her. She is showing herself when she was alive, walking through a dark bar and picking up this male spirit there, like he attached to her and came home with her. She says that she was dealing with a childhood tragedy at the time. I think she was a victim when she was younger."

"Ah, can I say something?" John interrupted. "Sadie, well, she had talked to me about something like that a week before she died," John explained. "She said that she had been sexually, you know, when she was a kid, and that she wanted to tell me. That it had been a secret for her entire life. So, yeah, she told me, and I listened. I knew she was dealing with it. I thought that was the problem."

"I think it was part of it, but not the cause. When I see her walk through the bar, I see her feeling vulnerable. Like because she was dealing with processing the attack as a kid, it left her energetically open. The hard part here is that I think she was open in the wrong place at the wrong time, running into this male spirit that wanted to cause someone harm."

"Sadie is saying something else too," I continued. "She is telling me that she not only struggled with depression around this but that she would go from one to ten with her emotions in two seconds flat. That she bounced back and forth with her emotions with such force that she feels bad that it affected you. But she says that you were amazing. You never got angry with her. She says she didn't deserve you and that you had more patience with her than you should have, considering the circumstances."

"I never got mad at her. I only wanted her to get better," John said.

"She knows that. She is also saying how sorry she is that she didn't find another way out. She says she just didn't know what to do to make him go away, to make the pain stop. She is really sorry." I paused for a moment to give John the space he needed to absorb what Sadie was saying. "She also wants you to know that nothing is going to happen to you. She says that you are worried about dying right now because you're worried that the kids would be left without any parents."

John nodded in agreement just before he dropped his head into his hands.

"Sadie says that you don't have to worry about that," I continued. "She wants you to know that you will be alright. Plus, she says, she doesn't want her mom to have custody over the kids because her mom is not a nice person at all."

John looked up at me and stared into my eyes for a moment before answering. "Ah, you could say that," John said, quickly and quietly.

"One more thing and then Sadie wants me to go upstairs and get rid of this guy," I said, as I looked into John's eyes. "She wants to thank you for giving her daughter the ring."

John sat upright in his chair. "Man! Yes. That's what I did. She saw that?"

"Looks like she did," I said.

"I gave our daughter Sadie's wedding ring," John explained. "I was torn between leaving it on Sadie's finger when she was buried and taking it off."

"Well, looks like you made the right decision," I wrapped up the conversation.

I told John and Paula I needed to take care of the male spirit upstairs by myself. Alone, except for Sadie, who was now by my side and just as determined. I turned the corner to the bedroom and saw him standing on the other side of the bed, looking directly at me. There was no longer anything intimidating about him, he seemed more ready to talk than anything else. Our eyes connected, I squared off my stance, and readied myself for what I expected would be an intense conversation. I took a full breath while I thought about what to say or ask. He slowly moved toward me while still keeping enough distance between us to not feel threatening. The tension I had expected to be between us just wasn't there. This once aggressive male was now cautious and in deep thought.

His eyes began to dart around the room, as if he was searching for answers to the questions I hadn't even thought up yet. It was like he was processing through the intents I held in wanting him to move on, like he was having a discussion with me without me even participating. I watched this process for several moments. Then, just when I thought he was moving in the right direction, I saw hesitation come back into his being. He bolted backwards as if to break through the back wall of the room and run away from a decision all together. Inches before he hit the wall, however, white light poured into the room, wrapped around him, and engulfed him. As it circled, I saw him lighten. The remaining bits of fear and hate poured out of him and were absorbed by the light. He looked at me once more, his eyes relieved and his posture more upright, as feelings of love and compassion settled into me. In a flash it was over. The room was empty.

Alone, I stared at the barren wall ahead of me and let the silence comfort me. I had witnessed his crossing. I felt the connection and I felt the release.

Sadie appeared by my side. She also now had relief in her eyes.

"I want to say goodbye to them," she said.

I called down to John and Paula to come upstairs.

"Does the room feel any different to you?" I asked them.

"Yes," said Paula. "Much lighter."

"The man is gone. Sadie is here and safe. She wants to say goodbye to you before she crosses over." I turned to Paula first. "Paula, she wants you to tell one of her friends that she is grateful for the time they spent together. That she loved collecting the small figurines with her."

"I'll tell her," Paula said. "I know who she means, and that is exactly what they did."

"And to you," I continued talking to Paula, "Sadie wants to thank you for your friendship. Your humor meant a lot to her and she is thankful to have someone like you, someone who is so straightforward and honest."

Paula nodded, as tears slid down her face.

I turned to talk to John. "Sadie wants to say goodbye."

"I'll head downstairs and give you a moment," Paula said to John, as she moved toward the door.

After Paula left, Sadie spoke to me again. "Beau, I just want to connect with him one last time."

"Okay, just tell me what to do," I said.

"I need you to hold the energy around us," she explained, as she showed me an image of wrapping the two of them in white light together. "Oh, and turn around to give John his space. He needs the privacy."

"Will do."

I explained to John that Sadie wanted to connect with him one last time and that I had to hold the energy in the room. I would turn my back and give him privacy.

"All you have to do is sit with her," I told him.

The once skeptical man nodded his head, and I turned around. I stood with my back to him for at least five minutes when I heard him break down and sob. It was then I knew they were connecting. The experiences of the entire evening fell away, leaving nothing but this moment of incredible beauty between husband and wife.

When it was over, John walked me out to the car and thanked me for helping. We spoke a little about the burden he was taking on and the love he had for his family. He shook my hand and shared with me his appreciation, followed with an apology for his skepticism. I told him not to worry about that. All that mattered was that we helped Sadie.

"We didn't help Sadie. You did," he said.

I drove home that night feeling overwhelmed. The car was empty—no Grandma, no Big Dog—just me, and somehow that felt right. I was left to myself to process the wonder and depth of death, and its journey.

I passed the exit to my house and drove instead to Joel's land

and the sacred circle. I was sure that his family was fast asleep, but I needed to connect with Big Dog in the circle.

My tires rolled slowly to a stop on the gravel driveway and I gently shut the car door behind me so as to not wake anyone. The moon was full and it lit the path to the circle. I didn't care about a flashlight or what might be lurking in the woods around me. Somehow this time I didn't need one. I knew I was safe. I entered the circle and settled into the imprints I had made over the last few months during my conversations with Big Dog.

"You there?" I asked into the wind.

"I am always here for you." Big Dog's voice resonated in my head, soothing my thoughts and warming my heart.

"Where are you?" I asked, as I looked ahead of me in the night air.

"Right next to you," he responded.

I turned to my right and locked eyes with the spirit guide who had now become my closest friend. *"That was a trip, man."*

"You could say that. Or you could speak of the significance of what you did."

"Don't think I'm up for speaking about significance. It feels pretty heavy, actually. Those children don't have a mom because of," I stopped short, choking back my tears.

"Everything that is supposed to happen, will happen. You, my friend, are there to help with the transition."

I looked up at the clear, bright, night sky, with its shimmering dots of radiant light. *"It's just hard to stomach."*

"I know."

We sat in silence for a while. All I wanted in that moment was to be there, surrounded by the circle of trees that had, over time, become my safe place.

Big Dog broke the silence, shifting his position to face me. "It is a gift to be able to work with you. I am excited to watch you grow. Look on and let me show you what you will do." He stood up and motioned for me to join him.

"Future stuff?"

He smiled, and I stared straight ahead. In front of me the fire pit and the wilderness floor faded away and before me stood an old hotel, five stories high. Out of the broken windows of the hotel poured hundreds of people, falling into a massive moat below them. I watched as they swam en masse toward me, each one struggling to stay afl oat. When they were close, just a few feet away from the ledge I was now standing on, each one reached out to me, begging for me to save them from drowning.

"This doesn't look good. What does it have to do with me?" I asked.

"You are seeing souls, trapped in their own in-betweens. They are coming to you because it is your job to help them cross over and complete their transition. You are a Collector," Big Dog explained.

"There's a lot of them." I ignored the word "Collector" and focused on the vision.

"Yes. Today, with the way man behaves, there are many reasons to be stuck."

"Wait. No. That's not my job," I protested. *"I'm not a Collector. A Collector is someone on the otherside, not me."*

"Yes, you are." Big Dog shifted slightly. "You are a Collector here on earth. Your job is just as important as the Collectors on the otherside. You work with them as a team. You are a Collector first, and a reader second."

"Them?" I repeated a familiar word. *"So this is the 'them' that Grandma spoke of?"*

Big Dog nodded. "'Them' consists of the Collectors, other higher beings, and me all waiting for you to step into your true line of work."

"So you want me to run around and help dead people cross over?" I complained slightly. *"No. I think I'll help more people if I keep doing readings. You know, make a bigger impact."*

"Without help to cross into the light, these souls are left to struggle." I could hear the heaviness in his voice. "Worse, because they have not completed their journey, the ones that they leave behind here on earth are not able to receive their guidance."

To my right another vision was unfolding. It was of a father floating above his son as his son attempted to maneuver through a forest blindfolded. The father had crossed over and completed his transition, and now watched over his son from the otherside. I watched as the father swooped in just as the son was about to collide with a tree, saving him from impact and getting him one step closer to the clearing that was waiting for the boy up ahead.

"I know that loved ones help us after they have crossed over. I knew that," I said with respect.

"Yes, but what you have not thought of is what happens when that boy does not have his father to guide him through the forest. His father, stuck in the in-between, is powerless to help his son. The father is one of the souls in the hotel, waiting for you to help him."

Big Dog paused. "People wonder why mankind is struggling. Well, this is why. Without our ancestors watching over us and guiding us along our path, we are prone to struggle and to never discover the beauty beyond the woods," Big Dog explained.

As I stood there in the cold night, I respectfully pondered what was being shown to me. I wasn't sure I was ready for what "they" were putting in front of me. Just two years into exploring my intuition and now I'm faced with "saving ghosts." Big Dog felt my apprehension.

"It's what you were meant to do," he reiterated. "They're drowning, and you are the one who knows how to swim. Don't you find it odd that crossing spirits has come so naturally to you?"

I looked down at my feet and shook my head from side to side. I didn't *want* to "swim." I wasn't ready for what he was showing me. I was still too new.

I felt the warmth of a hand on my shoulder and compassion wrap around me. The tips of my feet still hung over the ledge that circled the moat full of souls. I saw two new faces in the water, faces that were very familiar. Below me, desperately swimming to stay above, were my two sons, Michael and Max.

I reached down to the earth to grab onto the vision of my children, only to have it fade away, leaving the forest floor below me.

"Would you not swim for *them*?" Big Dog asked. "Each soul is someone's child, someone's parent."

I closed my eyes and took a deep breath.

"That's my girl," Big Dog said.

About the Author

Isabeau "Beau" Maxwell is one of the leading spiritual coaches in intuitive development today. Isabeau brings deep channeled knowledge and personal understanding to the field of spirituality. She has helped people connect to their authentic, natural intuitive abilities since 2006.

Isabeau is an internationally known medium, author and teacher, touching the lives of people across the world. Known for her compassion and accuracy, Isabeau brings peace and comfort to many through her energy work, transformative sessions and teachings.

The founder of The SAGE Method, a life-changing, intuitive training program that teaches people how to open to their intuition and live an authentic, blissful life, Beau is also the creator of The SAGE Circle, Discovery Meditation and the author of *Cracking Open: Adventures of a Reluctant Medium.*

Having earned a bachelor's degree from Minnesota State University with a major in mathematics and a minor in chemistry, Isabeau maintains a balanced perspective between this world and the next. Down-to-earth and easy to relate to, Isabeau offers safe space for students and clients to process the intuitive information they are provided.

Dive into your personal intuitive journey today by taking a free intuitive course, The Top Five Intuitive Tools. Visit OpenYourIntuition.com to get started.

Made in USA - Kendallville, IN
72813_9781735191195
01.25.2022 1457